At Western Kentucky University

Shelly Hampton Dantzler, Rita Jackson Dees, Betty Gentry and Suzanne Shurte

Thanks for your photos! Almost all those reproduced in this book were sent in by you, the '50s alumni.

Copyright© 1989
Turner Publishing Company

Information compiled and written by:
Fred Hensley

Fabulous Fifties book coordinator:
Lucinda F. Anderson

WKU Alumni Association Staff:
Jim Richards, Director
Ron Beck, Assistant Director
Lucinda F. Anderson, Reunion Coordinator

Created and designed by:
David A. Hurst, Publishing Consultant

This book may not be reproduced without the written consent of Turner Publishing Company.

Library of Congress Catalog Number: 89-50832

ISBN: 978-1-68162-236-1

Limited edition, 1989

Table of Contents

Dear Hilltopper of the Fabulous 50's:

It was a grand time to be at Western. From the class room to the dorms, to the soda fountain and the sock hops, we had fun as we prepared for life.

This book helps us relive those glorious times. It jogs our memories of people, places and events that meant so much to us.

I am proud to still be at Western directing the Alumni Affairs Office. It's still a wonderful place to be. I am also proud to be able to offer this book of memories to my colleagues.

Almost all the hundreds of photos in the book were sent in by you, alumni from the 50's. For this the Alumni Association and the university archives thanks you. The photos have been copied and placed in the archives since they had so few.

We had a difficult time deciding which pictures to use. There were so many exceptional ones. We tried to get a representative sample of the best ones. I am sure you will find yourself or someone you know as you look through the book.

As you read about the ballgames, beauty contests and class officers these people and events will pop back to the front of your mind. That's what this book is about—remembering a very important and influential period of our lives.

Well, that's enough from me. Thanks for your help with the book and thanks for the memories. Enjoy.

Sincerely,

Jim Richards

Jim Richards, Class of '54
Director, WKU Alumni Affairs

3

The Fabulous 50's

at Western

The 1950s represented growth, change and a renewed enthusiasm, not only on the campus of Western Kentucky State College, but on virtually every college campus in America.

It was the time of Rock 'n Roll, Thunderbirds, sock hops and juke boxes - it was known then and now simply as THE 50's.

Western Kentucky State College had risen from simple beginnings. Created by the Kentucky State Legislature in 1906 and incorporating the traditions of the Southern Normal School of Glasgow, Dr. Henry Hardin Cherry guided the development of the institution for its first 31 years.

During its development over more than 80 years, Western has made great strides in educating the citizens of the Commonwealth. Originally created as a teacher training institution, Western now is a multipurpose comprehensive university continuing to seek to expend its academic offerings.

No period in Western's past depicts the expansion and growth of the university better than the 1950s.

The college entered the decade under the leadership of Paul L. Garret, perhaps the least publicized period of any Western president. When Dr. Cherry died in 1937, there was much speculation among the faculty and citizens as to whom the successor would be.

Gov. A.B. (Happy) Chandler appointed Garrett who assumed the position saying "I know very well I cannot take his (Cherry) place...I simply want to do my best to carry on, and I hope I can do it in the manner he would want it done."

Though new at Western, Garrett was no stranger to the world of education. He had impressive credentials as a teacher. Appropriately for a leader, he started in a one-room school in Waddy and graduated from Shelbyville High School. He received his bachelor's degree in English and history and his master's degree in history and political science from

Georgetown College. He did post-graduate work at the University of Kentucky and the University of Chicago.

Garrett's presidency was marked by a lack of funds for expansion but as a period of continued dedication of purpose for Western.

Because of limited funds available for expansion, the physical appearance of the campus did not change greatly during Garrett's administration. The interior of VanMeter Hall was remodeled and the Kentucky Building and the music building were completed. McLean Hall was built for women's housing and Potter Hall was remodeled to serve as Western's first residence hall for men.

The building that now bears his name was opened during his administration in the fall of 1953. It was Garrett's plan to have a student union as a central meeting place on the campus - something that was lacking at Western up to that time.

During that same semester, Garrett suffered a paralytic stroke, which caused him to move his administrative work to his home. When he came back to his Van Meter Hall office during the spring of 1954, he fell and broke his hip. He died at his home on February 28, 1955.

While Garrett took Western through its most torturous times; through the post-Depression era of the late 1930s that sapped its resources, and a war in the 1940s that seriously jeopardized its student population, Dr. Kelly Thompson was president when the growth of the late '50s and 1960s took hold.

Thompson was appointed acting president when Garrett suffered a stroke in 1955. When Garrett died later that year, Thompson stepped into the President's office naturally, perhaps with little idea that the school he had worked for since 1929 was about to explode into a major institution.

Traditionally, Western had placed primary emphasis upon the needs of the individual student. From 1955-69, when the University experienced its most spectacular growth

Cherry Hall

and expansion, much care was taken to preserve this emphasis.

The Office of the Dean of Student Affairs was established in 1956. President Thompson initiated the first phase of student government at Western shortly after taking office 1955, calling the new organization the President's Student Advisory Council.

Enrollment soared on the Hill during the decade following President Thompson's election, and this growth was responsible for substantial changes in almost every phase of the institution's functions. The growth pattern was not unique to Western, but reflected a national trend that changed the face of higher education nationwide.

Reversing the decline in enrollment that began with the war years,

enrollment in 1955 started a dramatic climb that saw Western's headcount more than triple during the next decade. Enrollment in 1955 was 1,975 increasing to 2,161 in 1956, 2,351 in 1957, 2,546 in 1958, 2,917 in 1959 and 3,599 in 1960. As the 1960s began, Western had gained a prominent position in Kentucky higher education as the second largest state-supported university.

Thompson faced a major challenge early in his presidency as a result of the Supreme Court decision affecting integration. Kentucky's Day Law prevented the integration of schools for nearly half a century. However, that major challenge set the tone for the Thompson administration since the college was integrated without major incident and lingering effect.

Cafeteria capers after Saturday detail, Potter Hall. Kenneth Shore, Joe Jackson, Harold Phillips Virginia Arnold and Bill Faulkerson. April Fool's Day, 1950.

The Western Philosophy

Through the expansion and growth of the 1950s, Western never lost its direction or focus.

As stated by Dr. Henry Hardin Cherry, the Western's basic philosophy and principles are:

• To be a live school and to impart to its students a burning zeal to do and be something.

• To be progressive, to use modern methods and equipment, but reject all worthless educational fads.

• To let the reputation of the school be sustained by real merit.

• To seek recognition of the public to the extent the school deserves it.

• To fight against ignorance, and for higher education and the liberation of the human soul.

• To cooperate with all educational institutions that do honest work and bid them God speed in their efforts.

• To "ring the rising bell in the human soul" by inspiring all students who come in touch with the work of the institution.

• To teach that self-control is an imperative duty and the first great obligation that every person must fulfill, if he would succeed.

• To instill in the minds of the students the great truth that every person is created to do something, to be a producer.

• To teach students the power of earnestness and to warn them against all show and pretense.

• To make the school self-governing and to create a high moral sentiment among the pupils.

• To refuse to organize or permit the organization of any club or society that would foster care and destroy cooperation, but rather to teach that the good of one is the good of all.

• To recognize no aristocracy except that of work and character.

• To lead the student to understand that a broad and liberal education is essential to the highest degree of success in any endeavor of life and that unless he has a purpose in life and is willing to pursue it closely and courageously, he will fail.

• To lead students to see that success depends mainly upon his own efforts, and that he must discover the man in himself before he can become a being of power and influence.

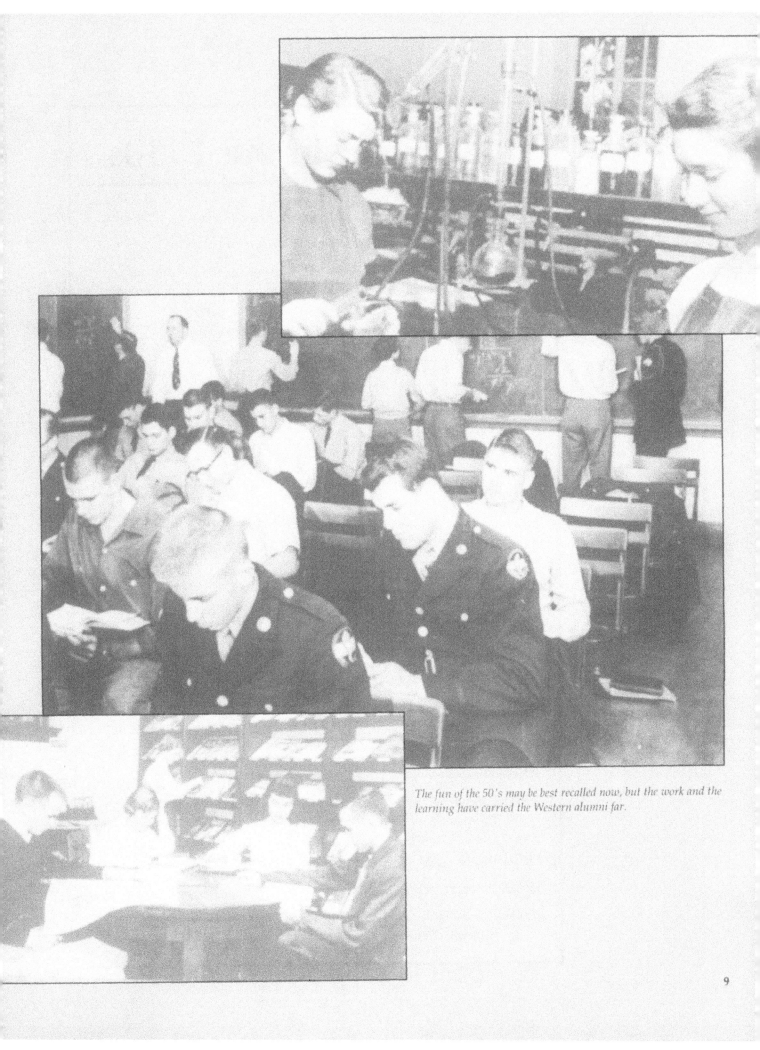

The fun of the 50's may be best recalled now, but the work and the learning have carried the Western alumni far.

9

Milestones in the 1950s

1950 Margaret Griffin first woman elected class president.

1952 Western defeats Arkansas State in Refrigerator Bowl.

1954 Dr. Stickles retires after 46 1/2 years as head of the Department of History, the longest tenure that Western has had for such a position and one of the nation's longest

1955 President Paul L. Garrett died.

1955 Kelly Thompson elected Western's third president.

1955 Fall enrollment - 1,648.

1955 Construction started on East and North Hall dormitories. Total cost, $260,000.

1956 Miss Margie Helm became Director of Library Services.

1956 3,000 high school seniors attended the first High School Senior Day since 1941.

1956 Senior class presented painting of Dr. Paul Garrett, by Mrs. Sara Peyton of Winter Park, Fla., to college.

1956 Student Advisory Council organized.

1956 Publication of Voices, literary magazine.

1956 First Summer Theatre Workshop held.

1956 Blacks eligible to enroll for the first time during summer session.

1956 Charles Keown appointed first Dean of Students.

1957 Baptist Student Center built.

1957 A contract was let for construction of Regents Hall (now Bates-Runner) at a cost of $600,000.

1957 TV sets installed in residence hall lounges.

1958 Coach E. A. Diddle was named Kentucky Press Association "Kentuckian of the Year".1958 - First formal use of the new electric organ in VanMeter Hall.

1958 Western gave credit for "Atomic Age Physics" TV course.

1959 Fall enrollment - 2,581.

1959 Coach Diddle won 700th game in the Sugar Bowl Tournament in New Orleans.

Friends

Memories of the Fabulous 50's at Western include many things, but the most enduring are friends.

Ann Duke and Cecil Schirtzinger

Birdie McCloud, Jeannie Warren, Pat Maestroleo, Betty Anne Dalton Bloss and friends at recess.

Clockwise from bottom: Bill Ploomis, Jim Sparks, Tony DeMarco, Bill Sanders and Jimmy Sacca

Western frosh, '53, in Chattanooga after initiation.

Ed Bridges, Bill Faulkerson, Gene Atkins, Virginia Arnold and Ruth Crews

Bill Stephens and Lynn Miller

Teddy Lou Johnson, Ina Thornbury, Mable Cheek, Dot Agew and Clara Ann____

Sunbathing beauties

Pat Cobb Strader and Barbara Morgan Rodgers

J. B. Sparks and Manuel Wilkerson

Waiting—a part of college life in the 50s.

Jacquetta Jackman, Mattie Mae Rherd and KatieToms.

Mister and Misses

1949-50

Mr. and Miss Senior - Arnold Robinson and Anne Ward Kleier

Mr. and Miss Junior - Bob Lavoy and Julia Smith

Mr. and Miss Sophomore - Jack Turner and Judy Pruett

Mr. and Miss Freshman - George Beard and Imogene Page

1950-51

Mr. and Miss Senior - Bob Lively and Wenonah White

Mr. and Miss Junior - John Q. Wesley and Sara Downing

Mr. and Miss Sophomore - Jim Olliges and Margie Berry

Mr. and Miss Freshman - Tom Marshall and Pat Horn

1951-52

Mr. and Miss Senior - Joe Kimbrough and Anne Hart Robey

Mr. and Miss Junior - Robert E. Simpson and Joan Curry

Mr. and Miss Sophomore - Bill Stephens and Tyler Diemer

Mr. and Miss Freshman - William C. Reynolds and Myra Mitchell

1952-53

Mr. and Miss Senior - Monie Beard and Betty Schroer

Mr. and Miss Junior - Bill Stephens and Tyler Diemer

Mr. and Miss Sophomore - Wallace Holleman and Lynn Miller

Mr. and Miss Freshman - Bill Jenkins and Jane Winchester

1953-54

Mr. and Miss Senior - Sam Fletcher and Helen Leet

Mr. and Miss Junior - Jim Callison and Lynn Miller

Mr. and Miss Sophomore - Scotty Carr and Jane Winchester

Mr. and Miss Freshman - Richard Knarr and Joyce Blackwelder

1954-55

Mr. and Miss Senior - Jack Sagabiel and Judy Koch

Mr. and Miss Junior - Bob Baggett and Mary Ligon Holloman

Mr. and Miss Sophomore - Wayne Duncan and Duraine Bailey

Mr. and Miss Freshman - Tony Fargnoli and Nita Chinn

1955-56

Mr. and Miss Senior - Jay Embry and Barbara Wilkins

Mr. and Miss Junior - Richard Knarr and Eva WIlson

Mr. and Miss Sophomore - Jim Owens and Martha Sue Fuqua

Mr. and Miss Freshman - Charles A. Miller and Marilyn Richards

1956-57

Mr. and Miss Senior - Paul Martin and Sally Reed

Mr. and Miss Junior - John Blair and Nancy Owen

Mr. and Miss Sophomore - Tom Emberton and Lady Henninger

Mr. and Miss Freshman - Fred Chelf and Jody Spradlyn

1957-58

Mr. and Miss Senior - Carroll VanHooser and Doris Havens

Mr. and Miss Junior - Delane Simpson and Marilyn Norris

Mr. and Miss Sophomore - Denny Wedge and Jo Ann Strange

Mr. and Miss Freshman - Fred Fish and Alice Chumbley

1958-59

Mr. and Miss Senior - Kenny Wright and Marilyn Norris

Mr. and Miss Junior - Tom Lynch and Bonne Drake

Mr. and Miss Sophomore - Tom Covington and Viola Jones

Mr. and Miss Freshman - Jack Poynter and Barbara Humphries

1959-60

Mr. and Miss Senior - Dan Brawner and Bonne Drake

Mr. and Miss Junior - Terry Ashbrook and Sandra Harrah

Mr. and Miss Sophomore - Carroll Harrison and Toby VanMeter

Mr. and Miss Freshman - Joe Burgess and Wanda Steenbergen

Mr. and Miss Senior, '59, Marilyn Norris and Kenny Wright

Mr. and Miss Freshman, '55, Ruthie Hutton and Harris Richardson

Queens of the 50's

Talisman Queen Mary Dean Pedigo being crowned by King Robert Simpson, '53

Mountain Laurel Queen Alice Chumbly, '58

Military Queens

1949-50 - Lou Nell Russell
1950-51 - Jean Amos
1951-52 - June Mitchell
1952-53 - Laura Stuart
1953-54 - Clara Lilly
1954-55 - Joan Graybruck
1955-56 - Jane Lovell
1956-57 - Michael Ann Ehret
1957-58 - Glenda Winn
1958-59 - Barbara Ann Humphries
1959-60 - Carolyn Turner

Talisman King and Queen

1949-50 Frank Cole and Betty Webb Cox
1950-51 John T. Johnson and Julia Smith
1951-52 Gene Rhodes and Sara Downing
1952-53 Robert Simpson and Mary Dean Pedigo
1953-54 Royce A Speck and Liz DeWitt
1954-55 Jerry Passafiume and Deborah Walters
1955-56 Jack Sagabiel and Jane Winchester
1956-57 Joe Cheatham and Dixie McGregor Duncan
1957-58 Owen Lawson and Sandra Fuqua Patterson
1958-59 Delane Simpson and Phyllis Robinson
1959-60 Jude Talbott and Rachel Chadwick Roll

Mountain Laurel Candidates

1949-50 - Dorothy Agnew
1950-51 - Julia Smith
1951-52 - Barbara Bates
1952-53 - Alice Allen
1953-54 - Kitty Buren
1954-55 - Sue Lynch
1955-56 - Margaret Pickens
1956-57 - Phyllis Dawn Robinson
1957-58 - Joann Faulkner
1958-59 - Alice Chumbley
1959-60 - Marilyn Ashby

Homecoming Queens

1949-50 - Teddy Johnson Bryant
1950-51 - Jean Amos
1951-52 - Nancy Atkinson
1952-53 - Tyler Diemer
1953-54 - Jane Winchester
1954-55 - Netta Oldham
1955-56 - Pattye Thompson
1956-57 - Shirley Barnes
1957-58 - Phyllis Robinson
1958-59 - Marilyn Norris
1959-60 - Alice Chumbley

Dorm Life

Sometimes we studied, sometimes we played, but we always had good times in those dorms.

Christmas Party, Third Floor, McLean Hall, '53

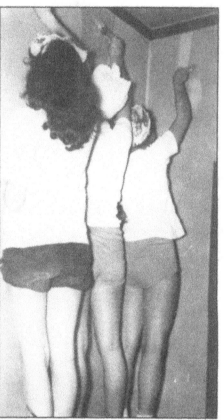

Renovating Potter Hall

Carol Cheal Mollyhorn studying in the Rock House, '54

Some members of the Red and Gray Orchestra performing for a Potter Hall party. Owen McPeek, David Livingston and Stan Grady.

Faye Weller, '57

McLean Hall's Fabulous Five—Joreen Hudson, Glenda Fowler, Judy Koch, Piatt Campbell and Anne Dawson

Privacy? Not in the dorm!

Margie Hina, '53

Potter Hall second floor gang

Nadine, Carol, Maxine and Peggy reading romance magazines.

Relaxing, a key to survival in the 50's

Coach Diddle, a Western legend, and Hardin McLane, '53 or '54

'57—Majorette Linda Newcomb and cheerleaders Rachel Chadwick and Alice Chumbly

'52-'53 band

Team spirit

Athletics

in the Fabulous 50's

Athletics played a major role in the resurgence of Western after World War II. Coach E.A. Diddle guided the Hilltopper basketball team through a glory-filled 1950s embellishing his reputation and the institution's image.

Between 1946-47 and 1953-54 the Hilltoppers won 202 games while losing only 40, an impressive 83.5 percent winning percentage. Diddle waved his red towel and he led the 1949-50 team to unreached heights. That team was the first to average 70 points per game and the 1952-53 team reached an 82.2 scoring mark.

The Hilltoppers played in the prestigious National Invitation Tournament in 1950, 1952, 1953 and 1954. Western teams annually made an eastern tour with regular season games scheduled in New York City, Washington, Philadelphia and other media centers. Coach Diddle's teams were usually ranked high in the national polls and their style of play pleased crowds wherever they went.

Bob Lavoy (1950), Rip Gish (1951), Tom Marshall and Art Spoelstra (1953), Tom Marshall (1954) and Ralph Crosthwaite (1958) received All-America status during the decade. The All-Ohio Valley Conference team included Johnny Givens and Lavoy (1950), Gish (1951), Marshall, Gene Rhodes, Art Spoelstra and Richard White (1952), Marshall and Spoelstra (1953), Lynn Cole, Marshall, Spoelstra and Jack Turner (1954), Forest Able and Ralph Crosthwaite (1955), and Crossthwaite (1958 and 1959).

Football played a prominent role in the 1950s as Coach Jack Clayton's team posted an 8-1 record in in 1952 and led by quarterback Jimmy Feix, defeated Arkansas State 34-19 in the Refrigerator Bowl in Evansville. Nick Denes assumed the football coaching spot in 1957.

Jimmy Feix (1952) and Jim "Yogi" Hardin (1957) earned All-America honors on the gridiron during the decade and more than a dozen players were named to the All-Ohio Valley Conference team including Hoyte Threet and Roy Hina (1950), Marvin Satterly, Lawrence Gilbert and Jimmy Feix (1951), R. E. Simpson, Satterly, Feix, Gene McFadden and Max Stevens (1952), Bill Ploumis, Satterly, Arnie Oaken, McFadden, and Stevens (1953), Walt Apperson and Tom Patterson (1954), Vernon Wilson and Bill Strawn (1955), Bill Holt and Jim "Yogi" Hardin (1957), Larry Nutter and Hardin (1958) and Herb Wassom (1959).

Football

1949-50

Louisville 47, Western 7
Evansville 20, Western 0
Western 19, Morehead State 0
Western 20, Union (Tenn.) 7
Western 20, Howard 0
Western 13, Georgetown (Ky.) 6
Delta State 13, Western 7
Eastern Kentucky 20, Western 7
Western 10, Murray State 7

1950-51

Western 13, Howard 0
Western 7, Evansville 7
Marshall 47, Western 13
Western 23, Morehead State 21
Western 41, Georgetown (Ky.) 13
Western 21, Tennessee Tech 0
Western 26, Delta State 7
Western 14, Eastern Kentucky 13
Western 27, Murray State 27
Stetson 41, Western 14

1951-52

Western 56, Bethel (Tenn.) 0
Western 41, Evansville 7
Marshall 35, Western 21
Western 20, Morehead State 7
Tennessee Tech 14, Western 7
Memphis State 38, Western 0
Western 46, Delta State 6
Eastern Kentucky 31, Western 7
Murray State 23, Western 6

1952-53

Western 33, Middle Tennessee 19
Western 39, Evansville 0
Western 39, Morehead State 7
Western 42, NE Louisiana 27
Tennessee Tech 21, Western 13
Western 35, Delta State 13
Western 48, Eastern Kentucky 6
Western 41, SE Missouri 0
Western 12, Murray State 7

REFRIGERATOR BOWL
Western 34, Arkansas State 19

1953-54

Middle Tennessee 13, Western 0
Western 32, East Tennessee 13
Stetson 18, Western 7
Western 48, Morehead State 0
Western 28, NE Louisiana 0
Tennessee Tech 34, Western 21
Western 21, Delta State 19

Eastern Kentucky 13, Western 7
Western 26, Evansville 13
Western 13, Murray State 7

1954-55

Western 32, Wittenberg 13
Western 24, East Tennessee 6
Western 7, Middle Tennessee 6
Western 19, Morehead State 13
Western 19, NE Louisiana 7
Western 32, Tennessee Tech 12

John "KoKo" Richardson and Ronnie Holtzweld

Western 25, Louisville 7
Eastern Kentucky 21, Western 0
Evansville 21, Western 13
Murray State 19, Western 0

1955-56

Western 20, East Tennessee 7
Middle Tennessee 25, Western 13
Western 12, Morehead State 7
NE Louisiana 21, Western 9
Tennessee Tech 19, Western 7
Louisville 20, Western 0
Eastern Kentucky 7, Western 0
Western 46, Evansville 6
Murray State 28, Western 12

1956-57

Western 12, East Tennessee 7
Middle Tennessee 7, Western 6
Western 26, Youngstown 9
Tennessee Tech 39, Western 26
Western 14, Eastern Kentucky 6
Memphis State 42, Western 0
Western 9, Morehead State 7
Western 14, Mississippi College 0
Murray State 34, Western 13

1957-58

Western 25, SE Missouri 20
Western 10, East Tennessee 6
Middle Tennessee 26, Western 7
Western 9, Youngstown 6
Tennessee Tech 27, Western 9
Eastern Kentucky 28, Western 0
Western 28, Morehead State 6
Western 28, Wittenberg 13
Western 7, Murray State 7

1958-59

Western 12, SE Missouri 0
East Tennessee 8, Western 0
Middle Tennessee 10, Western 7
Youngstown 20, Western 6
Tennessee Tech 7, Western 3

A tackle in '51

Western 21, Eastern Kentucky 14
Western 14, Morehead State 0
Western 34, Austin Peay 16
Murray State 12, Western 7

1959-60

Louisville 19, Western 0
Western 13, SE Missouri 8

East Tennessee 13, Western 7
Middle Tennessee 37, Western 2
Western 20, Austin Peay 12
Tennessee Tech 29, Western 19
Western 14, Eastern Kentucky 7
Western 27, Morehead State 14
Western 21, Murray State 6

Bill Ploomis, Marvin Satterly and Willy Watson

'53 managers—Lowell Stewart, Sterling Clark, John Garnett, John Richardson.

'57 football team before leaving Florida

Football Lettermen

Don Anderson - 1957-59
Walt Apperson - 1951-54
Jim Aurs - 1953-54
Rod Bagby - 1955-58
Norval Baird - 1956-57
Clarence Baker - 1956-59
Kenny Barrett - 1954-57
Sonny Berthold - 1953-55
Bob Bilyeu - 1950-53
Jack Binkley - 1951-52
Owen Blanton - 1949-51
William Bogdon - 1950
Billy Booker - 1958-61
Winton Boone - 1959-61
Bob Bradford - 1956-59
Jerry Brantley - 1954-56
Jerry Brewer - 1955-58
Dave Browning - 1955, 1959-60
Gary Brunson - 1959-61
Jim Chambliss - 1953-56
Don Chapman - 1950-52
Bob Clark - 1955-56
Sterling Clark, (mgr.) - 1953
Henry Cowan - 1947-50
Fred Culley - 1952-53
Joe Cunningham - 1954-57
Thomas Curley - 1959-60
Bill Curry - 1956-58
Jim Dailey - 1959-62
David Davidson - 1949-50
Charles Davis - 1954
Buddy Dixon - 1953
Ronnie Downard - 1957-60
Leon Dunagan - 1954-56
Wayne Duncan - 1954-56
Robert Elmer - 1949-51
Jimmy Feix - 1949-52
Fred Fish - 1957
Tom Fry - 1955-58
Robert Gerard - 1954
Lawrence "Butch" Gilbert - 1948-51
Melvin Gilbert, (mgr.) - 1959
John Gill - 1950
Gene Glod - 1947-50
Joe Goodman - 1950-53
Albert Green - 1947-50
Billy Griffin, (mgr.) - 1951
Kenneth Griffin - 1955-58
Jim Gunnell - 1952-54
Jim Hale - 1951
Jim "Yogi" Hardin - 1955-58

Joe Hardy - 1951-52
Roy Hina - 1948-50
Mark Hoffard - 1955-58
Billy Joe Holt - 1955-57
Ronnie Holzknecht - 1950-53
Jim Hughes - 1958-61
John Allen Hughes - 1954
Jack Jewell - 1958-59
Eddie Johnson - 1954-55
Jackie Johnson - 1953-56
Keen Johnson - 1959-61
Lewis Johnson - 1957-60
Larry Jones - 1957-58
Wayne Kelly - 1958
Billy Kinslow - 1954
John Lanier - 1949-50
Bill Lapadula - 1957-58
Buck Lawson - 1956, 1958
Ralph Madison - 1954-55
Leo Magers - 1948-49, 1951
Warren Mahan - 1950, 1952
Denny McAtee - 1959-61
James McChesney - 1950-51
Gene McFadden - 1950-53
Billy Meadors - 1957-59
David Miller - 1957-59
James Mitchell - 1956
Mike Moriarty - 1953-56
Doug Mumford - 1957-60
Lloyd Nash - 1959-60, 1962
Guy Newcom - 1950-52
Charles Newton - 1957
Larry Nutter - 1956-59
Ray Nutter - 1950-53
Arnie Oaken - 1952-54
Robert Osborne - 1949-50
Jerry Passafiume - 1951-54
Tom Patterson - 1952-54
Twyman Patterson - 1954-57
David Patton - 1952-55
Francis Payne - 1957-60
Bill Pegalusch - 1957-58, 1960
Frank Pettet - 1957-58
Jim Phifer - 1952-54
Bill Ploumis - 1950-53
Gerald Poynter - 1957-60
Jack Poynter - 1958-61
Willard Price - 1949-52
Ernest Rautter, (mgr.) - 1959
Ted Revack - 1955-56
Gene Robinson - 1953-54

Otho Robinson - 1950
Nelson Rue - 1950-51
Jimmy Sacca - 1950
Whitey Sanders - 1952-53
Marvin Satterly - 1950-53
George Sauer - 1950-53
Cecil Schirtzinger - 1950-51
Ronnie Sheffer - 1958-59
Millard Shirley - 1953-54
Sam Short - 1950-51
Delane Simpson - 1955-58
Robert "Bub" Simpson - 1949-52
Bill Smith - 1950
Don Sparks - 1951-54
Carroll Speer - 1953-56
Max Stevens - 1950-53
Lowell Stewart - 1950-52
Bill Strawn - 1953-56
Joe Talley - 1947-50
Bill Tate - 1950-53
Ed Tarter - 1957
Charles Taylor - 1958
Jack Theuerkauf - 1952, 1957-59
Hoyte Threet - 1947-50
William Underhill - 1959-60
Carroll Van Hooser - 1954-57
David Van Hooser - 1956-57
Melvin Vogel - 1958-59
Jack Waff - 1959-60
Mickey Walker, (mgr.) - 1958
Robert Wallace - 1953
Gordon Ware - 1951-52
Herb Wassom - 1957-60
Willie Watson - 1950-52
Lloyd Weaver - 1957-59
Raymond Weaver - 1950, 1955-57
Denny Wedge - 1956-59
Jerry Wilder - 1958-59
Vernon Wilson - 1952-55
Ed Worley - 1952-53
Bob Young - 1957-58

Jimmy Feix

Homecoming

A packed stadium in '53

'53 cheerleaders

Rock House decorations , '53

Frank Wallace was cagey in '51

"We Take Thee Tech"

Potter Hall float, '51

Reaching for the sky, '54-'55

1958 Cheerleaders

Hard play shows on the faces

Basketball

1949-50

Western 58, Morehead State 47
Western 89, Kentucky Wesleyan 45
Western 78, Bowling Green State 57
Western 59, Xavier 57
Western 67, Georgetown (Ky.) 48
Cincinnati 55, Western 54
Western 74, Canisius 61
Long Island 73, Western 66
La Salle 80, Western 69
Western 86, Eastern Ky. 61
Western 63, Xavier 51
Louisville 70, Western 59
Western 58, Murray State 52
Western 84, Cincinnati 59
Western 73, Evansville 69
Western 69, Eastern Ky. 51
Western 66, Miami (Fla.) 61
Western 78, Miami (Fla.) 61
Western 79, Tampa 59
Western 84, Louisville 62
Western 77, Morehead State 65
Western 103, Bowling Green State 87
Western 54, Murray State 50
Western 79, Miami (Fla.) 57
Western 83, Miami (Fla.) 47
Western 81, Evansville 56

OVC TOURNAMENT
Western 79, Tennessee Tech 60
Western 58, Murray State 54
Eastern Ky. 62, Western 50

NIT
Western 79, Niagara 72
St. John's (NY) 69, Western
(25-6)

1950-51

NAT'L CAMPUS TOURNAMENT

Bradley 75, Western 71

Western 73, SE Louisiana 59
Western 93, Georgetown (Ky.) 44
Cincinnati 70, Western 45
Western 74, West Texas St. 46

Western 103, Tampa 70
Western 77, High Point 64
Morehead State 70, Western 64
Western 73, La Salle 63
Long Island 77, Western 70
St. Bonaventure 62, Western 57
Western 79, Xavier 62
Western 75, Evansville 63
Western 65, Murray State 56
Western 89, Miami (Fla.) 47
Evansville 77, Western 46
Western 69, Bowling Green St. 68
Western 68, Miami (Fla.) 64
Western 67, Tampa 64
Eastern Ky. 84, Western 70
Western 75, Cincinnati 70
Murray State 77, Western 70
Western 86, Kentucky Wesleyan 62
Western 84, Eastern Kentucky 80
Western 95, Morehead State 73
Xavier 67, Western 64
Western 78, Bowling Green State 77

OVC TOURNAMENT

Murray State 78, Western 77
Western 72, Evansville 71
(19-10)

1951-52

Western 77, SE Louisiana 57
Western 89, Tennessee Tech 62
Western 69, Evansville 56
Western 89, Bowling Green State 57
Western 65, Morehead State 54
Western 76, Cincinnati 71
Western 76, Central Missouri 56
Western 92, Xavier 82
St. Bonaventure 73, Western 60
La Salle 67, Western 58
Seton Hall 77, Western 65
Western 77, Murray State 64
Western 64, Tennessee Tech 55
Western 69, Eastern Kentucky 63
Western 102, Miami (Fla.) 74
Western 82, Tampa 77
Western 79, Cincinnati 63

Western 76, Marshall 65
Western 80, Morehead State 72
Western 79, Tampa 70
Eastern Kentucky 73, Western 62
Western 87, Marshall 82
Western 97, Murray State 63
Western 92, Evansville 58
Western 94, Kentucky Wesleyan 68
Western 82, Bowling Green State 75

OVC TOURNAMENT
Western 83, Evansville 63
Western 89, Marshall 74
Western 47, Murray State 45

NIT
Western 62, Louisville 59
St. Bonaventure 70, Western 69
(26-5)

1952-53

Western 76, Kentucky Wesleyan 62
Western 87, Middle Tennessee 57
Western 56, Morehead State 33
Western 79, Morehead State 66
Western 77, Cincinnati 76
Seton Hall 77, Western 74
Western 88, St. Joseph's (Pa.) 83

ALL-COLLEGE TOURNAMENT
Idaho 75, Western 60
Western 79, Tulsa 70
Western 91, Penn State 78

Western 94, St. Bonaventure 63
Western 84, Cincinnati 76
Western 62, Murray State 57
Western 99, Tennessee Tech 61
Eastern Kentucky 78, Western 69
Western 98, Miami (Fla.) 56
Western 84, Loyola (La.) 75
Western 117, Tampa 58
Western 104, Tampa 56
Western 71, Bowling Green State 60
Western 88, Dayton 77
Western 86, Eastern Kentucky 76
Western 92, Loyola (La.) 67
Murray State 77, Western 67
Western 95, Middle Tennessee 57

Western 74, Tennessee Tech 61
Western 108, Kentucky Wesleyan 69
Bowling Green State 86, Western 82

OVC TOURNAMENT
Western 76, Morehead State 65
Western 70, Eastern Kentucky 60

NIT
Duquesne 69, Western 61
(25-6)

1953-54

Western 108, Belmont 75
Western 86, Kentucky Wesleyan 74
Western 90, Gustavus Adolphus 73
Western 84, SE Louisiana 60
Western 88, Middle Tennessee 80
Western 98, Morehead State 77
Western 74, Cincinnati 71
Western 78, St. Francis (NY) 55
Western 82, St. Bonaventure 76

KIT
Western 91, Houston 61
Western 81, Eastern Kentucky 78
Western 89, Louisville 71

Western 98, Middle Tennessee 67
Western 57, Murray State 43
Western 79, Dayton 75
Western 122, Eastern Kentucky 78
Western 62, Tennessee Tech 51
Western 63, Memphis State 53
Western 87, Regis 72
Western 94, Bowling Green State 82
Western 81, Stetson 63
Eastern Kentucky 63, Western 54
Western 88, Morehead State 75
Western 104, Murray State 68
Western 81, Kentucky Wesleyan 65
Western 108, Tennessee Tech 63
Western 92, Cincinnati 77

OVC TOURNAMENT
Western 97, Morehead State 79
Western 85, Eastern Kentucky 69

NIT
Western 95, Bowling Green State 81
Holy Cross 75, Western 69
Niagara 71, Western 65
(29-3)

1954-55

Western 90, Gustavus Adolphus 78
Morehead State 89, Western 79
Seton Hall 98, Western 85
LeMoyne 77, Western 75
Western 85, Cincinnati 75
Western 75, Colorado State 67
Western 86, Pacific 65

KIT
Eastern Kentucky 84, Western 81
Western 98, Murray State 89

Western 89, Brigham Young 78
Western 83, Middle Tennessee 71
Western 71, Murray State 70
Xavier 82, Western 80
Middle Tennessee 84, Western 77
Western 84, Eastern Kentucky 78
Dayton 91, Western 73
Western 81, Tennessee Tech 73
Western 89, Bowling Green State 69
Cincinnati 101, Western 92
Dayton 73, Western 67
Western 98, Eastern Kentucky 76
Western 80, Tennessee Tech 68
Western 85, Murray State 80
Western 71, Oklahoma City 59
Western 75, Xavier 72
Western 96, Morehead State 75

OVC TOURNAMENT
Western 80, Tennessee Tech 65
Murray State 77, Western 72
(18-10)

1955-56

Western 89, Gustavus Adolphus 62
Alabama 90, Western 85
Seton Hall 87, Western 85
Cincinnati 83, Western 54
Tulsa 67, Western 56
Oklahoma City 92, Western 87

KIT
Western 76, Ohio University 60
Western 86, Louisville 77
Murray State 74, Western 69

Western 73, Xavier 72
Western 88, Murray State 77
Memphis State 80, Western 64
Western 66, Midwestern 65
Western 73, Eastern Kentucky 67
Kentucky Wesleyan 70, Western 66
Western 86, Morehead State 80
Tennessee Tech 101, Western 79
Western 86, Middle Tennessee 78
Western 70, Bowling Green State 57
Western 93, Eastern Kentucky 92
Murray State 74, Western 70

Western 74, Xavier 65
Western 85, Cincinnati 74
Morehead State 73, Western 72
Western 86, Tennessee Tech 75
Western 100, Middle Tennessee 85

OVC PLAYOFF
Western 84, Tennessee Tech 80
Morehead State 84, Western 80
(16-12)

1956-57

Western 94, Gustavus Adolphus 55
Western 90, Kentucky Wesleyan 72
Western 95, New Mexico A&M 74
Seton Hall 78, Western 69
Western 61, San Francisco 57

ORANGE BOWL
Western 89, LaSalle 76
Pittsburgh 85, Western 81
Western 76, Stanford 66

Xavier 87, Western 79
Western 90, Murray State 78
Oklahoma City 85, Western 78
Western 91, Eastern Kentucky 71
Western 88, Tennessee Tech 74
Western 80, DePaul 76
Western 79, Middle Tennessee 72
Western 75, Eastern Kentucky 70
Memphis State 86, Western 84
Western 60, Murray State 58
Oklahoma City 96, Western 67
Western 82, Wichita 76
Western 97, Morehead State 81
Morehead State 87, Western 81
Memphis State 98, Western 82
Western 96, Tennessee Tech 85
Xavier 77, Western 71
Western 86, Middle Tennessee 82
(17-9)

1957-58

Evansville 105, Western 98
Western 85, East Tennessee 60
Western 101, Morehead State 70
Western 92, Hardin-Simmons 60
Western 101, Seton Hall 75

ALL-COLLEGE TOURNAMENT
Niagara 77, Western 74
Denver 84, Western 63
Western 78, Tulane 72

Murray State 57, Western 55
Western 70, Oklahoma City 56
Western 89, Eastern Kentucky 80
Tennessee Tech 84, Western 75

Richard White tosses in a winner, '53-'54

Xavier 102, Western 76
Western 69, Middle Tennessee 67
Western 83, Bowling Green State 65
Oklahoma City 67, Western 59
Western 96, Wichita 85
Western 77, DePaul 62
Western 70, Murray State 64
Tennessee Tech 85, Western 73
Morehead State 75, Western 60
Middle Tennessee 81, Western 75
Western 100, Eastern Kentucky 70
Western 100, Evansville 80
Xavier 100, Western 91
(14-11)

1958-59

Western 79, New Mexico A&M 60
Western 80, Mississippi Sou 56
Morehead State 86, Western 78
Seton Hall 73, Western 67
La Salle 84, Western 76
Western 76, Eastern Kentucky 73
Tennessee Tech 81, Western 73
Bowling Green State 76, Western 61
Western 86, East Tennessee 84
Western 87, Murray State 77
Western 89, Middle Tennessee 65
West Virginia 74, Western 72
Western 96, La Salle 74
Western 83, Tampa 64
Miami (Fla.) 109, Western 95
DePaul 80, Western 70
Western 94, Army 73
Tennessee Tech 83, Western 74
Western 89, Tampa 57
Western 88, Morehead State 74
Western 94, Xavier 67

Eastern Kentucky 72, Western 70
Western 75, Murray State 62
Western 82, Xavier 73
Western 110, Middle Tennessee 85
Western 84, East Tennessee 64
(16-10)

1959-60

Western 123, Union (Tenn.) 71
Western 89, NW Louisiana 60
Western 78, Seton Hall 69
Illinois 93, Western 80
Western 70, Morehead State 68
Western 103, East Tennessee 77

SUGAR BOWL TOURNAMENT
Western 61, Mississippi State 50
Western 71, Tulane 67

Western 86, DePaul 65
Eastern Kentucky 80, Western 73
Western 71, Tennessee Tech 67
Murray State 87, Western 72
Xavier 76, Western 66
Western 85, Bowling Green State 61
Marshall 100, Western 97
Western 76, La Salle 70
Western 109, Middle Tennessee 89
Xavier 82, Western 73
Western 85, Morehead State 72
Western 38, Eastern Kentucky 20
Western 65, Murray State 57
Western 85, Tennessee Tech 81
Western 109, Middle Tennessee 80
Western 69, Kent State 60
Western 83, East Tennessee 69

NCAA TOURNAMENT
Western 107, Miami (Fla.) 84
Ohio State 98, Western 79
Western 97, Ohio University 87
(21-7)

Basketball Lettermen

Forest Able - 1954-56
Alvin Almond (mgr.) - 1949-50
Eric Back - 1956-58
Monie Beard - 1951-52
Darrell Bicknell - 1958-60
Bernard Brantley - 1959, 1961
Billy Case - 1956-58
Buddy Cate - 1948-50
Ronnie Clark - 1955-57
Lynn Cole - 1953-55
Ralph Crosthwaite - 1955, 57-59

Billy Curry - 1957
Bob Daniels - 1954-57
Bill Delk (mgr.) - 1952
Eddie Diddle - 1949-51
Al Ellison - 1958-60
Rip Gish - 1949-51
Johnny Givens - 1948-50
Kay Greer - 1952-54
Montroe Holland - 1955-56
Joe David Johnson - 1945-46, 1950
Forbis Jordan (mgr.) - 1949-50
Dan King - 1952-54
Owen Lawson - 1956-58
Bob Lavoy - 1948-50
Tom Marshall - 1951-54
John McClearn - 1956-58
Bobby McGuire - 1949-50
Don McGuire - 1949-50
Hardin McLane (mgr.) - 1953-56
Pat Mezzanotte - 1949-50
Dencil Miller - 1954-55
Chester Montgomery - 1956-57
George Orr - 1956
Charlie Osborne - 1959-61
Don Parson - 1959-61
Gene Rhodes - 1949-52
Panny Sarakatsannie - 1958-60
Bill Scott - 1949-50
Dick Smith - 1951-53
Art Spoelstra - 1952-54
Jude Talbott - 1958-60
Jack Turner - 1949-51, 1954
Dyke Vest - 1951-53
Frank Wallheiser - 1950-51
George Warren - 1959, 1961
Richard White - 1951-53
Jerry Whitsell - 1954-55
Kenneth Wright (mgr.) - 1958-59

Coach Diddle

Alice Chumbly, basketball queen, on Senior Day, '58 with Hilltoppers Eric Black, Billy Case and Owen Lawson

Class Officers

1949-50

Senior Class
President - Fred D. Barlow
Vice President - Billy D. Adams
Secretary - Betty Webb Cox
Treasurer - Arthur Anderson
Sergeant-At-Arms - Alvin Almond
Sponsor - Dr. Earl A. Moore

Junior Class
President - Bob Lavoy
Vice President - Tom Redford
Secretary - LaVerne Van Cleave
Treasurer - Julia Smith, Owensboro
Sergeant-At-Arms - Hal Taylor
Sponsor - Dr. H. L. Stephens

Sophomore Class
President - Margaret Griffin
Vice President - Joe Kimbrough
Secretary - Judy Pruett
Treasurer - Sara Downing
Sergeant-At-Arms - Dewey Smith
Sponsor - C. A. Loudermilk

Freshman Class
President - George Beard
Vice President - David Davison
Secretary - Alma Penick
Treasurer - Don Walker
Sergeant-At-Arms - Allen Philpott
Sponsor - E.H. Canon

1950-51

Senior Class
President - Bill Dolan
Vice President - John T. Johnson
Secretary - LaVerne Van Cleave
Treasurer - Wenonah White
Sergeant-At-Arms - Stanley Grady
Sponsor - Earl A. Moore

Junior Class
President - Margaret Griffin
Vice President - John Quentin Wesley
Secretary - Rosemary Johnson
Treasurer - Claude Pickard
Sergeant-At-Arms - Eurie Wallace
Sponsor - H. L. Stephens

Sophomore Class
President - Jim Olliges
Vice President - Margie Berry
Secretary - Mary Lou Rogers
Treasurer - Gene Croft
Sergeant-At-Arms - Richard White

Sponsor - Charles A. Loudermilk

Freshman Class
President - Tom Marshall
Vice President - Bobby Bilyeu
Secretary - Patricia Patterson
Treasurer - Jewell Dennison
Sergeant-At-Arms - Carroll Elliott
Sponsor - E. H. Canon

1951-52

Senior Class
President - Margaret Griffin
Vice President - Gene Rhodes
Secretary - Anne Hart Robey
Treasurer - Betty Jo Clifton
Sergeant-At-Arms - Maurice Hale
Sponsor - Joe Howard

Junior Class
President - Robert E. Simpson
Vic President - Jerry Cohron
Secretary - Nancy Atkinson
Treasurer - Betty Ann Schroer
Reporter - Macon Ray
Sponsor - Dr. H. L. Stephens

Sophomore Class
President - Bill Griffin
Vice President - Tyler Diemer
Secretary - Nadyne Ryle
Treasurer - Helen Leet
Sergeant-At-Arms - Douglas LaNeave
Sponsor - Charles Keown

Freshman Class
President - William C. Reynolds
Vice President - Billy Joe Wilson
Secretary - Ruth Mulins
Treasurer - Albert Feix
Sergeant-At-Arms - Gordon Ware
Sponsor - E. H. Canon

1952-53

Senior Class
President - William E. Bivin
Vice President - James Olliges
Secretary - Nancy Atkinson
Treasurer - Betty Schroer

Junior Class
President - Bill Stephens
Vice President - Tyler Diemer
Secretary - Helen Leet
Treasurer - Paul Koenen
Sergeant-At-Arms - Dan King

Reporter - Lois Harmon

Sophomore Class
President - Wallace Holleman
Vice President - Tony Robert DeMarco
Secretary - Lynn Miller
Treasurer - Gay Lorraine Lively
Sergeant-At-Arms - Sterling Pitts Clark

Freshman Class
President - Stanley Street
Vice President - Van T. Vance
Secretary - Charlotte Smith
Treasurer - Ellen O'Keefe
Sergeant-At-Arms - Jim Robey

1953-54

Senior Class
President - Bill Stephens
Vice President - Tom Corum
Secretary - Elizabeth DeWitt
Treasurer - Martha Gray

Junior Class
President - Jim Callison
Vice President - Lynn Miller
Secretary - Jean Akin
Treasurer - Felix Schneider
Sergeant-At-Arms - Sterling Clark

Sophomore Class
President - Lacy Wilkins
Vice President - Virgil Vertrees
Secretary - Mary Ligon Holloman
Treasurer - Shelly Hampton
Sergeant-At-Arms - Spero Kereiakes

Freshman Class
President - Richard Knarr
Vice President - Lynn Habacker
Secretary - Tom Watson
Treasurer - Elaine Carroll
Sergeant-At-Arms - Wayne Duncan

1954-55

Senior Class
President - Jimmy Daniel
Vice President - Bill Bell
Secretary - Patty Harrah
Treasurer - Owen Arnold
Sponsor - Lisle Sherrill

Junior Class
President - Lacy Wilkins
Vice President - Naomi Jones
Secretary - Jane Winchester

Treasurer - Margaret Pickens
Social Chairman - Joan Graybruck
Sponsor - H. L. Stephens

Sophomore Class
President - Dewey Bratcher
Vice President - Victor Harned
Secretary - Pattye Thompson
Treasurer - Bob Daniels
Sergeant-At-Arms - Lynn Habacker
Social Chairman - Mary Way Drew
Sponsor - Charles Keown

Freshman Class
President - Jim Owens
Vice President - Charles Roberts
Secretary - Shirley Barnes
Treasurer - Jeanne Jones
Sergeant-At-Arms - Bill Jacobsen
Sponsor - E. H. Canon

1955-56

Senior Class
President - Bobby Hensley
First Vice President - Jack Sagabiel
Second Vice President - Maurice Utley
Secretary - Mary Ligon Holloman
Treasurer - Ann Williams
Sponsor - Mr. Lisle Sherrill

Junior Class
President - Harry Gray
Vice President - Bill Short
Secretary - Joyce Wood
Treasurer - Doris Farris
Sergeant-At-Arms - Paul Martin
Sponsor - Dr. H. L. Stephens

Sophomore Class
President - Jim Owens
Vice President - Julius Rather
Secretary - Shirley Barnes
Treasurer - Martha Sue Fuqua
Sergeant-At-Arms - Owen Lawson
Sponsor - Charles Keown

Freshman Class
President - Charles Miller
Vice President - Jimmy Hardin
Secretary - Wanda Pack
Treasurer - Marilyn Richards
Sergeant-At-Arms - Bobby Pace
Sponsor - E. H. Canon

1956-57

Senior Class
President - Harry Gray
First Vice President - Paul Martin
Second Vice President - Wayne Duncan

Secretary - Shirley Barnes
Treasurer - Jeanette Yohe
Sponsor - Lisle Sherrill

Junior Class
President - Jim Owens
First Vice President - Gregg O'Neil
Second Vice President - John Blair
Secretary - Jane Lovell
Treasurer - Martha Sue Fuqua
Sergeant-At-Arms - Ray Weaver
Sponsor - Dr. H. L. Stephens

Sophomore Class
President - Tom Emberton
Vice President - Al Crowder
Secretary - Patricia Pulliam
Treasurer - Ronnie Jones
Sergeant-At-Arms - Mike Hook
Sponsor - Hugh Johnson

Freshman Class
President - Fred Chelf
Vice President - Tom Lynch
Secretary - Shirley Shields
Treasurer - Anna Stiefrater
Sergeant-At-Arms - Ken Hightower
Sponsor - E. H. Canon

1957-58

Senior Class
President - Greg O'Neil
Vice President - Carroll VanHooser
Secretary - Carole Snyder Walker
Treasurer - Sandra Fuqua Patterson
Sponsor - Lisle Sherrill

Junior Class
President - Tom Emberton
Vice President - John Earl Schneider
Treasurer - Allen Hilsmeier
Secretary - Glenda Winn
Sergeant-At-Arms - Hardin Thompson
Sponsor - Dr. H. L. Stephens

Sophomore Class
President - Tom Lynch
Vice President - Dan Brawner
Secretary - Mary Ruth Grise
Treasurer - Rachel Chadwick
Sergeant-At-Arms - Chapman Burnett
Sponsor - Hugh Johnson

Freshman Class
President - Roger Davis
Vice President - Henry "Buddy" Messer
Secretary - Alice Chumbley
Treasurer - Elizabeth Wheeler
Sergeant-At-Arms - Shelby West
Sponsor - E. H. Canon

1958-59

Senior Class
President - Chester Montgomery
Vice President - Junior Wortham
Secretary - LaDonna Thrapp
Treasurer - Marilyn Norris
Sponsor - Lisle Sherill

Junior Class
President - Mary Ruth Grise
Vice President - Rachael Chadwick
Secretary - Pat Stiff
Sergeant-At-Arms - Dan Brawner
Sponsor - Dr. H. L. Stephens

Sophomore Class
President - Tom Covington
Vice President - Sandy Harrah
Secretary - Alice Chumbley
Treasurer - Diana DiOrio
Sergeant-At-Arms - Francis Payne

Freshman Class
President - Richard Turner
Vice President - Carol McCormack
Secretary - Anna Jo Brown
Treasurer - Clarice O. Brown
Parliamentarian - Joan Terry Ray
Sponsor - E. H. Canon

1959-60

Senior Class
President - Ronnie Sheffer
Vice President - William McCoy
Secretary - Bonne Drake
Treasurer - Louie Guthrie
Sponsor - Lisle Sherrill

Junior Class
President - Tom Covington
Vice President - Minnie Lou Toll
Secretary - Alice Chumbley
Treasurer - Dianne DiOrio
Sergeant-At-Arms - Ray Sutherland
Sponsor - Dr. H. L. Stephens

Sophomore Class
President - Pat Richards
Vice President - Roberta Johnson
Secretary - Martha Johnson
Treasurer - Dianne Robinson
Sergeant-At-Arms - Dennie McAtee
Sponsor - Hugh F. Johnson

Freshman Class
President - Norman Childs
Vice President Joe Burgess
Secretary - Dianne Winkler
Treasurer - J. Marshall Hughes
Sponsor - Dero Downing

Music

The band entertained during football games

From the sock hops to the orchestra pit, music played a major role in college life in the Fabulous 50's.

The Barbettes performed four-part harmony in the early part of the 50's. The original group is pictured, Phyllis Blakeman, Neva Kennon, Lois Harmon Poteet and Joyce Brooks Palmer.

The Red and Gray Orchestra, '53

Theatre

The Western Players and audiences alike escaped into many worlds as the theatre troup performed dozens of plays in the Fabulous 50's.

"The Taming of the Shrew"

Western Players Awards Banquet, Richard Smith, Carol Cheal, Paul Martin, Shirley Chandler, Russell Miller and Susie (Snyder) Walker

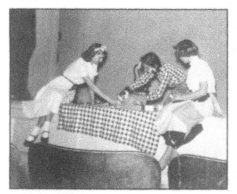

"Picnic"

"Lost in the Stars"

"Two Blind Mice," '51

Behind the scenes, the prompter

"The Night of Jan. 16"

Russell Miller, director, discusses the upcoming season with the Western Players in '52

Who's Who

1949-50 -Dot Agnew, Fred Barlow, Carolyn Boyd, Buddy Cate, Fred Clayton, Frank Cole, Greg Colson, John Givens, Nancy Good, Omer Gosnell, Dennis Lilly, Albin L. Lee, Charles Lively, Alice Meyer, Josephine Rigsby, Ben Sanders and Frank Wallheiser.

1950-51 - Thomas Beard, Ruth Bilbrey, Wilma Jean Depp, Eddie A. Diddle Jr., Raymon Gish, Judith Griffin, Ruby Hawkins, Douglas Hensgen, Roy Hina, John T. Johnson, Leta Kerr Perkins, Grace Lane, Robert Lively Jr., David Livingston, James McChesney, Ed Minor, L. A. Morgan, Homer Nation, Hugh Noffsinger, James Pickens, Sam Potter Tom Redford, J. D. Sigler, Eugene Steinquest, Vernon Stone, Hal Taylor, LaVerne Van Cleave and Louella Wycoff.

1951-52 - Evelyn Bailey, Carolyn Ridley Botto, Elizabeth Cherry Boyd, Nancy Lee Buren, Raymond L. Cravens, Billy R. Delph, Betty Dittbenner, Sara Downing, William Ford, Martha Helen Garrison, Margaret Griffin, Robert Maurice Hale, W. Wallace Hunt Jr., Rosemary Johnson, Joe Kimbrough, David H. Mefford, Gene Rhodes, Anne Hart Robey, Roger Sumner, Eugene P. Tanner, Ina Thornbury and J. Wellington Young.

1952-53 - Alice Allen, Nancy Lee Atkinson, Charles Ball, Monie Beard, William Bivin, Joan Curry, Jo Ann Dent, Mary Jo Diddle, Jim Feix, Mary Alice Hanson, Dottye Lindsey, Don McGuire, Marilyn Miller, William Miller, James Olliges, Roger Otten, Mary Dean Pedigo, Bob Richardson, Mary Lou Rogers, Robert E. Simpson, Seymour Spiegelman, Willard Price, Eurie Wallace and Richard White.

1953-54 - Bobby Bilyeu, Mac Caldwell, Betty A. Dalton, Billy H. Darke, Liz DeWitt, Sam Fletcher, Hack Garr, Russell Garr, Kenneth Gordon, Martha Gray, Kay Greer, Lindy Gunderson, Suzanne

Higgason, Pat Horn, Helen Leet, Tom Marshall, Glenn Massengale, Dale Mitchell, Jerry Parker, Shirley Risher, Bill Stephens, Max Stevens, Tyler Taylor and Catherine Winfrey.

1954-55 - Nancy Jean Akin, Catherine Hopper Allen, Walter Lee Apperson, Owen Arnold, William D. Bell, Eugene Bewley, Nancy Bewley, Ray Buckberry, James O. Daniel, Charles F. Dyer, Frank J. Groschelle, Charles H. Hood, Christine Forsythe Hood, Judy Koch, Gaye Lively, Sue Carolyn Lynch, Helen Vanover Oliver, Jerry Passafiume, Roxie Strouse, Ralph W. Posey, Ann Boyd Roberts, Bettye Sims, Jane Skinner, Shirley Smith, Pat Stagner and Deborah Walters.

1955-56 - Forest Able, Robert Baggett, Don Bell, Scott Carr, Lou Mae Davis, James C. Embry, Wayne Everly, Elizabeth McWhorter, Shelly Hampton, Mary Ligon Holloman, Kemble Johnson, Beverly Farior Jones, Emmalene Jones, Wanda Kirkham, Gerald Nassana, George Orr, Helen Orrender, Margeret Pickens, George Reecer, Rosemary Richardson, Norma Jean Ruble, William R. Sumerhill Jr., Jane Winchester, Pattye Thompson, Glen Vale, Shirley Walter, Jo Ann Fisher Whitsell, Barbara Wilkins and Lacy Wilkins.

1956-57 - James H. Atchison, Shirley Barnes, Bennett D. Baird, Mary Alice Black, Alice Mason Bradford, Elaine Carroll, Frances Hooks Catlett, John M. Chamberlin, Jim Chambliss, Carol Anne Cheal, Wayne M.Duncan, Betty Gardner, Bertha Gibson, Harry Gray, Marilyn Harrison, Charlotte Harwood, Nancy Hightower, Virginia Holloman, Jeanne Jones, James C. King Jr., Richard Knarr, William M. McCormack, Ann Meredith, William F. Mohr, Twyman Patterson, Sally Reed, Betty Roth, Jane Stewart, Joyce Wood and Lloyd Young.

1957-58 - Eric Back, Jerry Brantley, William Case, Paul B. Cook, Wade Allen Crowder, Joe Cunningham, Betty Zoe Douds, Sandra Fuguq Patterson, Doris Ann Gaines, Sara Helen Gleaves, Joan Heltsley, Billy Jane Lovell, Patsy Hooper Reca Ann Lynch, Owen Lawson, Barbara Dianne Michael, Don E. Michael, Ann Miller, Judith Anne Moore, Bradford E. Mutchler, Nancy Lee Owen, Jim Owens, Alice Faulkner O'Neil, David M. Prow, Jeanette Rider Sallee, Barbara Shelton, Carol Snyder Walker, Carroll VanHooser, Betty Spradlin, David VanHooser, George C. Moore, Shelby G. Tilford and Ray Weaver.

1958-59 - Cluster Belcher, Herman A. Blair, Vivian Marie Booker, Wanda Carman, James G. Chapman, Carl P. Chelf, Martha Ann Combs, Maomi Dempsey, Sandra Dempsey, James E. Greer, Allen E. Hilsmeier, Billy Joe Hoagland, Martha Sue Holland, Jeff Harlin Jenkins, George A. Kinslow, Anita Lane, Laska Ann Lsman, Anna Leach Long, John McClearn, Mary Lou Miller, Chester M. Montgomery, Joyce Mount Oden, Phyllis Dawn Robinson, John E. Schneider, Richard Smithson, Bonnie Thomas, Hardin Thompson, Francine Walker, Don S. Wood, F. E. Wortham Jr., Kenneth E. Wright and Mark L. Hoffard.

1959-60 - Nancy Lee Baugh, John Boyd, Dan E. Brawner, Eddie B. Copas, Mary ann Copas, Lerond Curry, Margaret Darragh, Sandra Dunham, John L. Foe, Mary Ruth Grise, Anita Fay Harper, William Hibbs, Ken Hightower, William Houston, Nancy Hughes, Pat Ireland, Archie Jordan, Bobby Leisure, William McCoy, Janice Walter Miller, Larry Nutter, James Rather, Doris Reed, Beverly Belcher Ritchie, Robert Ritchie, Rachael Chadwick Roll, Betty Ruble, Anne Shaver, Ronnie Sheffer, Mary Lou Tilford, Herbert Wassom and Clarence Wolff.

Sadie Hawkins Day

For one crazy day, the ladies took over and we all took leave of our senses.

Jeannette Homra

An odd couple!

A shotgun wedding with William Frank Smith, Dorothy L. Wilder, Allen Medus, Jewell R Coles and Neil R. Phelps

William J. Crowe, Jean Martin, Donald R. Riley, Patricia Louise Gauntt and Charles "Dutch" Isert

What a crew!

All sizes enjoy Sadie Hawkins Day

Nancy Good and Dot Agnew

Activities

The queen and her court

Bill Bivens, Joe Kimbrough, '51

Susie Snyder and "T" Whistle, '56?

Military Ball

The 13'ers

After the formal in 1954

Baron's Club, '52

Baron's Club

Baron's Camp, '56

Playing around

"Zeke" Nicar

At Mary Dean's stone house

Music Department Christmas party

Sigma Phi Alpha party, '58

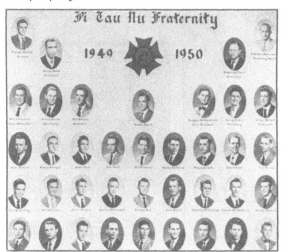

Pi Tau Nu

Pledging, Kenneth McClanahan

Greek Life

Beta Omega Chi, '59

Ragland Library Club, '52-'53

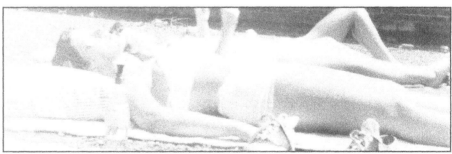

Sunbathing on the roof of West Hall, '53

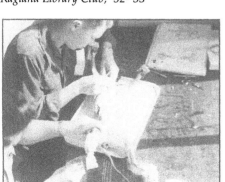

Cutting up cats

ROTC

Weddings, too—Mr. and Mrs. Scott Ford

Places

McLean Hall, the new girls' dorm.

The Cedar House, used for recreation in the 50's.

The Goal Post was a favorite hangout after classes for sodas, music and lots of talking.

Lewis E. Smith atop column

The Rock House

Jean Wimpy, Norma Wielman, Norma Cullen, ?, Sheila Peters

The Gymnasium in the early 50's.

Winter

Friendship will keep us warm—Jackie Berger, Margaret Ross, Allyne Holliday and Mary Ruth Page

Kitty Hunter

Jean Newcombs and Margaret Hicks, '51

Winter fun

Left, Bill Ploumis, Bobby Hensley and Joe Taborek, '56, Above, Winter of '56. Right, Bobby "Fodder" Sexton

Biographies

BEEGIE (LONG) ADAIR, Class of 1958, Music Degree, currently living in Franklin, TN.

I continued my education with graduate piano study at George Peabody College. Currently I am studying with a vocal coach.

I am vice president and co-owner of ABS Music Productions, Nashville. We write and record music for radio and TV commercials.

Other important positions include co-leader of Adair-Solee Jazz Quartet, Staff Musician—WSM-TV ('63-69), and Staff Musician—The Nashville Network ('83-85). I am now making phonograph recordings and TV appearances.

I am affiliated with Recording Musicians Association, American Federation of Musicians, National Association of Jazz Educators, and National Board of American Federation of TV and Radio Artists.

I am married to William Adair, a jingle producer and contractor.

My memories of Western include Sadie Hawkins dances, Student Center bridge games that lasted for hours, calling the Music Building "Spider Hall", and Mrs. Nelle Travelstead "Mom" Drew, and McLean Hall gab sessions.

I loved Western and still retain friendships with people I met there including teachers. I am active with animal rights groups, do seminars and clinics at colleges and universities on vocal and instrumental music, and collect antiques.

I am a member of many jazz groups including The Hank Garland Quartet, The Jazz Corporation Big Band, The Nashville Jazz Machine, Gyroscope, The Beegie Adair Trio, The Andy Goodrich Quintet, Orchestra XII, 2002 Jazz Sextet, and The Adair-Solee Quartet. I have recorded with Henry Mancini, Al Hirt, Jerry Reed, Connie Francis, Wayne Newton, Tennessee Ernie Ford, Ronnie Milsap, Perry Como, Johnny Cash, Chet Atkins, J.J. Cale, Englebert Humperdink, and Roger Wittaker. I have recorded on movie soundtracks including "Every Which Way But Loose," "Smokey and the Bandit," "The Villain," "Nashville 99," and "The Night the Lights Went Out in Georgia."

GENE C. ADKINS, Class of 1951. Upon graduation I was employed with Armco and worked in Open Hearth Office. My responsi-

bilities included computing tonnage production and also recording standard costs. I stayed at this position for about two years.

I was then transferred to the Accounting Department for Armco with responsibilities of the payroll section for approximately two years. I left Armco and went on the staff of Kelley & Galloway, CPA (1954-1960). I taught "Principles of Accounting" at Ashland Community College (UK) for one year until replacements for retired teachers were found.

In 1960 I joined Howard M. May, CPA. I worked for that firm for 17 years.

I then went on to form my own Public Accounting Firm (not CPA) Community Business Service, which I currently operate.

I have participated in Career Days at Fairview High School which involved speaking with students about careers in Accounting and am an active member in N.A.S.E.

I have four children, Steven 36, Jonathan 34, Denis 33, and Rachel 31. Rachel works as a senior accountant in my firm.

I also have three wonderful grandchildren: Michelle 14, Sara, nine and Katie, four.

My past activities include: Deacon in the Presbyterian Church, Sunday School Superintendent, and member of the choir. In scouting, have been assistant Cubmaster, Scoutmaster, Instructor Representative, Troop Committee, District Committee Chairman and various other scouting functions. I was awarded District Award of Merit and Silver Beav. among other numerous awards and recognitions. I was a recipient of Woodbadge Beads which inducts one into Lord Baden Powell's Troop #1 at Gilwell Park, England. I am also a vigil member of Order of the Arrow.

DR. J. ESTILL ALEXANDER, received my B.S. in 1952 in Elementary Education, and my M.S. in 1953 in Administration and Supervision, currently living in Knoxville, TN.

I continued my education at the University of Kentucky receiving an Ed. D in Curriculum (Reading Education). Currently I am a Professor at the University of Tennessee in Knoxville. My job responsibilities include the Director of Reading Center, and Coordinator of Elementary Education.

Other important positions include: Teacher at Wayne Co.,(KY) Schools, Teacher and Principal at Daviess Co., (KY) Schools, President of Daviess Co., (KY) Education Association,

Associate Professor at Kentucky State University, President of Tennessee Reading Association (State Organization), Coordinator of Tennessee Reading Association (six years), Board of Directors of Tennessee Reading Association (current), President of College Reading Association (National Organization), and Board of Directors of College Reading Association (current).

In 1984 I received the John Tunstall Award as outstanding professor in UTK's Department of Curriculum and Instruction (1st recipient).

In 1982 I was a nominee for the Board of Directors of International Reading Association.

I served on editorial review boards of several national journals and also served on several national committees in the International Reading Association and the College Reading Association.

I was co-author (co-editor) of seven books including **Diagnosing and Correcting Classroom Reading Problems** and **Teaching Reading**, 3rd ed. I was also author or co-author of about 55 journal articles and chapters in books.

My memories of Western include friends, basketball team, the faculty interest in students, and the PRIDE of students in WKU.

My hobbies now include traveling and reading.

MARGARET SIMONS ALFORD, Class of 1952, Biology Degree, currently living in Owensboro, KY.

I continued my education in Microbiology receiving a M.S. from the University of Kentucky. Currently I am a homemaker.

Other important positions include teaching Microbiology at WKU ('59-60), and at Auburn University ('61-65).

My activities include: President of Friendship Force of Western Kentucky ('86-87), and President of West-Central Kentucky Family Research Association (1986).

I am married to Henry C. Alford, a veterinarian.

Henry and I have three children. Sue, 28, received her B.A. and M.A. from Western, now teaching Art in Livingston County. Linda, 25, received her B.S. from Western (honor graduate), and now a Senior at University of Louisville, Med. School. Steven, 21, is a student at University of Kentucky.

My hobbies now include traveling, reading, genealogy and sewing.

ARTHUR N. ANDERSON, JR., Class of 1950, currently living in Hopkinsville, KY.

I continued my education by entering the University of Louisville Dental School in the fall of 1950. I graduated with a D.M.D. degree in 1954. Currently I have a private practice in Hopkinsville.

While at Western I played two years on the tennis team ('48-50). Since then I have helped coach the tennis teams at some of the local schools and helped in founding the local tennis club to support and promote tennis in our community.

In 1950 I married Sue Hilliard and we had three daughters and one son; Polly Sue Anderson, teacher, (deceased 1984); Clareesa A. Wright, physical therapist; Arthur Anderson II, dentist (in practice with me); and Judith Ann A. Greene, physical therapist.

I have one granddaughter, Catherine Anne Wright and one grandson, David K. Greene III.

SUE HILLIARD ANDERSON, Class of 1950, currently living in Hopkinsville, KY.

Currently I am teaching four year old preschool at First Baptist Church, Hopkinsville, KY.

Other important positions include: Teaching school in Bullitt County and in Jefferson County for four years.

I have been active in First Baptist Church teaching Sunday School and working with youth groups. I have also been active in Christian County Homemakers.

Last November I received the award as Kentucky State Mother for 1989, awarded by the American Mothers Association, an organization whose purpose is to promote and strengthen the moral and spiritual foundation of the home.

I married Arthur Anderson in 1950 and we had three daughters and one son; Polly Sue Anderson teacher, (deceased 1984); Clareesa A. Wright, physical therapist; Arthur Anderson III, dentist; and Judith Ann A. Greene, physical therapist.

I have one granddaughter, Catherine Anne Wright and one grandson, David K. Greene III.

ALLEN ANTHONY, Class of 1953, A.B. Degree in social science, currently living in Fort Davis, TX, population of 900.

I continued my education with a M.A. and Ed.S. Degree from George Peabody College and a Ph.D. Degree from North Texas State University.

I taught on the junior high level at the West Louisville School in the Daviess Co. (KY) School System for two years and then was an instructor at Sue Bennett College in London, KY for six years. Since 1965 I have been on the faculty at Sul Ross State University in Alpine, TX where I am presently professor of geography and history. My teaching assignments also include courses in sociology.

I am a member of the Kentucky Historical Society as well as being a member of the National Council for Geographic Education.

I have presented a number of papers of various professional meetings and have written in different journals including **The Register of the Kentucky Historical Society, The Filson Club History Journal,** and **The Kentucky Folkfore Record**. I have recently authored a book entitled **River at the Door: Unusual Experience in Remote Areas**.

I met the former Elizabeth Thomas while we were students at Western. After we married in 1953, we lived in Alaska for two years while I was in the service.

My memories of Western include living in Potter Hall, participating in Noonday Devotionals and Vesper Services in the Library Building and never seeing Western lose a basketball game during my four years on the campus.

I am active in my local church and also enjoy walking, mountain climbing and teaching courses in a nearby Elderhostel program.

ELIZABETH THOMAS ANTHONY, Class of 1954, B.S. Degree, currently living in Alpine, TX.

In 1967, I received my Masters from Sul Ross State University.

All of my career, I have been an elementary teacher. After teaching in Kentucky, Alaska, and Tennessee, my last 20 years have been spent as the first grade teacher in Fort Davis, a small resort town in far west Texas. It has been a lot of fun watching my students grow up.

My church has been my chief outside interest and I have served in many offices on local and district levels. I am a life member of NEA and have served as both president and treasurer of the local TSTA.

I transferred to Western from Bethel Women's College in Hopkinsville. On my first night there, I met Allen Anthony, my husband. We were in the old cafeteria in the basement of Potter Hall. My roommate, Janet Cooper, introduced us, both Janet and Allen were from Okolona. Allen and I have been married 35 years.

We have two children, Thomas Hudson Anthony, a dental laboratory instructor at the University of Texas, Health Science Center in San Antonia; and Susan Anthony Hinkle, an elementary teacher, in Lawton, OK. Both children are married and we have two grandchildren.

My memories of Western include walking everywhere. There weren't many cars on the campus in the early 50s. I also remember how hot the classrooms and dorms were in the summers. During my last semester there, I had to substitute a physics course for a physical science course and I was the only girl in the class with 39 boys. I'll never forget how kind Mr. Sadifur was to me in that class.

NEIL ALLEN, Class of 159, B.S. Business Degree, currently living in Bowling Green, KY.

I am currently the executive vice president at First Federal Savings and Loan of Bowling Green, KY. My job responsibilities are as acting president.

Another important position included serving on the Board of Directors for the Savings and Loan League of Kentucky.

I was the past president for the Kiwanis Club.

I am married to Rachel Allen who is assistant professor at Western Kentucky University. I have two children Michael, 28, and Steven, 20.

My memories of Western include a lot of pleasant memories and friends who have lasted for many years.

RACHEL (SMITH) ALLEN, Class of 1957-60, received B.A. and M.A. Business Degrees, currently living in Bowling Green, KY.

I continued my education at Peabody College.

I am currently assistant professor at Western Kentucky University of Bowling Green, KY. My job responsibilities are in administrative office systems.

Other important positions include president of Alpha Chi Corporation of Alpha Omicron Pi Sorority.

I received a 25-year service award from Western Kentucky University.

I am married to Neil Allen, an executive vice-president for First Federal Savings and Loan in Bowling Green, KY. I have two children Michael, 28, and Steven, 20.

My memories of Western include a small student body where you were friends to everyone.

MARIE (FINN) ARNEY, Class of 1955, B.S. Elementary Education, currently living in Franklin, KY.

I continued my education at Western Kentucky University. I received a M.A. in 1969 and a Rank 1 in 1977.

I am currently the principal at Franklin Elementary School.

Another important position included teaching grades 4, 5, and 6 in Simpson County Schools.

I am married to John Arney, a farmer and retired rural carrier. I have one daughter, Jana Hammock, and one son, John M. Arney. I also have one grandson, Dustin Hammock.

IMOGENE (YOUNG) ASHBY, Class of 1950, B.S. Degree Home Economics, currently living in Greenville, KY.

I continued my education at the University of Kentucky with correspondence courses during one summer.

I am currently a homemaker.

Important positions included teaching school for 11-1/2 years.

I am married to Norman H. Ashby who is the assistant manager for the Texas Gas Transmission Corporation of Owensboro, KY. I have two children Paul D. Ashby, 31, Joe E. Ashby, 28. I have three grandchildren Ross Tyler Ashby, seven, Katelynn Marie Ashby, one and one-half, and Joseph Scott Ashby, two.

My memories of UK are spending a lot of hard hours in the Home Economics Dept. where the maid, Sylvia, was a dear. Also, I developed friendships which continue. Wilson Wood, France Richards, and Helen Sydnor were inspiring.

My hobbies include volunteer services with Greenville United Methodist Church. My family enjoys trailer camping and traveling. Also, I'm finally learning to swim!

In July 1986 our house exploded with me in it. I spent nine weeks a the Humana University Hospital in Louisville, KY, recovering from 1st and 2nd degree burns over 40% of my body. Recovery continued through vigorous exercises, and I emerged with scars that can be hidden and not handicapped.

PAUL G. AUSTIN, Class of 1958, B.S. Agriculture Degree, currently living in Muncie, IN.

I continued my education at the Command and General Staff College, and National Defense University in Washington, D.C., for the U.S. Army Reserve.

I am currently agent/owner of the State Farm Insurance, Muncie, IN. My job responsibilities include operating a multiple line insurance agency.

Other important positions include Battalion Commander, Infantry BN, U.S. Army Reserve, completed 29 years reserve service effective Oct. 1, 1988.

I am a retired Lieutenant Colonel of the U.S.A.R. and affiliated with the Lions and Kiwanis Clubs as a member in Muncie, IN.

I am married to Sandra Leigh Austin, who is a secretary for State Farm Insurance Co. I have one son Bradley, 14.

I have fond memories of the Duck Inn Cafe off College Ave. and the old boarding house I stayed in during my tenure at WKU plus many good times watching WKU basketball.

My hobbies include gardening, automobiles, traveling, and the U.S. Army Reserve Lions and Kiwanis Clubs.

RICHARD BAKER, Class of 1955, Industrial Arts Degree, currently living in Paris, KY.

I continued my education with various work related engineering courses and USAF flight related courses.

I am a staff engineer for IBM, Lexington. My job responsibilities include product engineering support for IBM electronic typewriters at the Lexington plant and customer service worldwide.

Other important positions include Lt. Col. USAFR retired, instructor pilot, flight examiner, and wing chief of standardization and evaluation prior to retirement.

I have three children, Richard, 29; Susan, 27; and David, 25.

My memories of Western include friendly fellow students, helpful instructors and administrative officials, and being the "man in the hall."

JAMES R. BANTON, Bowling Green, KY. I took the teacher's examination in 1932, for my first certificate to teach. Entered Western second semester 1934 to renew certificate. Teaching seven months and going second semesters, got my BA, math major, English and biology minors in 1940, and my MA 1952, major in guidance and administration, and my Rank I 1962.

A native of Simpson County reared on the farm. Spent 40 years in the field of education, class room teaching, administration, and counseling in both public and private schools in Kentucky and Tennessee.

Attended Southern Baptist Theological Seminary 1941-42; pastored churches in Kentucky and Tennessee; retired from teaching July, 1975, and from pastorate May, 1983.

I married Minnie Edith Shanks of Warren County in 1942. Have one son, two daughters and five grandchildren.

I am now a volunteer: Chairman Welfare Board, hold offices RTA, AARP, Hospice and Arthritis, work with cancer, heart and blood-

mobile; teach Sunday School and belong Senior Adult Fellowship of First Bapti Church, Bowling Green.

Have had surgery several times includin open heart and appendectomy. My philoso phy, "Master situations don't let situatio master you." Keep busy serving others.

CHARLES J. BASSETT, Class of 1953, B.! Degree in Agriculture. Currently living i Drakesboro (Muhlenberg Co.,), KY.

I began my study at Western the fall of 194 I lived in Vet Village with my wife, Gladys M formerly "Hill" and our one year old daughte Sandra Lynn. There were several veteran with families from Muhlenberg County livin in the village.

We enjoyed the great basketball teams, th football games between Western and Louis ville, and the precision of the Western R.O.T.C Drill Team.

I could not say enough about the faculty. am especially indebted to Miss Emma Stith my English instructor; Mr. C.P. McNally Chemistry Department; and Mr. Ly Lancaste Zoology Department.

I received my B.S. in 1953, worked wit National Life & Accident Insurance Compan as an agent, Sanitarian with the Taylor Count Health Department, Muhlenberg Count Health Department, and City County Healt Department of Evansville, IN. For the past 2 years I have worked as an investigator for th Cabinet for Natural Resources, Division o Water, Madisonville, KY.

Returning in 1985, I have earned my privat pilot's license. I enjoy flying, Genealogy Re search, bass fishing, spending time with ou daughters and grandchildren, Alecia C. (16) and Scotty J. Taber (13) of El Paso, TX.

CLYDE T. BAUGH, B.S. - '57. The 50s a Western was the era of era's. Long registratio lines for desired classes and instructors. Th routine begins. It's toast, jelly and coffee at th Duck Inn Cafe. Then classes, bobby socks basketball (the first televised games) fast cars the '57 Chevy, loud pipes and my '47 Modifiec Mercury Coupe.

I married my high school sweetheart, Jolene Epley. We had two sons, Clyde Kimble anc Michael Joe. Both attended Western. Kim diec 1984 at age 26 with cancer. Mike has workec with me as Farm Bureau Agent for nine years

My career began as teacher at Paducah Tilghman. In 1958 I became Agency Manage for Farm Bureau Ins. Co. pursuing this caree for 30 years to date, having received the com panies top sales honors on several occasions.

received the SME Distinguished Sales Award in 1986. I refused promotion offers to top sales management position with Farm Bureau to stay in Logan County.

I have been married ten years to the charming Carolyn Sue Wagoner. We now reside in Russellville, KY. I continue to enjoy hobbies of fishing and classic cars. Carolyn and I are members of Second Baptist Church. I truly believe **"The Spirit Makes the Master."**

AARON E. BEALS, Class of '58, Agriculture. Currently living in Paducah, KY.

I furthered my education with a masters in Agriculture Education at UK; Rank 1, WKU and PhD Ag Ed, Purdue, 1974. I am currently a teacher of Vo-ag at Paducah Tilghman High School and Coordinator of Horticulture Programs there.

I am president of Kentucky Vocational Agriculture teachers Association, member of Resolutions Committee, NVATA. I am affiliated with PEA, KEA, KVA, KVATA, NVATA, AVA and a deacon at Broadway Baptist Church.

I am married to the former Ina Louise Price, a homemaker. We have three children: Dennis, Steven and Karen and three grandchildren, Mark and Jason Beals and Melissa Kay Little. Gardening is my hobby.

Memories of Western include playing softball for Cherry Country Life Club and helping build the winning float in 1956 Homecoming—theme "Plow 'em under Big red."

JOAN DIENES BEAN, B.S. Physical Education class of '47.

My first teaching job was at Fort Knox, KY. I married Red Bean, from Madisonville, KY. Neither of us had ever been to Florida, and we both wanted to go. Red's first teaching job was in Fernandina Beach, FL. It was easy to move, 'cause we loaded everything we owned in the car. We stayed here and raised our family - which is a big one. We have nine children and seven grandchildren.

I took dancing all my life - I was still taking lessons when I was at Western. I taught dance classes all over town - in the Rec Center, the church hall, the hotel, etc. And then in 1986, when I was 60 years old, we built our own dance studio. It has really been a dream come true. And when you think that's crazy, remember Colonel Sanders opened his first fried chicken place when he was 60!

My mom, Anne Dienes, lives about six blocks away, and comes every morning to wash the dishes and the clothes, and to do the mending. She's 88 years old, and is a legend in her own time around here. Life's been good - the best thing that ever happened to me was meeting "Red" Bean, and since that happened at Western, WKU will always have a special place in my heart.

Incidentally, one of my first jobs in 1946 was as a lifeguard at the pool - under the supervision of Dero Downing.

LEWIS "RED" BEAN, Class of '50, B.S. Industrial Arts, M.A. Administration. I came to Western in the fall of '46 to play on the first football team Western had after the War. (There was no football during WWII.) I had transferred from U.K. where I played under Bear Bryant.

I accepted my first job in Fernandina Beach, FL, and after 38 years, we're still here! I've been classroom teacher, coach, assistant principal, Director of maintenance for the county, ran all the adult and vocational programs for our county–you name it, I've done it. I retired in '84, ran for the city commission and was elected. I served on that board for three years. Then, in 1986, I built a dance studio, which keeps me off the street and out of trouble. (Because there's always something to do [or something to fix.) My wife, the former Joan Dienes, and both our daughters teach at the studio.

Joan and I have nine children, (the last one is a senior in college), and seven grandchildren. I still remember the Lettering and Engrossing

course I took under Dr. Craig. I letter diplomas, certificates, plaques, awards, etc., and I've taught several classes in calligraphy. (Thanks to that course).

I'm building furniture right now - thanks to the expertise I received from L.T. Smith, Nalback, and Mr. Barnes! - at the I.A. Building.

JOSEPHINE LEATHERS BENSON, Class of '54, BS Education, currently living in Murray, KY. Graduate work at University of Illinois.

My husband, Cedric and I co-own Benson Sporting Goods in Murray. I have also taught regular and special education in Illinois for 16 years and am a member of the Council of Exceptional Children.

Cedric and I have two children, Eric and Debbie, and four grandchildren.

I remember playing the clarinet at football and basketball games, my love and respect for Pres. Garrett, Dean Griss and the faculty and the many activities with fellow students.

KERMIT BINKLEY, Class of 1955, A.B. in English and M.A. in Secondary Education, currently living in Concord, MI.

I received an AB degree with a major in English and minors in History and Art in 1950, and a masters degree in Secondary Education in 1955.

I have completed 30 semester hours at Michigan State University in Guidance and Counseling.

I began my teaching at Houston High School, Houston, MO, in 1951-52. I moved to Concord Community School, Concord, MI in 1953 and after teaching English for a few years, I became the High School Counselor until I retired in 1986. Since then I've been an Instructor in AARP's 55/Alive Driver Education Program.

Memories of WKU include: fond memories of Dr. Gordon Wilson's all men English classes, seeing my first football game, Dr.

Russell Miller and playing parts in plays he directed (in Van Meter), West Hall being built, long meal lines at Potter Hall, Mr. Ivan Wilson's and Miss Ruth Temple's Art classes, especially, going to Western—U of L. basketball game on my 1st wedding anniversary, and studying very hard to keep up in Dr. Wilson's fast paced classes.

OWEN LEE BLANTON JR., Class of 1951, A.B. in Math and a M.A. in Education, currently living in Rome, GA.

I continued my education in Guidance and Counseling (Education Specialist) for six years.

I am currently retired from Rome City Schools. My job responsibilities, were a Football and Basketball coach, Math Teacher, and a School Counselor. At the present, I am active in the Rome Exchange Club.

I am married to Pat who is a school secretary. We have three children, Mike 35, Mark 31, and Lee Ann 28. We also have two grandchildren.

My memories of Western include beating Easter 14-13, in the last few seconds of the game at Home Coming-(1950); and also watching Eddie Diddle, count or talley Bert R. Smith's saying "AND WITH THAT" during class.

At this time my current hobby is playing golf.

BETTIE (DALTON) BLOSS, B.S. in Music. Currently living in Evansville, IN.

I am currently a housewife. I am director of Sr. Adult Church Choir, a soloist, and accompanist for Adult Church Choir.

I am married to Bryant A. Bloss, we have two children; Cathy, 32 and Hal, 30; and two granddaughters, three years and three weeks.

My memories of Western include wonderful and caring professors: Gertrude Bale, Claude Rose, and Dr. Gordon Wilson, in particular. I had the most fun singing in Madrigal Group.

I have enjoyed my music training in many ways for all these years. I have especially enjoyed my traveling with the Sr. Adult Choir (ages 55-94). I also like to play tennis.

MARIE HORD BLOYD, Class of '57 and '62, BS and MA plus 39 hours, History and government Education, currently living in Greensburg, KY.

I am head of the science department at Green County High School. I was the outstanding Social Studies teacher in '78 and '88 and in '89 honored as such for the entire fifth district.

I am widowed and have two children and two grandchildren.

My days on the hill were the best of my life. It was most stimulating and produced many lifelong friendships.

I still enjoy classes in US History and Government, but my hobby is my grandchildren.

ARTHUR W. BOONE, Class of 1950, B.S. in Commerce (Bus. AD). Currently living in Somerset, KY.

Currently, I am Purchasing/Insurance Manager at Southern Belle Dairy Co., Inc. My job responsibilities are Purchasing, Insurance, and Transportation Management. I am also Commissioner of Public Housing Authority.

I am married to Billie S. Boone. We have two children; Dr. Whit Boone, 31 and Mary Jean Boone, 28.

I attended and graduated at B.U.

My hobbies include woodworking and antique furniture restoration.

CHARLES H. BOZARTH, JR., Class of 1955, B.S. in Ag. Currently living in Hopkinsville, KY.

I am currently retired from TVA in Knoxville, TN. My job responsibilities included appraising TVA Real Estate and buying land. I also spent four years in Acquisition of LBL (TVA).

My wife, Sylvia Green died in 1984. I was remarried in 1988 to Eva Holloman.

I have two children; Danny G., 40 and Marty G., 36. I have one grandson, Nathan, three.

As I look back on the days at Western, very pleasant memories are brought to mind.

RICHARD G. BRANDON, Class of 1954, B.S. Degree in Agriculture, currently living in Louisville, KY.

I am currently a Transportation Analyst for Ford Motor Company in Louisville. My wife, the former Margaret Roberts received her BA in 1954. I have two children; Richard II, 31; and Dan, 29. I also have a granddaughter, Megan, two.

IDA FRANK BUTTON BRATTON, Class of 1959, AB in Math and English, currently living in Louisville, KY.

I am a teacher for the Jefferson County Board of Education in Louisville. I am a Math and English teacher and advisor for a group of 9th graders.

I have taught in the Advance Program 20 of my 30 years. I am featured in the following: **The World Who's Who of Women, Who's Who in the South and Southwest, Who's**

Who of America, Whose Who in the World. I am a member of the following: American Association of University Women, NEA, KEA, and JCTA.

My husband is Robert F. Bratton, who is career postal employee. I have one child, Timothy A. Bratton, 16 years of age. My son has made Country Day honor roll (Headmaster's Award annually since 6th grade) and is preparing for a career in medicine.

Memories of WKU include: many laughs at the many small town and country people who were attempting to be "big shots" on a college campus in another country town, Bowling Green.

My hobbies include extensive travel, crafts, decorating my large two story home, shopping trips to large cities, and collecting antiques.

DOROTHY (ROGERS) BRENT, Class of 1957, Secretarial Science. Currently living in Pewee Valley, KY.

I currently am a secretary for the Crestwood State Bank. My job responsibilities are correspondence, secretarial duties.

I am active in reading, crafts, and boating. I also enjoy being with my family.

I am a housewife. I am married to Robert A. Brent who is the manager of purchasing programs at General Electric. We have three daughters and five grandchildren.

My memories of Western include the teachers, my friends, the parties, dances, and the ball games.

JAMES D. BRENT (DON), Class of 1958, B.S. in Ind. Arts. Currently living in Frankfort, KY.

I furthered my education by attending numerous courses and seminars sponsored by the International Right of Way Association (IRWA), The Institute of Real Estate Appraisers, and Transportation Cabinet.

Currently, I am Right of Way Supervisor with the Kentucky Transportation Cabinet in Frankfort. My job responsibilities are to assign and supervise statewide the court appraisal witnesses in all right of way acquisition condemnation trials in Kentucky Circuit Courts.

Other important positions include past president of Kentucky Right of Way Agents Assoc., past president of Chapter 25 and past Region Chairman (seven states) Int. Right of Way Assoc. Commander, Capital City Squadron, Civil Air Patrol (Aux. USAF).

Honors that I have received include Outstanding Jaycee in 1968—Fleming County Jaycees, listed in 1970 edition of Outstanding Young Men of America, Chapter 25 IRWA Professional of the Year 1975 and 1983, currently candidate for Professional of the Year—U.S. and Canada.

I am married to Eva Joyce. We have two daughters, Traci Elizabeth, 24, and Laura Barington, 17.

My fondest memories of WKU are visiting (loafing) with friends at Snack Bar after classes and games, AFROTC, dorm life, and social life as a member of 13ers Fraternity.

My hobbies include aviation and weekend farm management of farm my two brothers and I own in Trimble Co.

R.A. BRENT, Class of 1952, Business Administration, currently living in PeWee Valley, KY.

I have continued my education through classes and seminars sponsored by General Electric.

I have worked for General Electric for 36 years where I am Manager of Purchasing Programs. My job responsibilities include purchasing support to new models and manufacturing locations. Other important positions include quality control engineer, and purchasing agent.

I am married to Dorothy Rogers Brent, who is a secretary at Crestwood State Bank. We have three children and five grandchildren.

My memories of WKU are of friendly students, helpful and professional faculty, going to the ballgames, the snow storm and sledding in the '50s.

My hobbies are fishing, farming and family.

EDWARD S. BRIDGES, Class of '52, A.B. Music Education. In the fall of 1948, I left my hometown of Hopkinsville, KY and entered Western. Apparently, I felt driven to sample as much of college life as possible, for the 1952 Talisman index contained 16 listings by my name: track team, Air Force ROTC, chorus,

orchestra, band (drum major), **Herald** and **Talisman** staffs, religious council, etc. I combined my music degree and Air Force commission for a career as an Air Force band director. I married a Western girl, and we had five children.

Retiring from the Air Force, I completed doctoral studies at University of Georgia, and became music department head and director of bands at Georgia Tech in Atlanta. My children are all grown, three are married, and I have five grandchildren.

I am presently director of music for a large, urban Catholic Church, as well as conductor of a community band, which I founded ten years ago. In 1979, I married Joyce, a young Georgia nurse, who joined my band to play oboe. We reside on a 15-acre horse farm south of Atlanta, where we swim and ride.

My Western memories include Coach Diddle's red towel, David Livingston's Red and Gray dance orchestra, Jimmy Sacca and the "Hilltoppers" singing "Trying," working in the college cafeteria in the basement of Potter Hall, and living in the attic of President Garrett's home (currently, the Alumni building).

BETTY (KOCK) BROCK, Class of 1959, B.S. Elementary Education. Currently living in Rockville, MD.

I am currently employed as an Assistant Sales Rep. for N.V. Ryan in Silver Spring, MD.

I am married to John Brock who is a Labor Relations Manager at Bechtel Corporation. We have two children, Scott, 26, and Craig, 24. We enjoy travelling.

My memories of Western include Mom Drew, my friends, the basketball and football games, and hours of playing bridge in the student union building.

BILL BROGAN, Class of 1957, A.B. Music Ed. Currently living in Glasgow, KY.

I furthered my education and received a M.A. in Music Ed. in 1968. I taught 27 years as high school Band Director—Caverna, Greenville, Franklin, Simpson, and Glasgow.

Currently I am Field Sales Manager at Q.S.P. Inc.—Readers Digest. My job responsibilities include Fund Raising with School Groups, initiating Educational Programs related to Drugs, Alcohol, etc. in schools, and Reading Programs.

Other important positions include past choir director—Glasgow Baptist Church (seven years), Music Coordinator, Glasgow Highland Games, and Community Choir Director in Glasgow.

Honors, Activities, and Affiliations include: Outstanding Young Men of America, National Band Parade Championship, St. Petersburg Festival of States, Honorary SunCoaster—Festival of States.

I am married to Betty Brogan, who is Administrative Assistant at the Chamber of Commerce. We have one son, Keith, 25 years old.

My memories of WKU are starting at W. Kentucky State College with less than 2000 students in 1952, the closeness of all students, (especially in Music Dept.), the good band program, and great basketball teams.

My hobbies include boating, fishing, travelling, and music.

ROBERT RUSSELL BROWN, June 1954, BA Music Education. I stated at Western September, 1950. Spider College (the music department) was usually my main hang-out. Being a music major meant I had to learn to play a stringed instrument. After receiving lessons on the bass viol, I sometimes "borrowed" a bass fiddle from the band hall in order to play in a dance band, either at the Boots and Saddle Club or with the Red and Gray Orchestra, which was co-owned by Pat Maestroleo and me during our senior year.

I got my BA in music education; taught school one year in Frankfort, KY; Entered the

US Air Force because of my AFROTC commitment; Retired 20 years later as a Lieutenant Colonel with 7000 flying hours.

I have three boys, Brian (33), Ben (15), Beau (11). The last two require me to be working forever. Since my Air Force retirement in 1975, I have worked as an advertising account executive for a newspaper, a personnel director for an oil company, and for the last five years as an Executive Director for an United Way alcohol and drug treatment facility.

PATSY RITTER BUNCH, Class of 1953, BS in Education, currently living in Waterford, WI.

I received my Masters in Education at the University of Wisconsin-Whitewater.

I am currently teaching the second grade in Mukwonago, WI. I was selected as Mukwonago Elementary Teacher of the Year, 1979-80.

I am married to Roy Bunch and we have two sons Jeff, 29, and Mike, 27.

I remember the fun we had at Rockhouse dorm, the basketball games, the Goal Post, and Western Players.

I enjoy playing golf and tennis.

LELIA ANN (LEE ANN) HOLEMAN BURROW, Class of 1959, BS in Biology, currently living in Radcliff, KY.

I received my MS from Western in 1962.

I have been a Biology teacher at Fort Knox Community Schools for 30 years, and I am the Junior Class coordinator.

I am a Charter member of Alpha Sigma Chapter of Alpha Delta Kappa (Educator's sorority) and a member of National Association of Biology Teachers.

I am married to Bob Burrow, (Assistant Superintendent of Fort Knox Schools) and we have two sons. Brent, 25, at the University of Kentucky Law School and Grant, 21, at the University of Kentucky.

I remember studying all night for finals and going out to breakfast; "Frog Room" at Snell

Hall; Beta friends and parties; great friends at McLean Hall; Dr. Steve and Dr. Sumpter.

GLENDA FOWLER BUSSELL, B.A. in Social Science, currently living in Columbus, OH.

I received my MSSW from the University of Louisville in 1965.

Since 1974, I have been the Executive Director, at North Central mental Health Services, a comprehensive center providing mental health counseling and other services to Columbus residents.

I have also been a teacher at Fern Creek High School, Flight attendant, Eastern Airlines, Atlanta, GA; Social Worker and Clinical Director, Department of Mental Health and Lake Cumberland Comprehensive Care Center Somerset, KY; Social Work Supervisor Adolescent Services, Children's Hospital Columbus, OH; and Assistant Professor, College of Social Work, Ohio State University, Columbus, OH.

Honors that I have received are Phi Kappa Phi, Kentucky Colonel, Who's Who in American Women. I am a member of Academy of Certified Social Workers, National Association of Social Workers, Mental Health Corporations of America, Columbus Metropolitan Club, Board Member-Mental Health Corporations Enterprises, President—Franklin County Federation of Mental Health Service Providers, Board Member—Ohio Association of Mental Health Administrators. I am a licensed Independent Social Worker and Certified Mental Health Administrator.

I have one child, Scott, 22, a graduate of the University of Denver, CO, now studying acting at the Academy of Dramatic Arts, Pasadena, CA.

My memories of WKU are; "Mom" Drew and McLean Hall, The Fabulous Five, The Ninnuts, Beta, Beech Bend, and The Goal Post.

My hobbies are traveling and reading.

GILBERT T. CALHOUN, Class of 1955, B.S. Geography. Currently, an Associate with Booz, Allen, and Hamilton, a management consultant firm in Washington, D.C. I recently retired from the Central Intelligence Agency where I served as an official in the Directorate of Science and Technology. Prior to my CIA experience, I spent seven years as an officer in the United States Air Force.

During my career I traveled and worked in various parts of the world. My geography training at Western served me extremely well. Whatever I have accomplished in life, I owe in some measure to those great years at Western.

My wife, the former Merrillyn Clark, a educator in the Fairfax County School System and I have two children, Catherine and David Cathy is an elementary teacher and David is systems manager with Federal Express.

When possible I log hours as a glider pilo and enjoy the peace and tranquility of the skie over the mountains and valleys of Virginia' beautiful Shenandoah Valley. Also, Merrilly and I are avid hikers.

Remembrances — The bridge games be tween classes at the Student Union; basketba games at the big red barn featuring Marsha Spoelstra, and company; Saturday afternoo football games; the Goldpost; the "Hilltop pers" military balls; and homecoming dance

AUVERGNE CROWE CARNEAL, M.A Degree in English, Education, and Frenc currently living in Madisonville, KY.

I furthered my education with a Master' Degree. I am a Kentucky Colonel and a mem ber of the Eastern Star.

I am retired. I taught in two one-roon schools from 1923 - '24 and from '24 - '25. taught in Nebo High School from 1931-1951. was principal at Nebo High School from 1951 1971.

I was married to the late Walter Carneal, mailcarrier. We have three children and si grandchildren.

My memories of WKU include completin high school at Western in the spring of 1922 and since teachers were scarce, I was solicite to teach three months before my 18th birthda in spring of 1923.

Hobbies include my three sons and si grandchildren, attending Sunday School an Church, Delta Kappa Gamma, Retired Teach ers, BPW Club, and Senior Citizens.

JAMES AUSIE CARPENTER, Class c 1954, AB degree, currently living in Bowlin Green, KY.

I received my M.A. from WKU—Ed

School Administration at Peabody-Vanderbilt University.

I am currently retired. I was the USAF ROTC Instructor at WKU. I was also the Director of South Hall, Director of College High School, Director of Teacher Admissions, Director of Teacher Placement, and Associate Professor of Education at WKU.

I am married to Evelyn Yates Carpenter who is a writer. We have a daughter who has a BA from WKU (Class of 1964).

My years at WKU made the difference in my life. My greatest challenge there was the training of young men to be USAF officers—many other challenges also. The third president of WKU was my mentor. Being director of College High School was one of my greatest challenges.

JOHNATHAN C. CARPENTER, Class of 1951, Physical Education Degree, currently living in Albany, NY.

I continued my education and received my M.A. in Education from Western in 1953, after being recalled to two years active duty in the Air Force.

During the next 12 years I was head of the athletic program of Mohawk Valley Community College, Utica, NY. In addition I coached basketball and tennis. During this period I also served as Regional Director for the National Junior College Athletic Association. During a reunion of the founders of the NJCAA I was honored at Hutchinson, KS in March 1981.

In 1966 my career changed from education to business when I continued my father's restaurant business located in downtown Albany, NY—close to the State Capitol building. For the next 18 years my wife Sheila and I hosted the famous and near-famous in New York politics, in addition to area and national celebrities. We sold the business in 1984 and I'm currently involved with historical and genealogical research.

In 1985 I retired as a Lt. Col. after a 40 year association with the military. I received my

commission from Westerns' Air Force ROTC program.

I have three daughters Jan Sheetinger, Dianne Carpenter and Gail Gygax, a son Jonathan and grandson Alexander Gygax.

Among my 50s flashbacks—that incredible aura of foreboding doom as I hand "my" cause of study to Prof. But. R. Smith, ping-pong at the Cedar House, "Crunch-time" on the baseline bleachers at the red barn, after standing for a rousing rendition of the "Fightsong", and last, but most memorable, the **Western spirit**—that wonderful, glorious state of euphoria which remains with you forever.

JANE WINCHESTER CARR, After graduating from Western in '56 with an AB in English, I married Scott B. Carr, also class of '56. Presently, I am in my 27th year of teaching English, five of these at Lafayette High School in Lexington, KY, and the rest at Blacksburg High School, Blacksburg, VA.

While teaching and serving as head of the BHS English Department, I completed a Masters in Education at Virginia Tech (VPI&SU) in 1976.

Active in the local education association; Delta Kappa Gamma Society International for Women Educators; the Blacksburg Christian Church; and an extension homemakers group, I have held various leadership positions in each of these organizations. I presently serve as a consultant to a committee of the National Council of Teachers of English (NCTE) and was awarded one of the first VA Association of Teachers of English (VATE) Service awards. I am also a member of Phi Kappa Phi.

My finest accomplishment is rearing, with their fine father, two children, Beth and Ron, each who has continued with brief stints of teaching. Beth is now rearing two wonderful grandsons for us, and Ron is the assistant basketball coach here at Virginia Tech (VPI&SU).

Much of what I am today can be directly traced to the academic and social opportunities I enjoyed at Western. There are too many memories for me to single out specifics, but enjoying Hilltopper basketball and working in the cafeteria were "special."

SCOTT B. CARR, I graduated with a BS degree in agriculture in 1956 and married Jane Winchester, also Class of '56, before serving in the U.S. Air Force for three years. Following a tour of duty with the 587th Tactical Missile Group in Sembach, Germany, I taught biology and math at Boone County High School, Florence, KY, for one year.

I then earned a MS and PhD from the University of Kentucky in Dairy Nutrition. I have been at Virginia Tech as a professor in Cooperative Extension Services since 1967, working in the areas of forage and animal production in the Dairy Science Department.

I enjoy gardening, some woodworking, a little golfing, and following my favorite basketball team, which presently has to be the Virginia Tech Holies as my son Ron is the assistant basketball coach here. I also have a daughter Beth, who lives in Martinsville, VA, near enough to Blacksburg for me to spoil my two grandsons.

I have many fond memories of Western.

BILL CASE, Class of 1958, B.S. Degree in Physical Education, currently living in Paris, KY.

I continued my education with a Master's Degree from Eastern Kentucky University, and Rank I, Eastern Kentucky University.

I am currently a head teller at Bourbon Agriculture Deposit Bank.

I am married to Virginia Ann Case, who is the assistant office manager of Claiborne Farm (home of race horse Secretariat). We have two children, Kim and Tim, and have two grandchildren, Jennifer and Katherine.

My memories of Western include Uncle Ed, Hilltoppers, good times, and friends.

I entered WKU in the fall of 1954 on a full basketball scholarship. The highlight of my basketball career was scoring 14 straight points against Murray. It was an honor to play with players like Abel, Crosthwaite, Daniels, Lawson, Burk, and many others. I taught and coached at Meade County, Jessamine County, and Bourbon County High Schools. I served as principal of Bourbon County High School from 1976 to 1985. I recently retired after 29 years in secondary education.

I am a retired major in the Army Reserves. I have a three handicap in golf and play about 10,000 holes yearly. I have a dog named Topper and recently lost an 18-year-old registered dog named Ed Diddle.

I have been blessed with the greatest wife, lovely daughter, and a mentally handicapped son, Timmy, who has given real meaning to my life.

CHARLIE CAMPBELL, Class of 1958, B.A. Degree in Economics, currently living in Fort Myers, FL.

I am currently the Regional Manager of Firestone/Dayton Tire. I am responsible for sales and distribution in Southeastern U.S.A. and Puerto Rico.

Other important positions include Director of Training at Cooper Tire and Rubber Co. 1969-1972; Training Director at Dayton Tire; and Marketing Manager at Dayton Tire.

I was honored by being chosen National Sales Manager in 1986.

I am married to Nancy Campbell, housewife, and have two children, Chuck, 28, who is a graduate of WKU, and Jeff, 25, who is a graduate of University of Southern Florida.

My memories of Western include "Max's" on the Barren River, "Omakrons," Uncle Ed Diddle, and the Hilltoppers.

I have played golf in all 50 states and in eight countries.

ANN BETTIS CLARY, Class of 1959, B.S. in Elementary Education, currently living in Stone Mountain, GA.

Western University certainly gave me a solid foundation for a full life ahead! "Life after Western" was spent traveling around the world with a military husband for 22 years. We retired in Alaska. I taught school, worked in retail stores, and pursued an interest in sports. Several years were dedicated to competition—skating, 10k races, and jazz clogging .

I have three children. A son, daughter, and a grandchild live in Anchorage. The youngest child lives in Atlanta. I am teaching 3rd grade in DeKalb County and plan to complete my masters degree at Mercer University.

Yes, I recall those times at Western which shaped and helped me realize my dreams ahead.

WILLIAM B. CATE (BUDDY), Class of 1950, B.S. Degree in Physical Education, and Industrial Arts, currently living in Bowling Green, KY.

I continued my education at Murray State in 1951 by receiving my M.S.

I played one year of professional basketball with the Waterloo Hawks, Waterloo, IA.

I am currently a private businessman with my own building supply business.

Other important positions include coaching

ten years in high schools in Alabama and Kentucky, and seven years at Tennessee Wesleyan College, and played four years at WKU '47-'50 on the team that played in three straight NIT tournaments.

Selected for the TWC Hall of Fame in 1988.

I am married to Joy Davis Cate who received a B.S. in 1950 and taught secondary education for ten years in Alabama, Kentucky, and Ohio, and was Health Services Coordinator in the Bowling Green City School System for six years.

Memories of Western include many memories of Coach Ed Diddle and playing under him from 1946-50.

JOHN M. CHAMBERLIN, Class of 1957.
Condensing my memories of Western reminds me of some other difficult tasks. Like the time I spent all night writing a term paper for Gordon Wilson, or worked too long on a quintic equation for Hugh Johnson, slaved over Gabrielle Robertson's impossible tests, lived in the lab to complete Glenn Dooley's quant unknowns, or struggled through Joyce's **Ulysses** under Justine Lynn. They asked too much — but I wouldn't trade what I gained.

What meant most to me at Western was knowing many wonderful people. Eating together, sharing casual moments between classes, bull sessions about everything under the sun, walking downtown on a date, and singing, praying and studying the Bible together.

After getting a Ph.D. at Duke University, I went back to Western to teach in the Chemistry Department Here I met my wife, Jan, who was teaching French at Western and now teaches Spanish at BGHS. Our daughter studied music at WKU, and she now works for a computer firm.

I enjoy swimming, camping, biking, hiking, and canoeing. Through these and other activities I try to share with the boys in my church the one who has been and is the central reality in my life: Jesus Christ.

DONALD A. CHAPMAN, Class of 1953, B.S. Social Science, Henderson, KY.

This year, 1989, marks my 36th year of teaching. Following graduation from Western I taught and coached at Henderson High School in Henderson, KY until 1959, at which time I became a teacher, coach and later principal at Fort Knox Dependent High School. During the summer of 1964 I completed a Master's degree in education at WKU. In 1968 I returned to Henderson County High School as principal and in 1969 became a teacher and counselor at Henderson Community College where I am now a Professor in the University of Kentucky Community College System.

Both professionally and personally I have remained involved in sports and physical fitness. My hobbies include tennis and fishing. My wife, Betsy, is an R.N. at Community Methodist Hospital in Henderson. Together we enjoy gardening, bicycling and our three grandsons.

My fondest memories of Western are of the camaraderie among the small student body; philosophizing with Mr. Diddle; Coach Jack Clayton with rolled-sleeves and starched collar; and the fruit provided by Mr. Diddle to the football team as we travelled to out-of-town games. Looking on this time in my life—I wouldn't change a thing!

MARION E. CHESNUT, Class of 1955, BA Degree in English, currently living in Orlando, FL.

I am now a retired Officer of the United States Air Force. My career was cut short when I developed Multiple Sclerosis in 1964. I helped Lee Robertson organize the WKU Alumni Club of Central Florida and was the first President.

My wife is Mary Ward Chestnut, graduate of Morehead State University and Masters at University of Central Florida. She is a special Education teacher in Orlando.

I have one married daughter, Diane Asher,

San Diego, CA. WKU MEMORIES: I feel very privileged to have played on four straight WKU Ohio Valley Conference Tennis Championship teams in 1952, '53, '54, and '55. I have fond memories of the many trips and humorous coaching stories and experiences with coaches Hornback and Diddle. I remember vividly what the Western Campus looked like when I was a student. I am completely astonished at the growth and size of WKU today.

I enjoy playing golf and travel experiences throughout the world, whenever possible.

BILL AND MYRNA (CHEW) CHUMLEY, Class of 1953 and 1955, B.S. Degrees (both), currently living in Owensboro, KY.

Bill is a Radiologist, Radiology PSC in Owensboro, KY. My responsibility is the provision of radiology services at Owensboro-Daviess County and Mercy Hospital. I was the past president of the Kentucky Chapter of American College of Radiology.

Myrna, a housewife, was a past Trustee for the Board of Directors of Paducah Community College.

We have two children Marsh William, 31; and Warren Franklin, 18.

We are involved in numerous professional and medical societies.

WKU MEMORIES: We have many fond memories, Billy Vaughn and the Hilltoppers, Coach Diddle's red towel, teachers (Lancaster, Stevens, Sumpter, Gabriella Robertson).

JEAN JEWELL CLAIBORNE, Class of 1955, B.S. Degree in Health and Physical Education; M.A. Degree in Education, currently living in Owensboro, KY.

I am married to George E. Claiborne, a retired school administrator. We have two children: George E. Claiborne, 25; Brent Smith Claiborne, 18.

I taught health and physical education at Daviess High School. I am now a realtor (on leave) with Century 21 Partners.

MEMORIES OF WKU: Thoughts of Western always bring back warm memories of years spent "on the hill" in Bowling Green. What a happy time college years truly represent. I love to remember those times and renew old friendships.

JOAN (GRABRUCK) CLARK, Class of 1957, B.S. Physical Ed. Currently living in Franklin, KY.

I continued my education getting a M.A. in Education in 1958 and am a P.E. teacher for first grade in Franklin, KY.

I am active in tennis, musical productions, football games, and basketball games.

I am married to Ronald W. Clark who is a president for a bank. We have two children, David 28, and Karen, 27.

My memories of Western include leading cheers for the Hilltoppers.

RONALD W. CLARK, Class of 1957, B.S. in Geography, currently living in Franklin, KY.

I furthered my education by receiving a M.A. in Education in 1960. I also received Educational Leadership in 1964.

I am presently the president of Franklin Bank & Trust. I am the Chief Operating Officer. I have been a member of the Board of Regents at WKU since 1974. I have also been a member of the Board of Directors at Franklin Bank & Trust since 1973.

My wife is Joan G. Clark and she is a P.E. teacher. We have two children: David, 28; Karen, 27.

MEMORIES OF WKU: I was fortunate to have been awarded a basketball scholarship and had a great time with all my teammates at Diddle Dorm. I enjoy basketball and tennis.

W. FRANK COLE, JR., Class of 1950-1964, BA-MA History, currently living in Salem, IN.

I continued my education with an EDS at Indiana University. Currently I am retired.

Some important positions that I hold include: President, Washington County Actors Community Theater, past president of the Salem Teachers Association, and I am also a member of the Board of Directors of the Salem Chamber of Commerce.

Past honors which I have held are: I am a Retired Colonel in the United States Air Force, Talisman King in 1950, Vice Commander of the 434th T.C. Wing, Member of WKU golf team, Golf Coach at Salem High School for 20 years, and Executive Officer (AFROTC) Battalion.

I have been married to Joanne (Puckett) Cole for 39 years. She is currently a teacher at East Washington School.

I have three children which are all WKU graduates. Deborah (Cole) Stout, Leslie Cole, and Julia (Cole) Hodges. I also have two grandchildren; Emily Stout and Meghan Stout.

My memories of Western include basketball games in the Old Red Barn, dances played by the Red and Gray, Military Balls, Talisman Balls, crisp autumn afternoons on the Hill, football in the stadium, spring evenings and walks by the Kentucky Building, Ed Diddle and his red towel!

I have many hobbies. I like golf, travel, gardening, acting in Summer Stock at Spring Mill (Mitchell, IN), grandchildren, and community work.

GINGER PALMER COLLINS, Class of 1956, B.S. Degree in Music Education, currently living in Jacksonville, FL.

I graduated from College High in 1951 and went right on to Western, starting in summer school. I was all set to graduate with the class of 1954 but married and wound up completing Dr. Willey's and Mrs. Travelstead's classes by correspondence.

I continued as a symphony cellist and as organist and teacher until my husband and I parted in 1970.

I'm currently a Collection Representative for Continental Cablevision, enjoying all the benefits of working outdoors.

My memories of Western include: hearing the Hilltoppers practicing "Trying" before they made their hit recording; practice teaching was a thrill not since equaled; unlike some I loved chapel; I played clarinet in the band and enjoyed marching and playing for the games; and most important my friends, teachers, and my fellow students. There's something about college life that leaves one with a wonderful feeling that never goes away.

BILL COOK, Class of 1954, B.S. in Geology/ Geography, currently residing in Kennesaw, GA.

I received commission into the Air Force. My first assignment was at Dobbins A.F.B., Marietta, GA. This is where I met my wife, Bobbie. We were married in 1957. In 1958 I went to U.S.A.F. Academy. We were there until late 1962, when I returned to Marietta and entered the mobile home sales and parks business.

At this time I am the owner of the **A Bar G Mobile Home Sales**, and the Vice President-Sales.

I received the Commendation Medal while in the United States Air Force. I am married to Bobbie, she is a Homemaker. We have four children, Billy, 27; Tracy, 26; Randy and Renee, 21 (twins).

My memories of Western include playing basketball, living in Ed Diddle's house, ("dorm"), Baron's Club parties and dances.

My hobbies include coaching midget football 13 years, and playing golf.

S. JOHN COOMBS, Class of 1959, currently residing in Bowling Green, KY.

After graduation I spent three years in the United States Marine Corp. Two of those years were in Hawaii. I then taught school and coached football and track in Ormond Beach, FL.

I worked for a short time with Texaco, Inc. and then owned a business, Moutardier Resort and Boat Dock in Edmonson Co., KY.

After selling my portion of the business I

moved my family back to Hollywood, FL and worked for a Quaker State Oil District for 15 years. When the company was sold I decided to move back to Bowling Green, KY.

I am now the District Manager for Citgo Petroleum and service the states of Kentucky and Tennessee.

I have three children, Terri Lynn, 30; Meredith Ian, 21; and Jonathan Charles, 17.

Golf is what I like best when I have the spare time to enjoy the game.

My days at Western are memorable ones. I'll never forget the track team and Coach Turner Elrod, the OMA KRON Fraternity, Potter Hall, working in the snack bar, and basketball games in the Old Red Barn. The greatest thing of all is the friends made during that time.

To me Western in the 50s was the greatest.

GRACE MARIE COPAS, Class of 1950, BS Degree in English.

I taught 44-1/2 years which included grades one through senior high school. Forty-two and a half years were taught in Barren Co., KY and two years in the west.

I enjoyed dormitory life having stayed in Potter Hall, West Hall and McLean Hall. My favorite was Potter Hall.

I liked the chimes although they made the hours slip by so fast. I liked all my teachers. I was in Dr. Gordon Wilson's last class. I liked all my roommates at the dorm. I got my M.A. in 1959.

I liked the song, **College Height on Hilltops Fair.** My favorite line in the song is "Service ever is thy goal, Thy spirit ever new."

I also liked the song, **Believe in the Power of the Blue and the Gray.** My favorite lines are "For there dost inspire with knowledge and truth, all the daughters and sons of the hill."

I am proud to be a "daughter of the hill."

GARLAND C. COTTRELL, Class of 1953, awarded the B.S. and M.A. Degrees in '53 and '57 respectively. Received the Ed. S. Degree from George Peabody College in 1961.

After I had completed military assignments I settled into a career in public school administration in Hart and Hardin Co., KY. I served as an elementary and high school principal, also as assistant superintendent.

My wife, Verna Dean, and I are the parents of seven children. Five of them, Gary, Joe, Cindy, Patty, and Ann have been awarded degrees by Western. Ted and Ben, the youngest, are pursuing their interests elsewhere.

I have been a member of and held offices at various levels in several professional organizations. I am active in church work and support youth groups by volunteering for service.

Western has furnished me with a long list of cherished memories involving classmates, faculty, weather and events. On cold snowy evenings a slip of the foot on College Street often meant an unscheduled trip downtown.

Since retiring from public school work I have become a Seasonal Park Ranger at Mammoth Cave National Park.

BARBARA ASHBURY CRENSHAW, Class of 1956, B.S. Elementary Education, Louisville, KY. Further Education - MED in 1983, Specialty in Math. Current position - Middle School Math and Computer teacher - grades 5-8 - Kentucky Country Day School - Louisville, KY. Honors - Received the endowed chair in Mathematics and Computer - 1985-1987; received the Eric Davis Memorial Award for excellence in teaching - June, 1988. Spouse - Robert L. Crenshaw - Draftsman. Children: Lynda Fadler, Latin and History teacher in Orlando, FL; Betty S. Crenshaw - fifth grade teacher at Brandeis Elementary School here in Louisville. Grandchildren: Katey Fadler - age 18 months.

My first weekend on campus as a freshman, feeling very strange, not knowing my way around, my roommate and I headed for the cafeteria for supper. As we walked up the hill, a gentleman stopped us and asked us the way to Van Meter Auditorium. We had a hard time deciding which way to tell him to go but we finally managed to figure it out and instruct him. He burst out laughing and introduced himself. It was Coach Ed Diddle. Since I am 5'11" tall, he asked me if I would be interested in playing on his basketball team. From then on, everytime he saw me, he asked if I were ready to start practicing for the team. He certainly made me feel welcome.

My education at Western certainly prepared me well for my career. It instilled in me a love of learning, teaching, and children. These are still strongly felt today as I continue my career. My background in Education was outstanding as I began my career in 1956. I have never forgotten the interesting discussions in Dr. Cole's education classes and the beautiful paintings in Dr. Wilson's home. Mrs. Robertson made history come to life for all of us, and many other dedicated teachers were an inspiration.

CLAUDIA DISHMAN CRUMP, Class of 1952, B.S. Degree in Elementary Education, currently living in New Albany, IN.

I continued my education with a M.S. at Indiana University in 1957 and an Ed. D at Indiana University in 1969.

I am a Professor of Education at Indiana University Southeast, New Albany. My job responsibilities include being an instructor in general, Language Arts and Social Studies; Supervisor of Field Experiences.

Other important positions include author of Indiana Yesterday and Today (pupil and teacher texts), Silver Burdett & Ginn, 1985 (currently rewriting the text for next state adoption), author of Teaching History in the Elementary School (with John Hoge of University of Georgia), ERIC Clearing House for Social Studies, 1988; author of Teaching for Social Values in Social Studies, ACEI, 1972 (with Maxine Dunfee of IU).

My husband Stanley L. Crump is retired from E.I. Dupont.

My honors include Outstanding Professor, Indiana University, 1972; Sagamore of the Wabash (Governor's Award of the State of Indiana), 1987; currently secretary of The World Council for Curriculum and Instruction; presenter at four national and international conferences (National Council for the Social Studies, Orlando, November, 1988; Association for Supervision and Curriculum Development, Orlando, March, 1989; Association of Childhood Education International, Indianapolis, April, 1989; and World Council for Curriculum and Instruction, Netherlands, August, 1989).

While I was in Central South Africa I stud-

ied culture and education. I have conducted research in teacher questioning, values of education, history instruction in the elementary school and varying cultures (Amish, Shaker, New Harmonists).

My hobbies include photography, and Japanese landscaping (rock gardens).

ROBERT M. DALE (BOB), Class of 1959, B.A. Economics. Currently living in Brooklyn, MI.

I am currently a Sales Rep. for General Electric Co.

I am married to Nancie Dale who is a marketing specialist at WILX-TV 10. We have two children, Dierdre, 26, and Shari, 23.

My memories of Western include the 13'ers.

BOB DANIELS, Class of 1957, Geography Degree and Masters Degree in 1964, currently living in Versailles, KY.

I have been self-employed for 12 years at Bob Daniels Sporting Goods in Lexington, KY and Paintsville, KY.

Positions which I have held include: Basketball Coach at Sacramento High School from 1957-1960, Basketball Coach at Muhlenberg Central High School from 1960-1964, Basketball Coach at Kentucky Wesleyan College form 1964-1972, Basketball Coach at Marshall University from 1972-1977, Pitcher for the Pittsburgh Pirates Baseball Team from 1958-1960.

Accomplishments which I have made are that I coached Sacramento High School to State Basketball Tournament (1958), Pitched a no-hitter in Pittsburgh Pirates Minor League (1959), Coached Kentucky Wesleyan to NCAA Tournament (1965), Coached KWC Basketball Team to National College Division Championship (1967 & 1968), National Coach of the Year in College Division Basketball (1968), Outstanding Young Man—Owensboro, KY (1969), Coached Marshall University to National Invitational Tournament (1972).

I am married to Gayle (Bryant) Daniels who is a partner in our business. We have two children; Gay and Scott who both live in Lexington.

My hobbies include attending sports events and playing golf and basketball.

My memories of WKU are that it was a great place to get an education because of the friendliness of the people and the supervision and friendship of Coach Diddle.

GAYLE BRYANT DANIELS, Class of 1957, Home Economics, currently living in Versailles, KY.

I continued my education with a Masters Degree with an emphasis in Physical Education from Evansville University.

I am self employed at Bob Daniels Sporting Goods, Lexington, KY and Paintsville, KY.

Other important positions include, 1957-60 taught in McLean County at Salramento High; 1960-64 taught in Muhlenberg County at Muhlenberg Central; 1964-72 taught in Daviess County at Daviess County Junior and Apollo High School; and 1975-76 taught in West Virginia at Milton High School. I have been a Real Estate Salesperson, Welcome Wagon Hostess, coached a girls track team, and sponsored cheerleaders.

I have attended many basketball games with my husband coaching and a son playing. Our son Scott played at Eastern Kentucky University. I have done many hours of volunteer work and now I am a sustaining member of the Lexington Junior League. For the past three years I have worked with the Junior Miss Program of Woodford County.

I have two children, Gayle and Scott, both living in Lexington.

My husband and business partner is Bob Daniel.

Memories of WKU are going to the Goal Post and Student Union between classes, walking downtown to movies, going to basketball games in the old Red Barn and the many friends that I made. While we were attending Western it was small enough that you knew most people on campus.

My hobbies include collecting antiques, attending sporting events, and playing golf.

SHELLY HAMPTON DANTZLER, Class of 1956, B.S. Degree in Home Economics, currently living in Radcliff, KY.

After graduation, I taught in San Diego, CA; Fort Knox, KY; Fort Campbell, KY; and a Christian academy in Chicago, IL.

Since then I have been a full-time mother at home to three daughters. Becky is 28, married and has a degree in Child Studies from Colorado State University. She and her husband have a son, Jason. Sarah is 21 and is a May 1989 graduate with a Fine Arts Design degree from Eastern Kentucky University and Beth is 15 and a sophomore at North Hardin High School, Radcliff, KY. My husband, Dan, is a Clemson University graduate and is an education specialist in the Armor School at Fort Knox, KY.

Presently, I am a volunteer tutor in the Hardin County Schools. I also serve as an officer with Christian Women's Club.

My memories include vespers each evening at the library, as a freshman going to see my first football game, signing out and in at McLean Hall, curfew at 9:30 p.m., being called down by the office girl for singing in the shower (M-I-C-K-E-Y M-O-U-S-E); and watching the beautiful sunsets from the old stadium.

BERNARD D. DAVIS, Class of 1958, B.S. Commerce. Currently living in Bowling Green, KY.

I am co-owner of SpotCash Store, Inc., Bowling Green, KY. My responsibilities are buying, selling, bookkeeping, etc.

Other positions I have held are past president—St. Joseph PTA, past president—T.C. Cherry PTA, past director—B.G.-W.C. Jaycees.

I am married to Patricia L. (Perrone) Davis. She is a teacher. We have four sons; Scott, 27; Victor, 25; Steve, 23; Vincent, 21.

My fondest memories are of going up and down the hill from B.U. to WKU to pick up "friends".

PAT PERRONE DAVIS, Class of 1960, B.S. Area of Concentration Commercial Education, currently living in Bowling Green, KY.

I furthered my education in 1975, by receiving a M.A. in Secondary Ed./Bus. Education.

I am a substitute teacher and business teacher at Warren County and Bowling Green

City Schools and at Bowling Green Voc. School. I also teach classes for adults at night—typing and Accounting II.

I held important positions such as a business Teacher at Shawnee Jr. High; Durrett High 1960/61; Secretary Department Chairperson for ten years; Chairperson Bowling Green Junior College; business teacher—set up new business Clerical program at Great Onyx Job Corps, Mammoth Cave National Park; and business teacher—Butler County High School.

I am a member of the Holy Spirit Catholic Church Choir, Mount St. Joseph Ursuline Community Associate member, and received three outstanding teaching plaques from students.

My husband, Bernard D. Davis, attended the Bowling Green Business University and graduate in 1950. He is self-employed, operating a Men's and Boy's Retail Store. We have four sons—Scott (27), Victor (25), Stephen (23), and Vincent (21).

Memories of WKU include: President (walking up and down hill for business classes in ten minutes), Kelly Thompson "Spirit Makes the Master" dedication, Beta Omega Chi Sorority Sisters, Mr. Ivan Wilson's famous water color classes, working in Bob Cochran's public relations office, Coach Diddle's basketball games, and fraternity dances.

It truly was FABULOUS during my college years of 1956-60.

WALLACE D. DAWSON, Class of '54, BS Biology, Louisville, KY.

When I arrived at Western in September 1950 on the L&N Pan American and took up residence in Potter Hall, the male student body was still abundantly populated by World War II veterans on the GI Bill, serious about earning a degree and getting on with life. Few students owned automobiles, and the idea of a good time was hoofing it to Tandy's or Chick's for a few games of pool or out to Bill Hardin's or down to Hunt's Oyster Bar on South Main for a cold beer.

Bull sessions in the dorm rooms were common, and favored topics were politics and religion. This was the peak of the McCarthy era. A liberal was anyone who favored TVA. When Truman fired General MacArthur, many a heated debate followed. Of course, the WWII vets always had war stories to entertain us. My room mate had one about how he single-handedly captured a German Panzer tank. Others described the horrors of combat. Music preferences inclined to country and western - then called "hillbilly". This was the

heydey of Hank Williams, Ernest Tubb and Kitty Wells.

By the time I graduated four years later, a very different atmosphere prevailed. Ike was president; peace and prosperity reigned. The GI Bill students were gone. Younger students, who were teenagers in the post-war period, were not at Western. Concerns were superficial, a mood of levity pervaded the campus. The Student Union Building had been completed the previous year, and more of the social life centered on campus activities. Diddle's 1954 basketball team ran up a long victory streak and ranked in the top ten nationally. The first panty raid brought the state police to campus. Students with autos were no longer a rarity. The first hints of rock and roll were being heard arising from something called rhythm and blues or "race music". We were all very proud of our own "Hilltoppers" with Jimmy Sacca, then at the peak of popularity.

ELMER C. DAY, Class of 1953, B.S. in Math/Physics. Currently living in Gaithesburg, MD.

I furthered my education at Harvard University, M.S. Applied Math, 1955.

I am Engineering Mgr. at IBM Corp., Gaithesburg, MD. My responsibility is to manage International Air Traffic Control System.

I am married to Frances Day, who is an Executive Secretary. We have four children and two grandchildren. My daughter, Susan, graduated from Western in 1983.

I miss the crew from Potter Hall.

DOROTHY BROWN DOOR, Class of 1954. Being from Portland, TN I came to Western in 1952 from Martin College, Pulaski, TN. I lived in West Hall and McLean Hall, fond memories of both.

After receiving B.A. Degree in Library Science in 1954 I went to Chattanooga, TN to be librarian at Kirkman Technical High School for four years. Married Robert Door of Rhode Island in 1956.

IBM transferred us to Kingsport, TN in 1958, where we have remained, except for short special assignments. I attended East Tennessee State University Graduate School. Did substitute teaching 12 years at Dobyns Bennett High School. In 1981 I went with Sullivan County Schools as elementary librarian at two schools. Had three children in three different colleges that year—all three have now graduated from college, but I still go to two school libraries.

I was active for many years in the AAUW

and Art Guild, entering shows and sales with watercolor paintings. Sewing, knitting, church, and walking fill much time.

Traveling is a favorite pass time, three trips to Europe. The most memorable being a chaperone for high school band trip to Europe in 1981. We go to New England every summer.

Western has many memories. One of the fondest, and most surprising, was being chosen a "campus favorite girl" after being there just one year and a transfer student. Going to basketball games early for a good seat; the Hilltoppers first basketball game on TV; going to State St. Methodist Church to eat Sunday evenings; Religious Council; Cherry Hall chimes every 15 minutes==Memories==how they linger!

BEULAH W. DOWELL, currently living in Mayfield, KY.

My husband, Edward N. Dowell and I taught Agriculture and Home Economics in Marshall and Graves County from 1930 to 1960. After his untimely death in 1960, I continued to teach until 1965. I worked at Murray State as Hall Director two years when I retired to my home and farm. In 1977 I sold my farm and moved to Mayfield, where I now live.

We had one daughter and now I have two lovely granddaughters.

My health is fair at age 86, and I enjoy my home, hobbies, family, and church family.

I appreciate the good training I received at Western and am proud to have Western as my Alma Mater.

W.R. (BILL) DORRIS, Class of 1959, Major in Business. Currently living in Hopkinsville, KY.

I furthered my education at Murray State University, 15 hrs. MBA.

I am personnel Director at Western State Hospital in Hopkinsville, KY. My responsibilities include staff positions and payroll.

I am also Assistant Hospital Administrator, and Administrator WSH/ICF (Western State Hospital). I am also licensed with Kentucky Board for Nursing Home Administrators.

I am married to Faye M. Dorris, who is a school psychometrist. We have one daughter 22 years old, who is a 1988 graduate of the University of Kentucky.

ROBERT A. EIMER, Class of 1953, B.S. Degree in Physical Education, currently living in Dayton, OH.

I continued my education with military courses and real estate subjects.

I am retired with 26 years experience in the

Air Force (LTC) and ten years with a civilian company. My job responsibilities in the Air Force were Chief of Supply/Squadron Commander. My responsibilities in civilian life were Manager of Production and Inventory Control for a company located in the Dayton area.

I was selected as an Air Force Outstanding Supply Officer of the Year for four years.

I am married to Mary H., a housewife. My children are: Doug, 34, who is an IBM Engineer; Steve, 31, who is a Medical Technologist, and Mark, 26, who is an Engineer with the USAF.

My memories of WKU include playing football, running track, and living in Potter Hall. The camaraderie that existed was just great.

My hobbies include golf, bowling, and traveling.

SHIRLEY CARDEN ELKINS, Class of '54, B.S. Home Economics. After graduating from Western I began teaching Home Economics in the Daviess County schools in Owensboro, KY. I earned a Masters Degree in Home Economics Education at University of Kentucky in 1962. I continued teaching in Daviess County schools for 30 years, retiring in 1984.

My husband, James Elkins, earned his Masters degree at WKU, and taught journalism at Kentucky Wesleyan College and Owensboro Public Schools for 23 years.

We have three children. James Jr. is an insurance business in Bozeman, MT, Jamie Lenon a dental assistant in Paducah, KY and Lisa Elkins, who graduated from Western in 1984, is an interior designer for Broyhill Furniture Co. in Lenoir, NC.

Western holds many memories for me. Some of them are rushing to get in McLean Hall by curfew, and not making it a few times, being grounded for cooking in my room, and trying to walk "the hill" in all the snow and ice in the winter of 1950-51, falling down once, and Ed Diddle helping me up.

Since my retirement, we have moved to

Smyrna, GA. James is working as a church consultant for United Church Directories, and I am a "lady of leisure".

KENNETH R. FLEENOR, Class of '51, Agriculture/Biology, Selma, TX. I grew up on campus at Western, graduating from College High with the class of '47. After being commissioned through Western's AFROTC program, I entered active duty and completed pilot training. I graduated from numerous service schools, including the Armed Forces Staff College in 1967. After a very rewarding career, I retired from the Air Force, after more than 28 years of active duty, on Aug. 1, 1980.

Anne Read of Scottsville, KY and I were married while at Western in June of '51. We have five children, a son John and daughters Kathy, Patti, Kerry, and Kay, and nine grandchildren.

Since leaving the Air Force I have served as Regional Coordinator for the Texas War on Drugs Program and as General Manager of the San Antonio Stock Show and Rodeo. I have served on the Board of Directors of United Services Automobile Association, the Randolph Metrocom Chamber of Commerce, the Board of United Way, and am currently on the Board of USAA Federal Savings Bank. In addition to several private business interests, I am currently Mayor of the City of Selma, TX.

ANNE DAWSON FORD, Class of 1955, B.A. in Social Science, currently living in Owensboro, KY.

I furthered my education by getting a M.A. in Education in 1974.

I am a teacher at Daviess County, and currently teach English and geography at 6th and 7th grade levels. I hold important positions such as a homemaker, classroom teacher, and Sunday School teacher.

My husband is William E. Ford, Jr. and he is a retired Industrial Arts teacher and is now a very busy woodworker, carpenter, etc. We have two children, William E. Ford III (28) and Sarah Ford (24). We have two grandchildren, Lyndsay Ann Ford (four), and William E. Ford IV (five months).

Memories of WKU include:Life in McLean Hall, our many friends, eating at Hilltoppers, the fantastic basketball games, Mr. Cockrill's geography classes, walking everywhere, Homecoming activities, Bowling Green itself—loved it all!! Everyone was so friendly. We were like a big family!

ANN TAYLOR HARRISON (FORD), Class of 1958, Elem. Education (B.A.) and a M.A. in Elem. Education and Art in June 1977. I am currently residing in Bowling Green, KY.

When starting at Western in the fall of 1954 the student body was small enough that we knew most everyone on campus by sight if not by name. I've lived with a lot of W.K.U. history—from Kelly Thompson (then acting president) to Thomas Meredith (current president). The Western Spirit lives on! I even remember the words to "College Heights" thanks to Nell Gooch Travelstead's beating it into my head in student assembly.

I met my husband, Scott Ford, a Navy veteran at Western and we married in August of 1958. I was secretary to Dr. F.C. Grise until his retirement and then for Dr. Raymond Cravens until the birth of our first child in August of 1960. We lived in Vets' Village until June 1961 when my husband graduated with a B.S. in Biology and a teaching degree. After six years at Tulane, a Ph. D. in Medical Mycology and another child, we moved back to Bowling Green into faculty housing (across from Vet's Village—where we started).

My husband still teaches at W.K.U. in the Biology Dept. and I work part time at the local newspaper. Our children and their spouses all attended Western. Our son, Douglas 28 and his wife Debbie got their M.A.'s here. He's now a nursing home administrator in Orlando, FL. Debbie teaches dance and takes care of our first grandchild, Matthew. Our daughter, Laura Kirby 26, is an R.N. in the Medical Center in Bowling Green. Her husband, Ron Kirby Jr., is in the auction and realty business.

My hobbies are painting, reading, cooking and bowling. My husband is an avid golfer. We are active in our church and still see a lot of our old school friends, many at W.K.U. sporting events. We have a really good life—a lot of it has quite a bit to do with our experiences at Western.

WILLIAM E. FORD, JR., Class of 1955, B.S.

Industrial Education, currently living in Owensboro, KY.

I furthered my education by receiving a M.A. in Industrial Education in 1972.

I am a retired teacher from Daviess County High School and also retired as Lt. Col. from the USAF Reserves. I now own and operate a custom woodworking shop.

I am married to Ann Ford, who is a teacher at Daviess County Middle School. We have two children and two grandchildren; William E. Ford III, 28, and Sarah Ford, 24, William E. Ford IV, four months, and Lyndsay Ann, four years.

My memories of Western include basketball games, Industrial Arts labs, the town of Bowling Green and eating at Hilltoppers.

I received Outstanding Educator in 1979, Western Kentucky's Outstanding Air Force Academy Liaison Officer for 1979, KEA delegate several years, NEA delegate four years, Kentucky Colonel, Member Air Force Association Reserve Officer Association, National Education Association, Kentucky Education Association, Local Education Association, American Industrial Arts Association, and served on the editorial board of "Man, Society, Technology".

The years at Western were some of the best of my life.

I now enjoy working with my woodworking activities.

I enjoy going to some of the NASCAR Winston Cup Auto Races and cheering on my favorite driver, Darrell Waltrip—a former student.

LOUISE BARBOUR FORSYTHE, Morgantown, KY, BS '58 and MS '72. I first attended Western in the fall of 1952 and received a BS degree in home economics in 1958. During those years I also taught one year in Grayson County, one and one-half years in Barren County and one semester at Butler County High School, all in Kentucky. In 1972 I received a Masters degree from Western.

In 1956 I married Royce Forsythe, also a WKU graduate. We have two daughters, Kathy Forsythe Mills, age 29, and Rebecca Lynn Forsythe, age 24. Rebecca is also a graduate of Western while Kathy and her husband, James Cory Mills, are graduates of Campbellsville College. Cory is the son of the late George Mills and Martha Miller Mills Roberts, also Western students of the 50s. Kathy and Cory are the parents of our two grandsons, Daniel and Stephen Mills.

After teaching home economics for 28 years at Butler County High School in Morgantown,

KY, I retired in October 1987. While teaching, I was co-adviser of Future Homemakers of America and chaired the Vocational department the last four years of teaching.

At present I am thoroughly enjoying retirement and doing the things I always thought I'd do when I retired.

ROYCE FINLEY FORSYTHE, BS '55, Morgantown, KY. I, along with my twin brother Lanyce, started to school at Western in 1950 and received a BS degree in agriculture in 1955. In July of 1955 I entered military service where I served for two years.

On Dec. 21, 1956 I married the former Louise Barbour, also a Western graduate. We are the parents of two daughters, Kathy Louise and Rebecca Lynn. Kathy and her husband, Cory Mills, are parents of two sons, Daniel Page Mills, age four and Stephen Royce Mills, born Feb. 9, 1989. Kathy and Cory are with Grace Baptist Church in Evansville, IN where Cory serves as Minister of Music. Rebecca lives in Morgantown and teaches special education at Butler County High School.

Beginning in August of 1957 until I retired in the summer of 1985, I taught in the biology department at Butler County High School in Morgantown, KY.

MARCIE A. FRANKLIN, Class of 1954, B.S. in Elementary Ed. Currently living in Burkesville, KY.

I furthered my education by getting my M.A. from Western in 1957.

I am currently a third grade teacher in a self-contained classroom at Cumberland County Elementary School. I have taught for 42 years in Cumberland County.

I have received two outstanding teacher awards. One in 1974 and again in 1980.

My husband, Carl P. Franklin is deceased. I have one daughter, Charlene Rabold and one grandson David Paul Shoultz.

I enjoy reading, gardening, and managing my farms.

LAWRENCE R. FRENCH, Class of 1954, B.A. Math. While waiting for my Air Force assignment, I returned home to Elizabethtown and taught and coached in a Hardin County elementary school.

By 1985, the Air Force magically helped me program 41 years of duties into a 30 year career. These included 18 years as a pilot, 20 years in Weather Service, and three years of meteorology studies at Penn State University, (BS - 1962), and University of Oklahoma, (MS - 1968). We enjoyed great football, but missed Western quality basketball.

In 1956, I married Betty Sue Davis from Vine Grove, (now North Hardin), and WKU, (1952-54). We have two daughters, Suzanne and Lara.

We still live in O'Fallon, IL, 20 minutes east of St. Louis, where we retired from the Air Force. I am now a registered agent and representative of an international company, USPA and IRA. We do family financial programs.

I remember most the friendly helpful spirit of the 2,000 students and faculty as I walked the halls of Cherry, and the campus paths to the Western Lunchroom, Goal Post, McLean Hall, Red Barn and baseball practice. I jog for fitness now, but I remember sprinting up the hill from off campus many times for those early M-W-F classes.

PHILIP L. FUSON, M.D., Class of 1950, B.S. in Biology. Currently living in Morristown, TN.

I furthered my education at the University of Louisville, M.D. 1954, Certified American Board of Surgery 1964, General Surgery Residence—Affiliated Hospitals, Ohio State University.

Currently, I am in private practice at the V.A. Center in Dayton, OH.

Other positions include member and secretary of Board of Directors—Morristown-Hamblen Hospital (1970 to present), and member of Lakeway Medical Society, Tennessee Medical Association, and Knoxville Surgical Society.

I am married to Anne Fuson. We have three children; Rebecca Anne, Jennifer Lynn, and Philip L., III.

Memories of WKU include living in Veteran's Village in what was known as double trailer, outstanding professor Dr. L.Y. Lancaster, Coach Diddle and his great teams.

JACQUELINE (BERGER) GALLOWAY, Class 1952, B.S. Degree in Elementary Education, currently living in Altamonte Springs, FL.

I am retired from Nationwide Insurance Company of Columbus, OH.

My job responsibilities included coder-rater in Commercial Department of Insurance.

Other important positions included teaching in six states and a preschool substitute.

My activities include selling some paintings done in oils, Church Archives, volunteer in hospitals and schools.

I have three children and four grandchildren.

My memories of WKU are Coach Diddle, Hilltoppers, they played Jim Sacca, and Hilltoppers' records on a local radio station which plays music of 40-50-60s.

My hobbies include: Walking, swimming, painting, sewing, working part time, volunteering at the local church.

My time at Western was the greatest!

GLYNA (MEREDITH) GALLREIN, Class of 1959, B.S. Degree in Elementary Education, currently living in Anchorage, KY.

I continued my education with a M.A. in Elementary Education at WKU in 1962.

I am the owner and manager of rental properties in Louisville, KY.

Other important positions include ten years teaching experience in Jefferson County Schools.

My husband is David R. Gallrein. He is the Agency Manager of Jefferson Farm Bureau Insurance Company.

I have two daughters: Anne, 19, who is a sophomore at UK; and Caroline, 16, who is a sophomore at Kentucky County Day School.

My memories of WKU include: Very few students had cars so we walked everywhere, living in Potter Hall (two telephones in the whole dorm), student trips with the Education Department, four or five girls going home to Morganfield, KY with Charla Mauzy ('59) for weekends to visit her family. After 30 years, we still get together every two years and reminisce about our days at Western!

See photos on page 90.

BOBBY G. GARRETT, Class of 1950, B.S. Industrial Art. Currently living in Hanover, PA.

I am retired from Worthington Pump Co. in Taneytown, MD. I retired after 33 years of working in marketing and sales for Worthington Pump Co.

I am married to Mary Lou Garrett who is a housewife. We have two children, Mary Beth (32), and Barbara Jane (28).

My memories of Western include the spirit of the student body and their loyalty to Western.

VERNON L. GARY AND NELDA ANN BARNES GARY, Bowling Green, KY. I enrolled in Western Kentucky State Teachers College in the Summer of 1953.

I transferred to the Bowling Green College of Commerce of the Bowling Green Business University, which was later purchased by WKU.

On May 26, 1956 I married Nelda Ann Barnes, who was also a student at Western, from Beaver Dam, KY.

I received a B.S. degree in the Spring of 1960, after having alternating semesters with work and school, and also serving in the U.S. Military. Nelda received a Secretarial Science degree from B.U., but from the birth of our first child has been a full time mother and homemaker.

For 28 years I was a working partner in Gary Brothers Crushed Stone Co.

At the present time other than some commercial Real estate and some other investments, I am retired.

My wife Nelda and I have three married children, of whom they all and their spouses have graduated from WKU or at least will have after the youngest graduates in December of 1989.

We are members of the Twelfth Street Church of Christ, 213 E. 12th Street, here in Bowling Green.

LAWRENCE B. "BUTCH" GILBERT, Class of 1952, B.S. Physical Education. I spent eight years as a student at WKU culminating in a masters degree in Education in 1956. Those years shaped my views, my future and my memories.

As an undergraduate I remember the team spirit, and the camaraderie between the football players. One of the more unique memories is playing rook underneath the goal post.

In Professor Whitmer's anatomy class we really had to keep that dead cat greased down to find all those muscles we had drawn! And giving that speech to pass Dr. Russell Miller's speech class in Van Meter Auditorium, that an experience I never got over - all by myself in that big, big building.

I followed through with my love so sports by teaching P.E. and coaching football including 16 years as assistant coach with Jimmy Fix. Today I teach Phys. Ed. back at WKU.

My wife, the former Daphna Gabbard, and I have two sons, Larry and Steve and two wonderful granddaughters, LeeAnna and Kelly Gilbert.

I'm active in the American Football Coaches Assoc. and a lifetime member of the Kentucky High School Coaches Association.

PATRICIA (WOOSLEY) GILMAN,
Class of 1956, A.B. Degree in Social Sciences, currently living in Lecanto, FL.

I continued my education with a M.S. Degree at Indiana University in 1962.

I am a Sixth Grade Teacher at the Lecanto Middle School and have been for three years. My job responsibilities include Sixth Grade Reading and being the Team Leader.

Other important positions include seven years at Jefferson Co., KY. I moved to Florida in 1963 and taught in Tarpon Springs, FL for four years, ten years at Crystal River, FL.

My husband is Lloyd F. Gilman. He is the owner of Gilman's Custom Furniture and Cabinets.

I have two sons; Lloyd Stephen, 21, and Mark Christopher, 16.

My memories of WKU are all the fun and friends while living in McLean Hall.

LAURA PURCELL GLENN, a former
member of the Glasgow, KY, Kay Bledsoe Business and Professional Women's Club. I was the guest soloist at one of the Winter Board meetings at the Galt House, Louisville, KY (1973).

I received the Golden Poet award for 1988, in Anaheim, CA, August 26, 27, and 28. It was the Fourth Annual Poetry Convention 2,000 received such an award and I was one of the 2,000. (World of Poetry Convention)

I was also the Supervisor and Instructor at the Tinyman (Barren County) Park of the Glasgow Recreation Department and the Summer Food Program for three years, Southern Kentucky Community Action Agency Center Street Bowling Green, KY.

I received an appreciation award for the above positions.

A book of poems will be published soon. A poem, "Surviving in this Land" has been accepted by the Music City Song-Crafters, Nashville, TN, to be set to music I'm looking forward for it to become a "Hit" song.

I have three children; two sons and one daughter. Lucian is a Respiratory Therapist at Medical Center, Bowling Green, KY. Wm. Keith, is a Junior at the University of Louisville, majoring in P.E., and Donna Marie is a Freshman at Glasgow High School, Glasgow, KY. She made All District in the Glasgow Scotties Band—Clarinet.

I also taught (13 years) in the Chicago City School System, Chicago, IL.

I was Teacher of the Year, at the Glasgow Campus, Bowling Green Junior College, Glasgow, KY (the name was Wooldridge at the time).

Most of all I remember the beautiful Commencement at night—the beautiful lights and us marching in, a building is now on the spot, I think that it was near the Music Building, in front of the cafeteria, the families were sitting in the stadium (outside).

STANLEY H. GRADY, Class of 1951, B.S. in
Biology, currently living in Jerome, MI.

I furthered my education by receiving my D.D.S. at the University of Detroit School of Dentistry.

I am now retired.

My wife's name is Joyce and she works part time as a X-Ray Technician. We have three children; Ann (22), Mike (24), and Steve (26).

I play trumpet with various Jazz, Dance Concert and Show Bands.

I teach improvisation and Jazz history at Jackson Community College, Jackson, MI.

I am a past president of the Jackson District Dental society, and the Kiwanis Club of Addison, MI.

My memories of Western include: The Red & Gray Orchestra, and the friendliness of the instructors and students. My hobbies are music, golf, cross-country skiing, and biking.

LARRY GRAHAM, Class of 1952, B.S. in
Agriculture, currently living in Bowling Green, KY.

I am the owner-operator of Riverview Farms, Purebred Breeding Cattle (Charolais Cattle).

I am past President of Kentucky Charolais Association Member of American International Charolais Association, Executive Director of Kentucky Beef Cattle Association, Chairman of Research and Education Committee of the Kentucky Beef Cattle Association, member of the National Cattlemen's Association, member of (NCA) Research and Education Committee, and member of National Integrater Resource Management Committee.

My wife and partner is Beverly. We have four children and nine grandchildren.

My memories of WKU start with the first grade when we collected pennies for Dr. Cherry's statue and we perceived that they melted the pennies to cast the statue. (By high school I found that that was a false impression), Hardin's Bar-B-Que (at intersection of Russellville Road and University Boulevard—Southwest Corner where parking lot is located), the "Goal Post" and Rook Games during free periods.

CHARLE SNOW GUTHRIE, Class of
1958, degree in English. Currently living in Bowling Green, KY.

I continued my education at Western getting my master's in English, and my Ed. D at UK.

I am retired from the English Department at Western. I was an instructor at Cumberland County High School and also an Editor at Kentucky Folklore Records.

I am the author of **Kentucky Freemasonry, 1788-1978** and active in the Methodist Church, and Freemasonry.

I am married to Vera Grinstead, who is retired. We have two children, Teresa (22), and Troy (20). We also have two grandchildren, Justin and John.

My memories of Western include classes with Gordon Wilson Sr., and L.Y. Lancaster.

VERA GRINSTEAD GUTHRIE, Class
of 1953, Math-Library Science Major, currently living in Bowling Green, KY.

Received my M.S. in Library Science from U.K. in 1957, and my Ed.D from U.K. in 1973.

I am retired. I was a teacher in the elementary and secondary schools for six years, and Professor of Library Science, at WKU for 26 years.

I am Chairperson, Board of Library Certification of Kentucky; Chairperson Salvation Army Advisory Board, and President elect of Altrusa Club of Bowling Green.

I am married to Charles S. Guthrie and we have two children; Teresa Wissing, 22, and Troy Guthrie, 20; and two grandchildren, Justin and John Wissing.

My memories of WKU include Mr. Hugh Johnson standing before a math class and Dr. Gordon Wilson teaching poetry, Dr. Wilgus' folklore class, and senior reception at the President's home.

My hobbies are crocheting and quilting.

STOKELY B. HALL, Class of 1957 and 1965,
B.S. and M.A., currently living in Bowling Green, KY.

I have 37 hours above the Master's Degree at University of Tennessee, University of Kentucky and Western Kentucky University.

I am a Vocational Education Regional Coordinator for the Kentucky Department of Vocational Education Region IV. I am regional coordinator for vocational programs, services and activities in a ten county region.

I have also been a teacher for five years, worked in the insurance business four years, Guidance Counselor for seven years, and Regional Coordinator 17 years. I was in the Army from 1951 to 1953 during the Korean Conflict.

I am married to Anna N. Hall and we have three children and one grandchild. Gary (30), Anita (28), Donna (26), and Louise six months.

My memories of WKU include assisting Aubrey Hoofnel in guarding the Campus on Halloween, the uniqueness of Ms. Nell G. Travelstead and Dr. Mary I. Cole, and playing the guitar with "Wild" Bill Deweese in Potter's Hall Dorm. I still enjoy playing a guitar.

A.G. HAMILTON, currently living in Bowling Green, KY.

My wife is the former Janet Omer. We have one daughter, Linda H. McNevvin who lives in Florence, KY and three grandchildren, Kim, Kate and John Hart.

I am a retired Vice President of American National Bank and Trust Co., Bowling Green, KY. I was also the Manager of Kentucky Finance Co., Veteran of World War II serving three years in the South Pacific area with Air Force Engineers, and Superintendent of Kentucky Houses of Reform (Greendale), Lexington, KY.

I have served on the following Boards: member of First Christian Church (Disciples of Christ), past Chairman of the Board, Treasurer, and Elder; Civitan Club (30 Years) serving as President, Lt. Governor, and board member; Civitan "Outstanding Citizen" for 1968-69; Bowling Green Elks Lodge (24 Years); Bowling Green Girls Club (served as the first male president); Kentucky Consumer Finance "Man of the Year" award for 1963; Reedyville Lodge No. 438 F. and A.M. (49 years); City-County Planning Commission, (February 1967 to date) presently Chairman.

GRACE W. HARDIN, Class of 1950, Degree in Elementary Education.

I continued my education at the University of Louisville receiving my Masters in Education in 1953.

I audited 30 hours in 1982-83 being the oldest student on the campus. (I'm 88 years old and will be 89 in May)

After graduating in 1950 I moved to Jefferson County to teach. I retired in 1965 and was

fraternity house director for three years in Michigan.

I have two sons, Charles and Jim, five grandchildren and four great grandchildren.

My husband Leonard died in 1960, since then I have traveled, been a house mother at Adrian College in Michigan, and have done a lot of volunteer work.

In 1949 I went to Western and lived at Potter Hall for girls first part of the year. In August of 1949 my husband, Jim and I moved into Potter Hall for boys, to be director and manager. Dr. Garrett made me a little kitchenette, and Jim who was 12 yrs. old had the guest room. We really enjoyed it. Since I had been employed by Jefferson County Dr. Garrett hired us with an option of staying or leaving in January of 1950. I have a letter from Dr. Garrett praising us for a fine job. Leonard always regretted that we didn't stay.

I have such happy memories of Western, a spirit of the hill that is unlike any other institution. Dr. Cherry wanted it to be a place where anybody could go to learn, poor or rich. Somehow Western has always attracted the finest! I didn't have a teacher at Western that I didn't like—they were super.

JAMES "YOGI" HARDIN, Class of 1959, B.S. Degree in Geography, currently living in Dumfries, VA.

I continued my education at University of Virginia receiving a Masters Program in Human Resources.

I hold the position of Special Agent for the F.B.I. in Washington, D.C.

I achieved the rank of Major in the United States Marine Corp.

I am an honorary member of American College of Sports Medicine, and Little-All American Football team ('56-59). I am a Commercial/Instrument Rated Pilot.

I am married to Pat Stiff Hardin, who is Manager of Custom Decorating at JC Penney. Pat and I have two children, Pamela (28), and Valerie (27).

My memories of Western include courting Pat (my present wife), Coach Dennis kicking me in the shins for missing a play, and working at Gale Stiles Texaco.

My current hobbies include flying, physical fitness activities, sports and travel.

CLAUDETTE ROYSE HARRIS, Class of 1959, B.S. Biology. Currently living in Columbia, KY.

I continued my education at University of Louisville getting a degree in Med. Technology. I am currently employed part time as a Med. Technologist at Aaron Medical Center in Columbia, KY.

I am active in oil painting, quilt making, and gardening. My husband and I enjoy collecting and refinishing antiques. We also like boating and fishing when time allows.

I am married to Darrell E. Harris who is an employee at the Ford Motor Company. I have no children of my own. I have one step-son, Phillip.

My memories of Western include the "get-togethers" in the dorm, going to the basketball games and meeting with my friends at the "Gold-Post" before and after class.

NETTA OLDHAM HARRIS, Class of 1955, B.S. in Elementary Education, currently living in Owensboro, KY.

I am a retired Kindergarten Director and Head Teacher for 20 years. Currently I am a housewife.

I had the honor of being Football Homecoming Queen in 1954 while at Western.

I am married to Robert L. Harris, Manager and Chief Pilot of Texas Gas Transmission Co.

Robert and I have two sons who attended and graduated from Western. We also are proud grandparents of four grandchildren, three girls ages two, five, and six, and a one year old boy.

My memories of Western include being Homecoming Football queen in '54, The Goal Post, B.S.U. Cherry Hall, Chimes, McGlean Hall fun, basketball games and crowning, and the old gym.

My hobbies now include belonging to Kentucky Association of Children Under Six, South Association of Children Under Six, Womens Club of Owensboro, Love to cross stitch, and work with preschoolers at my church. I love to work in my herb and flowers.

CHARLES E. HARRIS, Class of 1958, M.A. in Education Administration, currently living in Somerset, KY. Further education includes Rank I.

My current position is as a Sales Representative for McGraw Hill Book Company. My job responsibilities include sales to elementary and high schools in Western Kentucky.

Other important positions include Child Abuse Commission ('84-89), Supt. of Schools ('85), and teaching. I was honored as the KASA Superintendent of the Year ('79).

I am married to Elizabeth Harris, a housewife. We have two children, Brent (31) AB Western 1980, and Brad (17).

My memories of Western include Tate Page, simplicity of the times, and the closeness of the faculty with the student body.

My hobbies now include golf and travel.

ROBERT LEE HARRIS, Class of 1954, B.S. in Geography, currently living in Owensboro, KY.

I furthered my education in the Air Force for four and one-half years.

My current position is Manager-Flight Operation with Texas Gas Trans. Corp. My responsibilities include managing Aviation Department at Texas Gas Trans. Co. I achieved the rank of Captain (Pilot-Company Aircraft BAE 800).

I am married to Netta Oldham Harris, a housewife, who is a retired kindergarten teacher. Netta and I have two sons who attended and graduated from Western. We also are proud grandparents of four grandchildren, three girls ages two, five, and six, and a one year old boy.

My memories of Western include basketball and football games, Goal Post, Hilltopper Cafe, and a very friendly campus.

I enjoy woodworking in my spare time.

HELEN PAULINE HARRIS, Class of 1951 and 1963, B.S./M.A. in Elementary Education, currently living in Drakesboro, KY.

To further my education I achieved Rank I status by obtaining 30 hours above a Masters Degree at Western.

I am a 5th grade elementary teacher at

Drakesboro School in Muhlenberg County. This year completes my 38th year in the classroom.

I also served as a part time secretary at Drakesboro First Baptist Church for more than 30 years in addition to full time teaching.

My activities are at Drakesboro School in Muhlenberg County. During that time I have coached nine students who have won the County Spelling Bee — three of those students have advanced to the State Spelling Bee sponsored by KEA. I am still hoping to get a state champion before I retire!

My memories of Western include being a student worker in Miss Etta Runner's office (part of President's office), serving as typist for Talisman, decorating old Western gym for Talisman Ball, education classes under Mr. Joe Howard and Dr. Mary I. Cole, Dr. Garret chipping ice off icy sidewalk steps after dark one night so girls could get from supper in Potter Hall Cafeteria to West Hall and new dorm (McLean Hall).

My hobbies include stamp collecting (an interest encouraged from being in college office with Miss Runner).

JULIA SMITH HAYDEN, Class of 1951, A.B. Degree in Elementary Education, currently living in Owensboro, KY.

I taught school for 16 years in the Owensboro City School system and then went to work in the office of the D.R. Hayden Oil Company, a business my husband and I owned. I continued working there until we sold it five years ago.

Since our retirement, we have continued traveling and playing golf, which we both enjoy.

I have many fond memories of Western and have kept in contact with many close friends from my Western days.

One of the highlights was living in McLean Hall (the first year it was built) and having Mom Drew as house mother.

GLENNIS NORVELL HENSLEY, Class of 1959, A.B. Degree in Library Science, currently living in Corbin, KY.

I furthered my education by getting my Master's Degree from Eastern Kentucky University, Richmond, and a Rank I Certification from Union College in Barbourville.

I am currently a teacher at Corbin Elementary School. I am the librarian for grades kindergarten through second.

I am married to William E. Hensley, who is a lawyer. We have three children. Our oldest is Nancy Hensley Haggerty, 27, who is a lawyer and an accountant. Next are William Alton, 22, who is a marketing student at the University of Kentucky at Lexington, and Cynthia Lynne, 17, who is a senior at Corbin High School.

WILLIAM E. HENSLEY, Class of 1958, A.B. Degree in English, currently living in Corbin, KY.

I furthered my education with an LLB from Cumberland University School of Law.

I am currently a self-employed lawyer practicing general law.

Other important positions include being District Judge for two years.

I am married to Glennis Norvell Hensley, who is a teacher. We have three children: Nancy Hensley Haggerty, 27, who is a lawyer and an accountant; William Alton Hensley, 22, who is a student at UK; and Cynthia Lynne Hensley, 17, who is a senior at Corbin High School.

JOSEPHINE RIGSBY HEPBURN, Class of 1950, A.B. Degree in English, currently living in Lexington, KY. I furthered my education with experience.

I am currently a substitute teacher for Fayette County Schools and a volunteer in Mission Presbyterian Church and have had posts in Alaska, New York, and Appalachia.

I do volunteer work with Compassionate

Friends, a group for bereaved parents, and am an Elder in the Presbyterian church.

I have three children, David, Mary H. Nicholson, and Jonathan (deceased). I have two grandchildren who are nine and four years of age.

My memories of WKU include Cedar House, football and basketball games, WKU orchestra, and many wonderful people.

I enjoy traveling and the freedom of substitute teaching and look forward to another Mission post in the summer. My grandchildren are also very important to me.

JAMES R. HICKS, Class of 1959, B.S. Elementary Education, currently living in Louisville, KY.

I received my Masters from Western Kentucky University in 1962. I continued my education at Mercer University, in Macon, GA.

I am a retired teacher and principal. I worked for the Jefferson County Board of Education for 27 years. I taught at Okolona for five years and served as principal for the Hawthorne, Prestonia, and Klondike Schools for 22 years.

I am affiliated with the American Numismatist Society, League of Kentucky Sportsmen, and National Rifle Association. I am on the Board of Directors for the Farmington House and the Louisville Zoological Society.

I am married to Barbara (Noel) Hicks who is a retired music teacher.

My memories of WKU include meeting my wife Barbara, room mates, South Hall, Vince Street Inn, basketball games, Dr. Cole's classes, Dr. Tate Page, and friends.

My hobbies include coins, antiques, guns, running, collecting Civil War materials, and reading.

ALLEN E. HILSMEIER, Class of 1959, B.S. in Physics, currently living in Delta, PA.

After attending WKU I went to graduate school at Vanderbilt University where I majored in Physics. I received my Masters in Theology from St. Mary's Ecumenical Institute of Theology.

I currently am a Health Physicist for the Philadelphia Electric Company, Philadelphia, PA. I am the Health Physicist at the Peach Bottom Atomic Power Station.

I am the owner of Paper Mill Farm's Restaurant, Hilsmeier's Auction Gallery, and Farmer's Market.

I am married to Margaret (Murphy) Hilsmeier. Margaret manages the businesses that we own. We have six children. They are Derek 27, Jeff 26, Damon 25, Todd 23, Sonya 21 ,and Kurt nine.

My memories of Western include George Paige, Mr. Sandefur (Physics), Mr. Johnson (Math), Jim Miller, Bob Thomas, and Luther Norene (fellow physics student).

My hobby is contemplating the meaning of Christ and life and finding God's love amongst the suffering.

JUANITA BROOKS HIRE, Class of 1958, B.S. Elementary Education. Currently living in Woodburn, KY.

I furthered my education and received my M.A. in 1961 and Rank I in 1963.

I teach a half load at W.K.U. (early retirement). I also taught ten years in public schools and 21 years at W.K.U. and have served as elementary, secondary, and college teacher and elementary, secondary, and college counselor.

I am a member of Delta Kappa Gamma and Kappa Delta Pi.

I am married to Lewis Hire, Jr., who is retired from Franklin Express Co. We have one son, Douglas Dickson. We have three grandchildren, Clayton, Emily, and Katie Dickson.

My memories of W.K.U. are working in Potter Hall Cafeteria (Ptomaine Hall), meeting at the Goal Post after class, the Hilltoppers, and hearing Mrs. Richards read poetry.

I like to cook, read, and attend church and community activities.

JEAN BOZARTH HITCHCOCK, Class of 1959, B.S. in Home Economics. Currently living in Evansville, IN.

I am a homemaker with the Indiana Extension Homemakers Association. I am a District Representative from Evansville. My responsibilities include serving on State Board and conducting district meetings. I am also an Extension Agent for the youth in Warren and Metcalf counties, and a Public Assistance Social Worker in Bowling Green.

I am married to Philip D. Hitchcock, who is a physician. We have one daughter, Holly Ann Hitchcock, 20.

My hobbies include needlecrafts, such as knitting, and participating in fairs and fashion shows.

ALMA JEAN (RENDER) HOCKER, born Dec. 7, 1930, Logansport, KY, Butler County.

Parents: Anna Mae (Moore) and J.U. Render. My mother died when I was three months old, so we moved to grandparents, Mr. and Mrs. J.E. Render, and lived there with them and Uncles Dav and Aubrey and Nurse Ruth Campfield.

Education: First eight grades at Logansport one-room school; high school at Morgantown, graduating in 1948; freshman and sophomore at Western 1948, 1949, 1950; returned to W.K.U. 1958 for Saturday classes and summer terms until received B.A. Degree (English Major-Music Minor) in 1963; received NDEA scholarship to Peabody, 1966; completed M.A. (Education at W.K.U., 1969.

Teaching Career: Substitute in Butler County System 1956-58; English teacher at Butler County High 1958-1986. Retired in Spring 1986; sub since 1987-89.

Family: Married high school sweetheart, Hugh R. Hocker in 1949 (deceased 1988); have Mona (W.K.U. graduate, 1972), Hugh, Jr. (U. of Georgia Pharmacy, 1974), Laura (W.K.U. 1983) and Ruth (U.K. 1987).

Interests: Church history of First Baptist where I am a member, reading, photography, genealogy, travel, and four grandchildren.

Organizations: Past member of NCTE; KCTE; N.E.A.; TDEA; Past President, K.C.T.E.; Butler County Genealogical and Historical Society; DAR; W.K.U. Alumni.

MARY EDNA SANDERS HODGE,

(Mrs. Melvin B.) teacher, civic, and cultural leader, 2512 Ralph Avenue, Louisville. Born on July 28, 1909, at Priceville in Hart Co., KY, she is the daughter of Porter and Josie Mae (Avery) Sanders. She is an alumnus of Western Kentucky State College in Bowling Green, having earned the B.S. degree in 1950 and the M.A. degree in 1953. She married Melvin B. Hodge of Canmer, Hart Co., KY, on Dec. 26, 1931.

Mrs. Hodge has been teaching at the elementary school level for nearly 30 years. A life member of the Kentucky Parent-Teacher Association, she belongs to the National, Kentucky, and Jefferson County Education Associations. A member of the Louisville Poetry Club and of the Hymn Society of America, she has published a collection of ten hymns of which she is author and composer. She also belongs to the Filson Club of Louisville and fraternally, to the Order of the Eastern Star, in which she has held a variety of offices. Mrs. Hodge is a registered Democrat, though she prefers voting for the individual. She is active within the Southern Baptist Church. Mrs. Hodge has served as a Sunday School teacher, member of the choir, pianist, and in other capacities.

CARL D. HOLLAND, Class of '57, B.S. Biology-English.

After graduating from Western, Carl practiced social work with the Kentucky Department of Child Welfare in Hartford, Owensboro, and Louisville. After his first graduate degree from the University of Louisville, he

served as superintendent of Lake Cumberland Boys Camp at Monticello and administrator in child welfare and mental health in Owensboro. After further graduate study at the University of Illinois, he became professor of social work at Illinois State University where he continues to teach and to consult in the areas of health, developmental disabilities, aging, and international social welfare. His international presentations ranged from substance abuse in Spain, grief and bereavement in Canada, to aging in Mexico. His fourth book, Applied Social Services will be published in 1989.

Carl remembers the time when Marilyn Harrison and he accompanied Mark Brown to Nashville for a dental appointment. While racing back for a class, the 1948 Ford blew a radiator hose that resulted in more more missed class meeting. Irvin Bell had suggested that they take his 1952 Ford which had overdrive!

J. MARILYN HARRISON-HOLLAND, B.A. Elementary Education, Class of '57.

Marilyn Harrison graduated cum laude and taught in the elementary school in Owensboro, KY prior to moving to Champaign, IL in 1970 with husband, Carl Holland, and children, Timothy and Amy. She completed her M. Ed. at the University of Illinois in Urbana-Champaign and was employed as reading specialist for public schools. In 1987 she was awarded an Outstanding Teacher award. In 1985-86 she served as president of Illini Reading Council and remains active in the promotion of literacy.

She recalls the wonderful drives out Barren River Road with friends Mark Brown and Xexia Barnes. On one occasion, they had stopped in a farm road to observe the environs when suddenly a man appeared on the horizon with a gun. It was later - after a quick exit - that they discovered that the man with the gun was a friendly local hunter.

Marilyn enjoys reading for personal pleasure and reading to grandson Jonathon. She also teaches a women's class for her church. She serves a international trip planner when accompanying Carl.

OVA (McMILLIN) HOLLINSWORTH, Class of 1953, B.S. Currently living in Tompkinsville, KY.

I am retired from teaching. I taught for 37 years in elementary grades.

I am active in reading and needlework.

I have two children, Anthony and Marla, who are both Western graduates.

CARTER KOON HOOKS, Class of '56, '60. Currently living in Union City, TN.

After receiving my masters at Western, I continued my education at Indiana U, Oklahoma U and CID. I am now the executive director of the Obion Co. Industrial Development Board and Chamber of Commerce. Other important positions include administrative assistant to Gov. L.B. Nunn, regional VP Am. Econ. Dev. Council, Pres., TN Ind. Dev. and Southern Ind. Dev. Councils.

I am married to the former Sherry Lee Driver, dir. of Communications and Energy Services, Union City Electrical System. We have two children, Dana Jones and Carter Robert Hooks and one grandson, William Nicholas Maxwell.

I am a fellow member of the Am. Econ. Dev. Council and enjoy golf in my spare time.

Memories of WKU include the Hilltopper teams and singers.

SHERRY DRIVER HOOKS, Class of 1956/1960, B.A. and M.A. Degrees, currently living in Union City, TN.

I furthered my education by taking 30 semester hours above my M.A. at Western.

I am currently the Director of Communications and Energy Services at Union City Electric System. My job responsibilities include communications in-house, with service areas, TVA, appliance dealers, building contractors, etc. I coordinate special projects and direct the community leadership school.

I coordinate English, art, speech and drama departments at Briarcrest Private School in Memphis. I owned and ran a training and consulting firm for six years, and I am a real estate affiliate broker for NSUI, Tennessee.

I am married to Carter Hooks, who is the Executive Director for Obion County Chamber of Commerce. We have two children, Dana Hooks Jones (29), and Carter Robert Hooks (19).

My memories of WKU include Dr. Willie's

lass (where I met Carter), dorm memories, my roommate Wanda Kirkhaur (deceased), and Naomi Jones "Jonesy."

I love renovating homes, keeping up with the latest information and acting on it, playing bridge, reading, and traveling.

I taught for 23 years in both public and private school in both Kentucky and Tennessee. I served as chairman of the English Department and I sold real estate for three years in Nashville. For six years I ran a training and consultant firm doing training in areas of management, leadership, and customer service.

PAT I. HOOPER, Class of 1958, Degree in Mathematics, currently living in Bowling Green, KY.

I furthered my education by getting my M.S. from Purdue University and doing A.B.D. Doctoral work at Auburn University, though I did not complete my dissertation.

I am currently the Assistant Professor of the Math Department at WKU. I teach undergraduate math courses and train secondary math teachers.

Other important positions include being co-author of five precalculus math textbooks for MacMillan Publishing Company.

I am affiliated with MLAA, NCTM, and Phi Delta Kappa.

My memories of Western include working math problems on the steps of VanMeter while waiting for Russell Miller to yell for me to be on stage.

I own my family farm in Union County near Morganfield, where I spend vacations and summers playing in the dirt.

NANCY HAMMOND HUGHES, Class of 1956, B.S. Degree in Elementary Education.

After graduation from Western, I married Tommy Hughes and began teaching in the Bowling Green City School system. In 1981, I was named Bowling Green's Teacher of the Year and was runner-up for the Kentucky Teacher of the Year award.

We have a daughter, Amy, also a Western graduate, who is a social worker. She and her husband, Frankie Wood, have a son, Andrew Thomas, age three.

I retired from teaching in 1986 and I am enjoying the time I can now devote to hobbies, clubs, family, and friends. I enjoy photography, painting, and playing bridge. I am a member of Alpha Delta Kappa, Pierian Literary Club, Mabel Thomas Garden Club, Bowling Green Woman's Club, Bowling Green Homemakers Club and Whist Investment Club.

I am so glad that teaching was my career choice and that I chose Western to prepare me for my life's work. I cherish the memories of all the students that I taught and I treasure the wonderfully warm, rich memories of carefree campus life.

GERTRUDE HUMPHRIES, At age 16 I entered Western Teacher's College in 1927—deep depression days.

For two years I worked in class toward a Life Certificate and on campus at various jobs—waiting a football table, washing dishes, operating a bread salad and making salads.

In my junior year I began work toward a BS in home economics and more jobs—operating the hand powered ditto machine on which all tests were copied (I was bonded) and assisting Miss Mattie McLeon, Pres. Cherry's private secretary. Since there was no intercom system I RAN errands to all points on campus.

During my senior year I was assistant to Mrs. Penick, house mother, Potter Hall. After doing office work, four nights each week and socializing the other three, I weighed a hefty 87 pounds at graduation.

Teaching jobs were scarce but I went to a small high school in Christian County, Sinking Fork, to open its first home economics department.

At the end of four years I married Ira Humphries. We celebrated our golden anniversary in 1984 and still live in the same century and a half year old house. We had a son, Harold, who died of a heart attack at age 50.

In 1942 I went back to Sinking Fork to teach in a new home economics department. I had the same principal, Babe Hunt, a former football star and graduate of WKU.

In 1948 I transferred to Trigg County High and taught there 23 years. During my last year we planned a beautiful new department—large living and dining area, four class rooms, an observatory, office and workroom. Upon completion it was dedicated and named for me.

During our active years we were active in many organizations and officers in most of them. We are still active in our church and special groups such as Farm Bureau, Retired teachers and DAR.

We have a lovely daughter-in-law and two "grand" grandchildren.

EARL D. HUNTER, Class of 1957, B.S.-M.A. Elementary Education. Currently living in Bowling Green, KY.

I am retired from Bowling Green City Schools. I was the principal at T.C. Cherry

School for 30 years. I taught for four years in Owensboro, KY.

MARTHA HENRY HUNTER, Class of 1957, B.S. Degree in Home Economics, currently living in New Madrid, MO.

I am currently the head branch librarian for the New Madrid County Library. Had I known I would wind up a librarian, I would certainly have taken some Library Science while at Western!

I taught Home Economics for 18 years, but left to raise my two adopted children and never resumed teaching.

I have three grandchildren and spend my time outside the library sewing, doing crafts and researching my genealogy.

I came to Western in the fall of 1953 with my friend Joyce Littrell, also from New Madrid, MO. At that time, I believe we were the only ones on campus from Missouri and we got a lot of teasing.

We lived in West Hall. I later moved to the Rock House and was there when I graduated.

I was a Home Economics major so my "fondest" memories are of my days in the Home Management House trying to "learn" to be a good homemaker and mother.

I have only been to Western twice since graduation in 1957 and found so many changes I could hardly recognize the old campus.

I welcome you to stop in New Madrid to visit me. I'll tell you about the 1811-12 Earthquake!

RONDA (GRAHAM) IRACANE, B.S. Business. Currently living in Owensboro, KY.

I continued my education at Western getting a Masters in Business.

I currently am a teacher at Owensboro High School in Owensboro.

I am married to Joseph A. Iracane who is self-employed. We have two children, Amy 24, and John 18.

CORDELIA KING JACKSON, Class of '55, B.S. Elementary Education, Owensboro, KY.

The Fabulous Fifties began in January of 1950 as I entered Western. The Rockhouse, thanks to Mr. and Mrs. H.B. Clark and Randy, became my 'home away from home'. Next door was the Goal Post, Hub of the Hill, a place to eat breakfast, play pinball machines, and pass the time between classes not otherwise spent in the library. The jog down the hill to Western Lunch Room was refreshing and refilling. The sledding down College Street was exhilarating on snowy evenings.

While completing my B.S. in Elementary Education, who could forget working part time in the clinic with Ms. Redd, or attempting to take dictation from Dr. Gunderson, Head of the Music Department as well as the hours as hostess in the Cedar House. All were great fun!

I have taught in Owensboro City Schools and Daviess County Schools. I also taught in Rolla, MO while my husband completed his Petroleum Engineering Degree at Missouri School of Mines. I earned a M.S. in Education from Indiana University in 1968.

I am married to Louis Jackson, president of ReBart, Inc. We have one daughter, Leigh, who is planning to enter Western next year to study veterinary medicine. May her years at Western be even more rewarding.

Congratulations to a fine school and thanks for the memories.

GORDON R. JACKSON, Class of '56, B.S., Physical Education.

I started at Western in 1949, dropped out 1950-52 for a sabbatical to the Marine Corps, and returned in fall, 52. My most lasting memories are of the Barons, Moose Lodge, and Bill Hardin's. Graduated in 1956 with an Army ROTC commission, worked three years with GMAC and Standard Oil, then returned to active duty in 1959. Duty assignments followed in Germany, the U.S., and Vietnam.

Returned to civilian life in 1973 as a Management Instructor for University of Oklahoma, and later as Education Specialist for Dept. of Army at Ft. Sill, OK. Retired from USAR as COL in 1986, and will retire from DA in two years to devote serious attention to my golf game. Shirley and I were married in 1957 and have two grown children, Mike, 29 and Toni, 27, who also live in Lawton, OK.

NELDA MEFFORD JAMES, Class of 1950, B.S. Degree in Elementary Education, currently living in Drakesboro, KY.

I furthered my education by getting my Master's Degree and 31 hours above (Rank I) from Peabody College in 1968.

I run miscellaneous errands for needy friends.

I started at Western in 1946 and completed my B.S. Degree in 1950.

I taught school 29-1/2 years. Due to an auto accident, I had to retire in 1980.

In 1973, I was married to John R. James and lived a happy life with him until he died in 1979. I have two lovely step-daughters and their families; I also have a host of lovely nieces and nephews.

I enjoy socializing with my many friends and relatives.

My memories of WKU are life with friends in Potter and West Halls, basketball games, P.E. classes, and B.S.U. at First Baptist Church in Bowling Green, and homecoming events.

ISHMEAL E. JOHNSON, Class of 1951, A.B., currently living in Pensacola, FL.

I retired as District Manager of the Daytona Beach, FL area in 1982 after 29 years with the Social Security Administration. I also served as District Manager at Hazard, KY, and Meridian, MS.

My wife is Nannie Kelley Johnson, she is also retired. We have four children; Connie Champion, B.S. W.K.U. 1962, Nancy Clark, B.S. U.K. 1965, Theresa Cartell, A.B. Transylvania 1973, and Ishmeal, B.S. E.K.U.

The late 40s and early 50s are remembered as the GI Era. The camaraderie that existed between faculty members and student Vets makes the period most unforgettable. Also, it seems that the entire student body could be found at the "Goal Post" around lunch time.

RICHARD H. JOHNSON, Class of '55, B.S. in Geography, currently living in Lynden, WA.

After leaving ROTC at Western, I served 24 years in USAF, I retired in January 1979 at Lake AFB, AZ, participated in World wide service,

it was great! Currently I am Captain with San Juan Airlines, Bellingham, WA. I learned to fly at BWG. Worked my way through WKU working at an airport and as a radio dispatcher for Kentucky State Police.

My wife, Carole A. is a nurse and we have one son who is a sophomore at Western Washington University.

My memories of WKU are attending summer school to graduate in four years while working full time, people watching at "Goal Post", steps of Cherry Hall, Mr. Cockrell the WX Guy Col. Peterson and Capt. Lane and my TF-51 D rides—awesome—still. I am still a full time "airport bum" and love it!

SHELBY JOHNSON, Class of 1950, B.S. in Agriculture, currently living in Scottsville, KY. Masters in Public Health Administration University of North Carolina, 1957.

I am retired from F.D.A. Region II Atlanta, GA where I was the director of Milk and Food Program Region IV F.D.A. and from the Kentucky Cabinet for Human Resources Div. Consumer Health Protection, Dept. of Health.

My wife, Doris, and I have one daughter, Shelby Sue Burleson, and two grandsons; Scott T. Burleson Grad. Scholarship Math at Vanderbilt University Nashville, TN and J. Todd Burlesom Soph. at David Lipscomb University, Nashville, TN.

1967—Kentucky Outstanding Sanitarion Award; "Louisville Ambassador of Good Will"; 1971—"The International Sanitarion's Award"; 1974—"Russell E. Teague Award"; 1977—"Harvey U. Wiley Award".

Affiliations include: Kentucky Association of Michigan Food and Env. Sanitarion's President from 1964-64; Kentucky Reg. San. Examining Committee. Secretary 1967-77; Central States Association of Food and Drug officials, 1959-60 President, 1965-66 President; Association of Food and Drug Officials of the Southern States 1970-71 President; Interstate Milk Shippers Conference, Chairman 1967-69; 1969-71; Member of Advisory Committee to U.S. D.H.S. in the development of the U.S.D.H.S. milk ord. and code; Member National Conference on Product Safety Steering Committee to develop a National Conference on Product Safety for 1974-Served as Vice Chairman of the Committee.

My hobbies are fishing and horticulture activities.

My memories of WKU are of playing in the Pinochle tournaments in Veterans Village.

MARGARET BOSWELL JONES (PEGGY), Class of 1956/B.U., A.B. in Business Education. Currently living in Bowling Green.

I received my master's degree in education in 1966 from W.K.U.

I am married to Brewer T. Jones; we are both retired.

I taught business education for 28 years; nine years at Owensboro High School and 19 years at Bowling Green High School.

RAY KALDENBACK, Class of 1956, B.S. in Physical Education, currently living in Placentia, CA.

I furthered my education at California State University, taking advanced classes in Public Administration.

I am Parks and Human Services Director in La Verne, CA. I administer all facets of a Comprehensive Parks and Human Services Program. I am also president of Student Scholarship Services, a company which matches high school and college students to potential scholarships and grants.

I am a member of the Southern California Municipal Athletic Federation, the California Park and Recreation Society, and Pi Sigma Epsilon (a professional recreation fraternity).

I am married to Eleanor Kaldenbach, who is a secretary. We have two children, Kim, 25, and Ken, 22.

My hobbies include tennis and golf.

CHRISTINE RULE KOENEN, Class of '54, B.S. in Chemistry, currently living in Sawda, NC.

After graduation came marriage to a classmate, Paul Koenen, then two and a half years as a service wife, a baby and a move to Chicago where I worked for two years in analytical chemistry.

With time out for two more children I worked as Donations Librarian for Northwestern University Medical School for six years, a photo assistant for a food photographer for a year, then for nine years as a Business Librarian for American Hospital Supply Corporation.

In 1986 I received my MLS from Rosary College in River Forrest, IL. That same year I moved to Sawda, NC. I currently work as a Reference Librarian with Greenville County Public Library in Greenville, SC.

My most vivid memories of Western are of West Hall and Mrs. Reep waiting in the lounge when we came in from dates; the 10:30 "lights out" and no radio playing; the building of the new Student Union Building; Coach Diddle asking me when I was coming out for basketball; and going to every home basketball game

for four years and never seeing the Hilltoppers Lose!

PAUL R. KOENEN, Class of '54, B.A. in Art, currently living in Sawda, NC.

Within weeks after graduation I married one of my classmates, Christine Rule, and started a tour of duty as a Second Lieutenant in the Marine Corps. After my release from active duty I attended the American Academy of Art in Chicago for two years. My career as a commercial artist was spent in Chicago where I worked as a layout artist, designer and art director at a number of different studios. In 1969 I went to American Hospital Supply as Art Director, then became Director of Advertising and finally, Director of Marketing Communications.

All during my commercial art career I pursued a side-career as a watercolor artist, and in 1986 I quit commercial work to paint full time. I now live in Sawda, NC and paint and exhibit throughout the Southeast.

In 1977 I retired from the Marine Corps Reserves as a Lt. Colonel.

Favorite memories of Western include the gang at the Harmon House, being involved in Western Players, and dates with my future wife.

NORMAN D. LANE, Class of '59, B.A. in History, currently living in Cottontown, TN.

I received my Law degree from the University of Tennessee College of Law in 1960.

I currently practice Law with Hildebrand, Nolan, Lane, et al. in Nashville, TN. I was formerly Assistant to Governor of Tennessee, Captain in the U.S. Army, Judge Advocate General's Corps, Assistant U.S. Attorney.

Deeply involved with the Association of Trial Lawyers of America—Have held National Office.

I am married to Emily P. Lano and we have four sons: Nicholas, 26, Norman Jr. 23, Jason, 20, and Philip, 18.

My memories of WKU include snowfall on the Hill, Albino Squirrels, and Coach Diddle. I left Western in January 1957 but did not apply for my degree until 1959.

JUNE LINVILLE LANIER, Class of 1955 (BU), Degree Business Education, currently living in Greensboro, NC.

I am a former business education teacher and have also been a legal secretary. I am presently a homemaker and do volunteer work through the Charity League of Greensboro. I am a member of the Charity League and

Garden Club Pres. I am married to Thomas F. Lanier, Pres. Covington Diesel, Inc. (a Detroit Diesel distributor). Our children are Stephanie - age 34 and Thomas, Jr. - age 21. My hobbies include bridge, flower gardening and reading.

I transferred to BU from U. of K. in the spring of 1952 and lived at the Mac House for a year and a half. I later moved to the Boyd House on College Street. I have many good memories of my years at BU and am interested in renewing old friendships through the Alumni Association. I am particularly interested in knowing about some of the professors we had there in the 50s and their current whereabouts. I am originally from Somerset and have lived in North Carolina since graduation.

THOMAS FRANKLIN LANIER, Class of 1955, Degree in Accounting, currently living in Greensboro, NC.

I am President of Covington Diesel, Inc., in Greensboro, NC. I have the responsibilities of the entire operation of Covington Diesel which consists of 238 employees in four locations within North Carolina.

Other important positions include being on the Board of Directors of Branch Banking & Trust Company; Past President of North Carolina Chapter of Associated Equipment Dealers; and member of North Carolina Motor Carriers Association.

I am a member of Parkway Baptist Church - have held several positions there - currently am serving as a deacon, Sunday School teacher and member of Personnel Committee.

I am married to June Linville Lanier, a housewife. We have two children; Stephanie who is 34 is a business education teacher, and Tommy 21, is a senior at Greensboro College.

I have fond memories both in and out of the classroom. I lived across the street from BU at the "Poker". The memories I cherish most are of fellow classmates and professors. It was at Bowling Green that I had my first non-agricultural job, having been reared on a farm in

North Carolina. That job was selling ladies' shoes in a ladies' shoe store on the square downtown. I also ran a laundry route with a fellow classmate from Mississippi. The experience I received from those jobs has been invaluable throughout the years.

My hobbies are boating and water skiing, gardening, and jogging.

BONNIE THOMAS LAWSON, Class of 1959, B.S. in Chemistry, currently living in Bowling Green, KY.

I continued my education with a M.A. in Education from WKU in 1968, and a B.A. in Accounting from WKU in 1980; became a Certified Public Accountant in 1980.

I am a Senior Accountant at General Motors Corp. in Bowling Green. My responsibilities are that of managerial accounting.

I previously taught in both Chemistry and Accounting Departments at Western. I also worked as a CPA in public accounting.

I am a member of KSCPA, and AICPA.

I am married to W.B. (Buck) Lawson, Jr., a claims representative. We have a son W.B. (Chip) Lawson III. He has his B.S. and M.S. from WKU and is a loan officer with Farm Credit Services.

My memories of Western include Chemistry Labs in the basement of Cherry Hall, Beta parties, and many hours of studying.

My hobbies include following sports, especially basketball, walking, and reading.

W.B. (BUCK) LAWSON, JR., Class of 1960, B.S. in Physical Education, currently living in Bowling Green, KY.

I am a Claims Representative at Kentucky Farm Bureau Mutual Insurance Company in Bowling Green. I am a Senior Claims Adjuster. I have worked for the same company for 28 years.

My wife is Bonnie Thomas Lawson, who is a C.P.A. in industry. We have one son W.B. (Chip) Lawson, III, 27.

I like to travel and read.

ALBIN L. LEE, Class of 1950, A.B. Degree in History, currently living in Louisville, KY.

I continued my education with a M.A. at Western in 1955; and an Ed. D. at Indiana University in 1965.

Currently I am retired. Other important positions include: 1950-'53 and 55 I was a teacher at Hodgenville High School; February '53-February '55 I was in the U.S. Army; from 1955-'80 I was a teacher, counselor, assistant director, director, assistant superintendent at Jefferson County Public Schools. At various times from 1962 to 1981, I was a part-time instructor in graduate education classes for Indiana University Southeast, University of Louisville, Spalding College, and Murray State University.

I am married to Eva Rush, a retired educator.

Memories of WKU are working on The Talisman, classes with Dr. Stickles, Dr. Poteet, Miss Egbert, Dr. Moore, and Dr. Wood.

Professional memberships have included—at appropriate times—Phi Delta Kappa, American Psychological Association, National Education Association (Life Member), American Personnel and Guidance Association, National Vocational Guidance Association, and State and Regional Associations. I have served on a variety of state curriculum and certifications standards committees.

I am currently a member of Aedabon Baptist Church and teach a Sunday School class.

NANCY WILLIAMS LEE, Class of 1954, B.S. in Elementary Education, currently living in Louisville, KY.

I continued my education at Western receiving a M.A. in 1959.

I am a retired elementary teacher, working for Jefferson County Board of Education for 30 years.

I am married to William T. Lee, D.M.D., who is a retired Oral Surgeon.

C. DOUGLAS LENEAVE, M.D., F.A.C.R., Class of 1953, B.S. degree, currently living in Mayfield, KY.

I continued my education at the University of Louisville, School of Medicine, graduating in 1957.

I am a Medical Doctor and Radiologist working at Community Hospital in Mayfield.

I am a fellow American College of Radiology.

I am married to Del Rita Myers, who is a housewife. We have three children, Mark, 30, a graduate of Murray State University and St. Louis University; Jeffrey, 27, graduate of

Western Kentucky University; and Christopher, 23, a graduate of Western Kentucky University.

My hobbies include Private Pilot, Aviation Medical Examiner, Aircraft and Powerplant Mechanic, and Authorized Inspector.

BERNICE PIGG LIGHTFOOT, I quit Western in 1954 after receiving my Provisional Teachers Certificate in Elementary Education. I live at 150 Valleybrook Rd. in Bowling Green, KY with my husband, William.

I retired from South Central Bell Telephone Co. in 1983 after a 30 year career during which I started as an operator and eventually became a Group Manager, the position I held my last 12 years with the Company. After retirement I worked two years at Greenview Hospital as a switchboard operator. My husband is a retired First Sgt. in the U.S.M.C. and is currently President of the local branch of the Fleet Reserve Association. I am President of their Ladies Auxiliary. We both belong to State Street United Methodist Church. We have a trailor at Barren River Lake and love to putter around there and take the boat out. Bill loves to garden and I crochet. Our favorite activity is traveling and we are both enjoying our retirement.

DOTTYE NUCKOLS LINDSEY, Class of 1953, B.S. Elem. Educ. Attending Western during the years from 1949 to January '53 were some of the happiest years of my life. It was my student teaching under Miss Seward in Kindergarten that made me realize I wanted to pursue teaching as a career.

I attended the Business University after my graduation taking shorthand and typing. Till I could get a teaching position I worked as secretary at WAVE-TV. By January '54 I was given a teaching position and later returned to Western and received my M.A. in 1959 and my Rank 1 (30 hrs. above Masters) in 1974. I retired after 30 years of teaching in 1984 in the Louisville-Jefferson County School System. In 1980 I re-

searched and found all the Miss Kentucky's but one and had the first Miss Kentucky Reunion. I still keep in touch with many of them. Our first Ms. Kentucky 1935 now lives in Louisville. From 1984 I have modeled for Cosmo/Casablanca Modeling Agency. I was Treasurer for eight years for Metropolitan Louisville Woman's Political Caucus and I'm now Treasurer for Kentucky Women's Political Caucus. I'm Precinct Captain and Clerk on Election Day. I'm now working with A.L. Williams a financial and marketing company. I've enjoyed square dancing as a hobby the last four years. I was married to Willard W. Lindsey but now divorced and haven't any children.

CHARLES A. LIVINGSTON, Class of '53 B.S. Agriculture.

I started Western at midterm during '49-'50. There were no men's dorms then. About a dozen young men occupied a few rooms on the first floor in the rear of the agricultural pavilion just north of Vet's Village. Animals occupied the basement. There was a mini grocery on the east end of the pavilion and showers on the west end. The following year the men occupied Potter Hall at the top of the hill.

I got my B.S. in Agriculture in 1953; my masters in 1982 and have completed 21 hours of graduate work at UK. I currently teach industrial education in Drakesboro, KY and live in Central City.

On the side, I pursue my hobby, painting. I sell prints of my work from my home. One of the paintings, "The Old Fort" depicts the bridge and trench of the old Confederate fort preserved on Western's campus.

MARVIN L. LOGSDON, Class of 1950, B.S. Degree in Agriculture, currently living in Radcliff, KY.

I furthered my education with extension classes at University of Kentucky and Michigan State.

I worked as Superintendent of Hardin County Water District #1 until retirement. I now work part-time for the city of Radcliff as an Inspector of any new sewer lines being laid. I also am part-time field representative for an engineering firm in the city.

Other important positions I have held consists of being one of a three member team on the Executive Committee of the Radcliff Industrial Foundation, and Senior State Representative for the Central Kentucky Water and Waste Water Operation Association.

I am affiliated with the Optimist Club as a life member, Boy Scouts, and United Methodist Choir.

I have two sons Jam Dewaine who attended Western in the 60's, and Michael Ray who graduated from Western in 1977 with a B.S. Degree. I have one grandson and two granddaughters.

I met my wife while we were attending Western. I proposed to her on the steps of the Kentucky Building. We spent much of our time meeting and studying at the library. I lived off campus with my grandmother.

I hunt during the fall and fish with my grandchildren. I am a Steward in the Radcliff Methodist Church. I have worked with the Boy Scouts for 25 years. I am in the Optimist Club serving from President of home club to Lt. Governor for zone. *See photos on page 90*

ALICE CHUMBLEY LORA, (1957-1961), Toledo, OH.

Toledo, OH. Western has always meant people, and for me the two men who epitomized the Western spirit were Ed Diddle and Russell H. Miller. My freshman year Coach Diddle always introduced me as the cheerleader "from a town so far back in the hills they had to pump the sunshine in." By my junior year, Dr. Miller had introduced me to the "city lights" of Nashville and Louisville, through the Western Players.

The Western women were such wonderful Southern ladies: Frances Richards, our Shakespeare scholar and English Club adviser; Margie Helm, who knew every book in the library; and Ercell Egbert, whose history class gave me nightmares for years!

After Western, I got a masters degree at Duke U., and for 23 years I've taught journalism and English. I'm married to Ron Lora, a history professor, and we have four children: Leah Ray, a Gaines Scholar at U.K.; Jeff Ray, an athlete and French major at Miami of Ohio; Jackie Lora, a telecom major at Indiana U.; and Cynthia Lora, a high school senior.

BURLIN LOWRY, Class of 1954, B.S. Degree in Agriculture, currently living in Cary, NC.

I am a specialist at Carolina Power & Light Company in Raleigh, NC.

Important positions I have held are: a Major in USAF (Retired); and Chairman of the Board of Trustees at Pembrake State University.

I have three children 32, 30, 25; one grandchild eight years old.

Memories of WKU include the school spirit and a wonderful student body.

My hobbies include golf, hunting, and fishing.

DON MANSFIELD, Class of 1958, B.S. in

Biology, currently living in Stone Mountain, GA.

I received the M.D. from the University of Louisville Medical School in 1962.

I am a Board Certified Obstetrician and Gynecologist.

My present practice is at Donald Z. Mansfield, MD PC, in Stone Mountain, GA, in solo practice of OB-Gyn.

I am a Diplomat of Board of OB-GYN, member of AMA and American College of OB GYN, and member of the County Medical Society.

I have been married to my wife Janet for 30 years and we have three children; Denise, 29, Don, Jr., 25; Mike, 19.

My memories of WKU are Ed Diddle and the "Old Red Barn", and the Biology Club, spirit of Western with friendly atmosphere especially with faculty and many good friends—relaxed and informality making you feel at home. I loved my four years at Western and have many fond memories. I also remember Hugh Johnson, Math Professor and Dr. Sumpter in Chemistry.

FRANCINE WALKER MARKWELL, Class of 1959, A.B. in Music Education, currently living in Evanston, IL.

I continued my education at Western receiving my M.A. in 1970. Also studied at Northwestern University, Roosevelt & American Conservatory of Music/Chicago.

I am the Choral Director/Teacher at District #65 in Evanston, IL. I have the responsibilities of the general and vocal music for the Middle School, Grades six, seven, and eight.

Other important positions include member of Evanston Arts Council (Mayoral appointed position), member of Phi Delta Kappa, and soloist/member of Trinity Lutheran Church Choir.

I am married to Ron Markwell, High School English Teacher/B&B owner. Ron and I have two sons, Howard, 24 and Scott, 22.

My memories of Western include the Goal

Post and Western Hills Restaurant, Music Building "The Web", BSU Miss Bale-student teaching, Mr. Rose-theory, Dr. Whitmer-biology and 15 minute naps, the yearbook staff.

I have been editor of the middle school yearbook for the last three years, and have taught 24 years. I have a daughter-in-law from Shanghai, PRC.

DONALD GENE MASON, Class of 1955, B.A. Degree in English, currently living in Lexington, KY.

I am a Purchasing Supervisor of Cabinet for Human Resource, Frankfort, KY.

One of my job responsibilities includes supervising statewide procurement for cabinet.

Other important positions that I have held include: U.S. Marine Corps (Retired) in 1974 with a rank of Major, commissioned through the Army ROTC, and inter-service transfer in 1955.

My wife is Beverly (Seidel). She is a housewife, a mother, and a best friend.

I have two sons; Douglas, 28; Scott, 27; one grandson, Sean, three and one half.

Memories of WKU include working as a late-night disk jockey at WLBJ; taking requests from the "Hill," "Mason's Music Shop," and later "Norma's Night Watch." From 1953-'55 I knew virtually every student on the "Hill." Great Memories!!

CHARLA J. MAUZY, Class of 1959, B.S. Degree in L.S., currently living in Morganfield, KY.

I continued my education by receiving a Master of Arts Degree in August, 1975.

I am a school librarian at Union County Board of Education in Morganfield, KY.

Other important positions include: Head Cataloger in Lakeland Public Library in Lakeland, FL; Supervisor of an elementary school library in Henderson County.

My memories of WKU are the fun of living in the dorm, and acquiring life long friends.

My hobbies include bridge, culinary arts, and reading.

JOHN D. MCCLEARN, Class of 1959, Degree in Commercial Education, currently living in Madisonville, KY.

I continued my education with a Masters Degree in Administration at WKU in 1964, 30 hours (Rank I) Standard Leadership Certificate at WKU in 1970.

I am an Assistant Superintendent at Hopkins County Board of Education. My job responsibilities include personnel and instruction.

Other important positions include: being a retired Colonel from U.S. Army Reserve, a 28 year member; Madisonville Lions Club, for 20 years; and YMCA Board of directors, 14 years.

I have been married to Jean (Rudd) for 30 years. She is a secretary for the Hopkins County Board of Education.

We have two children. The oldest is Keith, 27, a CPT, Chemical School Instructor at Ft. Mc; and the youngest is Kevin, 24, Engineer, Tennessee Tech University, Kentucky Department of Highways.

Memories of WKU include: living in Diddle, fellow teammates, track meets, long bus rides to OVC, school dorms for four years, and ROTC outdoor drills.

BOBBY MCGUINE, Class of 1951, B.S. Degree in Physical Education, currently living in Decatur, GA.

I recently retired from Columbia Broadcasting System after 30 years with company's publishing division, Holt, Rinehart and Winston. I served as Vice-President for sales/marketing division.

In 1983 I was named as first recipient to company's Hall of Fame.

Previously taught and coached at Erlanger Lloyd High School and J.M. Atherton High in Louisville.

I served two years with 351 MASH Hospital in Germany.

My wife, Charlotte, teaches professional tennis and has been ranked as high as second in Georgia women's doubles.

My two sons, Brent and Patrick, both won college basketball scholarships. Brent attended Georgia State University and made All Sun-Belt conference; Patrick graduated from Georgia Tech and was named to All-Atlantic Coast Conference Team in his senior year.

Brent is married, has two children and teaches in the Atlanta school system. Patrick is a methods analyst with Delta Airlines in Atlanta.

The McGuine family enjoys boating, tennis, and traveling together.

I remember Western for wonderful life long friendships that began there...Coach Diddle and family...rooming with Eddie Jr...The Goal Post...Friday night pep rallies...Jim Pichens' humor...Potter Hall Meals...Aubrey...Talisman Dances...Dero Downing becoming president...Beech Bend Weekends...Winning Russell Millios' variety show contest in Van Meter Auditorium with Bill Birdwell...but most of all the spirit of the Hill that will never leave us.

HARDIN MCLANE, Class of 1956, B.S. in Social Studies, currently living in Elizabethtown, KY.

I continued graduate work at Western.

I am a Broker-Owner of Hardin McLane Realtors in Elizabethtown. I am a broker for Commercial and Residential Real Estate.

Other important positions include former Judge for city of Elizabethtown; Author of a book on basketball; Past President of the Elizabethtown Rotary club, also a Paul Harris Fellow Rotary; Past President of the Hardin County Board of Realtors; Former Director of the Kentucky Association of Realtors; Hardin County Realtor of the year; first President of Elizabethtown High School Academic Boosters Club; South East United States Coach of the year; distinguished Military Graduate from Western; and President "W" Club.

I am married to Marilyn Taylor McLane, who is also a Realtor. We have two children, Michelle, 25 and Mike, 21.

My memories of Western include basketball and baseball games with Coach Ed Diddle, and meeting Marilyn, my wife of 33 years.

My hobbies are mainly sports.

MARILYN TAYLOR MCLANE, Class of 1958, Majored in English, currently living in Elizabethtown, KY.

I am currently a realtor with Hardin McLane Realtors in Elizabethtown where I sell residential property.

I have been past president of Elizabethtown Junior Woman's Club.

I am married to Hardin McLane who is also a realtor. We have two children. Michelle who is 25 and Mike who is 21.

My memories of WKU include: Basketball games in the Old Red Barn, the only time girls wore blue jeans was on Saturday, and I remember my future husband, Hardin McLane, wearing white bucks.

I enjoy reading, needlepoint, designing needlepoint, and singing in the choir at Severns Valley Baptist Church.

DR. RONALD A. MEEKS, Class of 1952. Degree in Chemistry-Biology, Glendale, OH.

Received his Doctor of Veterinary Medicine Degree in 1956 from Auburn University, Auburn, AL. First Lieutenant, then Captain, US Army, 1957-1959. Came to Cincinnati and established veterinary clinic in 1959. Current position: Owner/Director of Springdale Veterinary Medical Clinic, Cincinnati, OH. Practice Small Animal Medicine and Surgery, Business Manager.

Other important positions include Elder, College Hill Presbyterian Church; Board Member, Cincinnati Inter-Faith City Gospel Shelter; Teacher, Bethel Bible Program, CHPC; Shepherd in Lay Pastor Program, CHPC; Board Member and Trustee, Greater Cincinnati Tennis Association; Board Member, Greater Cincinnati Platform Tennis Association.

Honors, activities and affiliations include Member and Past President, Greater Cincinnati Veterinary Medical Association; Member, Cincinnati Academy of Medicine; Member, Ohio Veterinary Medical Association, and the American Veterinary Medical Association, Member; Glendale Lyceum; Kentucky Colonel; Recently (February 1989) invited to and attended the Presidential National Prayer Breakfast in Washington, D.C.

I married Ernestine (Tina) Joiner, BGBU 1953. She is a homemaker and artist. We have three children and two grandchildren.

Memories of WKU: Walking under the old foot-bridge by the water tank; driving our dates to town and back on 25 cents worth of gas in an old Model A Ford which was owned by four of us; lifeguarding at the old swimming pool; sneaking in to the old swimming pool after "hours" (!); History under Dr. Stickles; the old chemistry labs in the basement of Cherry Hall; Biology under Dr. Lancaster; ping pong

in the Log Cabin; track, and trying to run "the mile" in under five minutes; the Hilltoppers (team and quartet); the "W Club"; Potter Hall; the Talisman Balls; getting voted "The Most Eligible Bachelor" in '52!

Hobbies: church and Christian related work and activities; Tennis; Platform Tennis; Gardening; Woodworking; and Traveling, seeing the world with my beautiful Tina.

ANNA F. CLEMMONS MEUNIER, Class of '57. AB Economics-Sociology. Now lives in Merritt Island, FL.

Presently, I am in my 26th year of teaching in high school. Three years were spent teaching in Kentucky, and the remainder in Brevard Co., FL. After moving to Florida, I did graduate work at Stetson University and Jacksonville University.

My husband, Ray, is a building contractor. Our daughter, Leisa, is employed by an astronautics company; our son, Marc, is with a construction company. (Both live in Florida.) We have a four-year-old grandson, Brenton Andrew.

My activities and interests are the Riverside Presbyterian Church, Alpha Delta Kappa International Honorary Sorority for Women Educators, and the Florida Teaching Profession-National Education Association. I enjoy many hours of playing with our grandson, walking on the beach, "shuttle-watching," sewing, helping my husband with his company, and reading.

Among the many memories of Western, I value the life-long friendships that I made while a student there.

MAE SWINNEY MEFFORD, Class of '57, B.S. Chemistry.

Currently, principal of Potter Elementary School, Bowling Green. Began teaching in Bristol, TN. After a brief stint in Virginia, returned to Kentucky. Earned Masters in Education at WKU, 1972.

My years at Western instilled a love of learning which I have nurtured and attempted to pass on throughout my life. My husband, David Mefford, associate director of admissions, WKU, shares this mission.

We have three sons. Jim's in computer management in Fort Worth, TX. Our second son, Jeff, heads the accounting department of a major factory in Nashville. Doug, our youngest, is a law student at UK.

My career and interests have made me active in the Delta Kappa Gamma Soc. for Women Educators, the Kentucky Assoc. of School Administrators and the Kentucky and National Association for Elementary School Principals. I'm particularly proud to have been named one of the Outstanding Educators in America.

When not attending to home and work duties I enjoy reading, sewing, ceramics and playing with our three grandchildren.

Those wonderful years at Western contain many memories, but I'll never forget the 9:30 curfew, the famous quote "Man in the Hall," the ten minute marathon from the third floor of Cherry Hall to Snell and wonderful professors like Dr. Gordon Wilson.

BENNIE S. MILLER, Class of 1959, Guidance Counseling-Political Science, M.A., currently living in Princeton, KY.

I have also completed 30 hours beyond the Masters.

I have retired after 28 years in Caldwell County School System as a Teacher, Counselor, and Principal and four years at Earl C. Clements Job Corps, Morganfield, KY, as Vocational Guidance Counselor.

My wife, M. Lucille Moore Miller, and I have one son, Bennie Dan Miller, and six grandchildren.

Memories of WKU include the basketball and football games, Coach Diddle throwing in the red towel, and my favorite instructors.

I have a US Patent on what is a TV Projector Scope (US Patent #3820885).

EDWARD O. MILLER, Class of 1958, B.A. in History, currently living in Louisville, KY.

I furthered my education through the school of hard knocks!

I am owner and president of Miller Co., Inc. located in Louisville, which is a copier and facsimile dealership with 50 employees.

I am a member of the Boy Scouts Executive Board, Finance and Administrative Board of Christ Methodist Church, and the Chamber of Commerce.

My wife June C. Miller is Vice President of

Miller Co. and also own's Jewels by June Inc. We have two sons Mark 30, and Scott 22, and one granddaughter who is one year old.

My memories of WKU include the Cafeteria where I worked, free food, Dorm's Red Barn and lots of friends.

My hobbies include golf, coin collecting and Florida vacationing.

NANCY ATKINSON MILLER, Class of 1953, B.S. Degree in Home Economics, currently living in Morganfield, KY.

After teaching home economics at Daviess County High School, Morganfield High School, and Union County High School for 30 years, I retired for three years then returned to Union County High School to supervise a special program in Parenthood-Education.

I am married to Charles E. Miller, a retired Agriculture teacher who is now chairman of the Board of Directors of Union Bank and Trust Co., Morganfield. Charles and I have two daughters, Mary Ann Collins of Morganfield and Cathy Parkey of Nashville, TN. We have three grandchildren one of whom is over six-feet tall at age 13.

My best memories of Western include the students themselves. Special people like Margie Berry Hina, Barbara Harrison Nation, Mary Dean Pedigo and Barbara Lamb will always be at the top of my list. I felt I knew every student while I was there and they were all great.

I loved having been chosen Homecoming Queen in 1951 and was proud to serve as secretary of my class.

All the athletic programs were our source of feeling the "Spirit of the Hill". I never missed a game! Uncle Ed could call most of us by our first name. I remember too that President Garrett knew us by our names.

Mrs. Helen Kelly was an excellent teacher, and Marie Adams gave us encouragement.

The Cedar House was the place to go after class for ping pong and cards.

Western was a great choice for me and I thank all who were a part of my life there.

CAROL CHEAL MOLLYHORN, Class of '57, B.S. Vocational Home Economics, 1983 Rank I Elementary Ed., currently living in Leitchfield, KY.

I received my Masters in Curriculum and Instruction at University of Tennessee at Martin in 1973, and Elementary Cert. added at WKU in 1976, then Rank I.

I am currently teaching the first grade at Clarkson Elementary School in Grayson County, where I substituted at the beginning

of my senior year at WKU. I taught high school at Hodgenville the last year before consolidation to Larue County. I worked in the Rural Development Program in Butler County four years and moved to Tennessee in 1963 to teach in Clifton and then Gleason. I returned to Kentucky in the fall of 1974 and to Grayson County in 1977 where I continued to teach. Every time I have changed teaching levels the new is "best yet".

I am active in Ed. Assn. and Alpha Delta Kappa in Tennessee and in KEA, Grayson County Historical society and Leitchfield Woman's Club.

I am divorced from D. Paul Mollyhorn ('74); and we have two sons; James Scott Mollyhorn, 29, and Jeffrey D. Mollyhorn, 25, student at WKU.

My memories of Western include the Western Players—I spent all my "spare" time at play practice or working in related activities as I was President Junior and Senior years and summer between. I remember watching the sign being assembled across from Rock House. So many memories—my four years on campus are still the best four years of my life. Once in class—Maybe 1955—Miss Evadine Parker even let me make a second lemon meringue pie; when before, everything had to be perfect the first time! Then while in Home Management House with her, two weeks before graduation, I sprained both ankles so I sat and ironed linens during Senior Chapel but I was graduated!

I'm beginning the second 30 years, but half way should be enough. I do enjoy seeing the first graders learn now.

CHESTER MONTGOMERY, Class of 1959, B.S. in Physical Education, currently living in Henderson, KY.

I continued my education receiving an M.A. in Education in 1965.

I am the Director of Scouting for the Cleveland Indians in Cleveland, OH. I direct all areas of scouting for the entire organization.

Other important positions I held was working with Pittsburgh Pirates as Scout ('62-67), also worked for Cincinnati Reds as Scouting supervisor and Eastern Coordinator of Scouts ('68-88).

I am married to Audrey Montgomery, a housewife. We have two children, Jeanette (29) and Robert (26) and two grandchildren, Natalie (eight) and Jessica (three).

My best memories have to be the many friends I made while at WKU. Both students and teachers still are very special to me. The leadership was excellent in every phase during the years I spent there. The highlight would have to be the association with the great Ed Diddle and Nick Denes.

SHIRLEY ENNIS MONTGOMERY, is a free lance writer and homemaker from Franklin, Tennessee.

A native of Kentucky, she taught in the public school system of that state for five years. She is a graduate of Campbellsville College and Western Kentucky University.

Montgomery has served as a conference speaker-leader across the United States in the areas of Ministers' wives seminars, stress conferences, and spiritual growth retreats.

She is a writer for Southern Baptist Convention youth Sunday School materials and other publications. She is author of A Growth Guide for Ministers' Wives (Broadman Press, 1984) and Winning Ways for Ministers' Wives (Broadman Press, 1987).

Her hobbies include bread baking, French cooking, yard work, knitting, and counted cross stitch.

Shirley is married to Felix E. Montgomery, a marketing specialist in the Church Administration Department at the Baptist Sunday School Board, Nashville.

JOHN F. MOORE, Class of 1957-1960, BS Degree in Industrial Arts and a MA degree in Secondary Education, currently living in Bowling Green, KY.

I received an Industrial Education Endorsement in 1986.

My current position is a Vocational Carpentry Teacher for Green River Boys Camp in Cromwell, KY. There I teach troubled youth the basics of the construction industry.

Another important position which I have held was in 1985 when I concluded a 33 year National Guard career, the last five years being assigned on Active Duty as the National Guard Bureau representative to Fort Knox, KY.

My wife is Mrs. Freida Moore. She is a housewife and secretary. We have two children. John Richard who is an electrical engineer in Wichita, KS and Randall David who is a computer programmer/analyst in Louisville, KY. We also have two grandchildren; Amanda who is five and Mark who is one.

I have many memories from those great years at WKU and I am proud to have been one of "Mr. L. T. Smith's boys".

When time allows I enjoy visiting with my children and grandchildren, canoeing, fishing, and doing woodwork at home.

JUANITA MORGAN MORRIS, Class of 1952, B.S. in Elementary Education, currently living in Caneyville, KY.

After working 30 years at Grayson County Board of Education, I am retired. I still keep busy being a substitute teacher and the secretary and treasurer for Morris Homes, Inc.

I have also been the Clerk of Grayson County Baptist Association for 18 years.

I am married to J.D. Morris, retired teacher, who owns and operates Morris Homes, Inc. We have three children. Eugenna Tabor, Pam Cartwright and Wendell. Eugenna has two children, Ingrid and Daniel. Pam also has two children, Brittany and Shawna, and Wendell is a coach and teacher at Raceland, KY.

I always loved Western. My memories include working in the cafeteria, growing close to many people, football and basketball, and chinies at Cherry Hall.

I enjoy quilting.

JACQUELINE (CHADWICK) MOSS, Class of 1957, B.A. in Mathematics.

Teaching mathematics at Paducah Community College for 25 years has been very rewarding to me through my contact with students and with mathematics. I was promoted to the rank of Professor in 1977. I have served 20 years as Mathematics Program Coordinator and three years as Chairperson of the Science and Related Technologies Division.

I received my Masters Degree from Murray State and have done additional graduate work at Western, Murray State, and Southern Illinois University.

I have been active in the Kentucky Mathematics Association of Two-Year Colleges and the National Council of Teachers of Mathematics. I served a term as Second Vice President of the Mathematical Association of America. I enjoy doing volunteer work in Sunday School, with 4-H, and with the handicapped adults in Paducah.

In 1977, I received the University of Kentucky Great Teacher Award after being nominated by the Student Senate at Paducah Community College. In 1985, I received the Paducah Community College Distinguished Service Award and also the Business and Professional Womens Club Achievement Award.

I married Bill Moss (class of 1957) in 1956. We have two children: Patricia and Ed. Patricia is married to Keith Feather, lives in Columbus, OH, and is a special education teacher. They have two sons, Brad and Bill. Our son, Ed, is a CPA and is a manager with the Price Waterhouse Accounting Firm in Orlando, FL.

My memories of Western are very special and I really enjoy visiting on the WKU campus.

WILLIAM E. MOSS, Class of 1957, B.S. in Agriculture, currently living in Paducah, KY.

After a brief stint in the military, completing Armor Officer Basic at Fort Knox, and receiving a Masters Degree in Animal Science at the University of Kentucky in 1959 we moved to Paducah, KY, where I have served as a County Extension Agent for 4-H for the University of Kentucky Cooperative Extension Service for 30 years.

After completing 34 years and five months with the Kentucky National Guard and the U. S. Army Reserve, I am currently retired from the U.S.A.R. as a Colonel. Most of this time was served in the Third Battalion, 389th Regiment, Second Brigade, 100th Division (Training) located in Western Kentucky.

Because of my career and interests, I have been active in the Kentucky and National Association of Extension 4-H Agents, serving as President of the Kentucky Association in 71-72. I received the Distinguished Service Award from the National Association in 1980. One of my most memorable experiences as a 4-H Agent was serving as a group leader for the 4-H Teen Caravan to Norway for the National 4-H Council in 1970.

I am married to the former Jacqueline Chadwick (class of 1957) and we have two children. Our daughter, Patricia, is married to Keith Feather, she is a special education teacher in

Columbus, OH, and has two sons, Brad and Bill. Our son, Ed, is a CPA for Price Waterhouse Accounting Firm in Orlando, FL.

JOSEPH A. MURPHY, Class of 1953, B.S. Degree in Geography, currently living in Augusta, GA.

I continued my education by getting a M. Ed. at Emory University and a Ed. D. at the University of Georgia.

I am currently the Dean of School Education at Augusta College. I am responsible for administering School of Education.

Other important positions held were being a school teacher, a principal, and an instructional supervisor.

I am married to Carlene, who is a school administrator.

All our children are grown.

My memories of WKU include great friends and great spirit.

ROBERT D. MURPHY, Class of 1958, B.S. in Agriculture, currently living in Fairfax Station, VA.

I am a Food Technologist for the United States Department of Agriculture, Washington D.C. I work in the headquarters office of Federal Meat and Poultry Inspection to correct inspection activities in the 7,500 plants regulated by U.S.D.A.

I have been honored by the Institute of Food Technologists.

I am married to Ann Murphy, a secretary. We have three children, Donna, Sharon, and Mike.

My memories of Western include the friendliness of students, teachers who care, Western spirit, brothers in 13ers, dancing at Macks, and beer and BBQ at Bill Hardins.

I now enjoy gardening, canning foods, and playing golf.

DEL RITA MYERS, Class of 1953, B.S. Degree, currently living in Mayfield, KY.

I am currently a housewife and mother.

I am married to Charles Douglas LeNeave, a medical doctor. We have three children. Mark (30) a graduate of Murray State University, Jeffrey (27) a graduate of Western Kentucky University, and Christopher (23) also a graduate of Western Kentucky University.

My husband and I have fond memories of WKU. It was a great place to receive an education and a fun place to live. My husband received a good pre-medical background and after graduating from the University of Louisville School of Medicine has become a successful doctor. I put my training to good use and taught school for several years before our children were born.

We shall always be grateful to WKU for our educational background and for a great climate to "meet your mate". My husband and I met at Western and one of our sons met his wife there also. She is a WKU graduate, also.

THOMAS J. NALL, B.S., Class of 1956.

I started at Western in the fall of 1952. The application form asked; "When did you first use a dial telephone?" and "Does your home have indoor or outdoor facilities?"

I roomed on the third floor of the President's House. I remember Dr. Paul and Mrs. Virginia Garrett well.

Working for Bob Cochran in the pressbox at football and basketball games, I carried the note to Coach Ed Diddle the night that Art Spoelstra was helped to break the record for individual scoring in a college game. I was up inside Cherry Hall chime tower the night of the ceremonial lighting of the tower dome. I relayed the "turn 'em on" signal.

I entered the Air Force in 1957 as an Officer from Western's ROTC program. I joined General Electric in 1960 and after 29 years am at my fourth GE location.

I have a patent with GE and belong to the American Mensa Association.

My oldest son, Brad, is a Petty Officer in the Navy. My other son, Tim, will finish Graduate School at Western in 1990. Marilyn and I live in Boone County.

I am proud to have graduated from Western in its Golden Anniversary Year!

EMILY HELM NAMKEN, Class of 1952.
Following my first year teaching music in Gideon, MO I went to Southwestern Seminary in Forth Worth, TX and received my Masters in Religious Education in 1955. In 1973 I graduated from RGBI Language School after a year of Spanish study. During the 70s I earned from Pan American University certifications for the teaching of Elementary Education and for the Learning Disabled.

In 1987 I retired from Mission Jr. High Mission, TX where I taught L.D. for ten years. Other places where I taught either music or elementary education were Naples, FL, Kelso, WA, Beeville, Donna and Edinburg, TX.

My husband, Calvin Namken, is a Baptist missionary to the Spanish speaking in Mexico and along the Texas-Mexico border. I have worked with my husband in helping to start over a dozen churches.

Our daughter, Robin, is a pastor's wife and our son, David, is attending Pan Am. Univ. We have two grandchildren, Kristofer and Nickole Chandler.

I thank God for the opportunity of going to Western. I lived just at the foot of the hill on Adams Street. Running up the hill to classes and BSU activities is something I won't forget. Much time was spent at the Music Building trying to learn to play the violin from my teacher, Mr. Adam Foster. Spanish was my minor. Classes with Dr. McChesney were fun.

I continue to express my love for music and Spanish through various church activities.

RANDAL E. NIX, Class of '59, BA English, currently living in Haines City, FL.

I am a visiting teacher and social worker in the Polk Co., FL school system. I have been an employee of the school system for 30 years and was recreation director for the city of Haines for 20 years.

Honors include being named Haines City Jaycees Citizen of the Year, and city employee of the year, 1986.

I am married to the former Anita Goodall, a claims representative for State Farm Insurance. We have one son, Clifton.

I have many, many great memories of Western. How about walking out to Hunt's Barbeque with the grand, enlightening conversation with Dr. Gordon Wilson, "the shot" by Frosty Able and the general feeling of closeness between the faculty and students.

CHARLES M. "TOD" OLIVER, Class of '54, B.S. Physical Education.

After serving two years in the army, I received an M.A. in Journalism (Univ. of Missouri), worked for six years as a sports reporter in Springfield, MO, and South Bend, IN, and taught journalism and English for three years at Mt. Vernon, IL, High School and Community College; since 1966, I have been on the English Faculty at Ohio Northern Univ., receiving my Ph.D. in English from Bowling Green (Ohio) Univ. in 1970.

For the last ten years I have been editor of The Hemingway Review a twice-yearly journal of interest to Hemingway scholars, and of The Hemingway Newsletter, published for members of The Hemingway Society.

My memories of Western are many, but I'll never forget writing a sports column for the College Heights Herald on sportsmanship, suggesting in passing that the water tower hadn't been "painted" recently, and being called in for a chewing out by Kelly Thompson the next morning because somebody had done it at a cost to the college for repainting of $4,000.

HELEN VANOVER OLIVER, Class of 1955, B.S. Elementary Education.

After leaving Western in 1955, I taught special education classes in Columbia, MO, South Bend, IN, and Mt. Vernon, IL, before moving to Ada, OH, where I have been employed with the Allen County Board of Mental Retardation/Developmental Disabilities for the past 18 years, currently as Director of the Case Management Division.

My husband (Tod) and I have three sons. Last year it was fun to take our twins back for a tour of Western's campus, and show them the statues still standing in the garden behind the old Snell Hall Building where Martha Gray and I spent one Saturday morning in 1952 with water buckets, brushes, and cleanser trying to remove the mold and grime from their forms. I also remember the smell of the lilac and magnolias on a warm spring night in West Hall, the late night fun in the dorm, and the visits in the homes of several favorite teachers.

Tod and I are using our hobby of used book collecting as a side line business, selling at book fairs under the name of "Oliver and Co. Books."

TWYMAN L. PATTERSON, currently living in Jeffersonville, IN.

In 1958-61 I was in the United States Army;

in '61-'72 I was a teacher; '72-present I am a counselor at Jeffersonville High School.

In 1961-1981 I was a football coach; currently on I.S.T.A. State Board of Directors.

I married Sandra Fuqua in 1958. We have one daughter, one son, and one grandchild.

In May of '88 I had open heart surgery (triple bypass); I have been bicycling since 1976 and in June of '83 I rode from Portland, OR to Jeffersonville, IN.

EDGAR R. PAYNE, Class of 1955, B.s., M.A., Rank 1, currently living in Lewisport, KY.

I have a major in P.E., and Biology, and a minor in English.

I am a retired elementary principal after serving 23 years for Hancock County Board of Education, I was a high school basketball coach for ten years-Bremen High School, two years, and Lewisport High School, eight years.

I am a Phi Delta Kappa member.

I have been named the Lions Club President, and Second District Elementary Principal President.

I am married to Shyrlon Horsley Payne, Elementary Librarian at Hancock County School. We have three sons and one daughter. We also have eight grandchildren.

When I think of Western, I remember when I was enrolled there were only 1300 students. We knew most everyone on campus. By 1955 the enrollment had increased to 13,000.

I enjoy golf and antique refinishing.

MARY DEAN PEDIGO, Class of '53, B.S. Economics. Currently living in Cookeville, TN.

After graduation, I taught Home Ec at Allen Co. High School in Scottsville where I met John Pedigo. We were married in 1955 and moved to McMinnville, TN, living there for 16 years before moving to Hendersonville, TN, where our family of five children grew up. During their collegiate education I taught science and home economics at Hawkins Jr. High in Hendersonville for 12 years.

Our oldest son, Al (B.S. Agriculture, '79, WKU) is a farmer in Fountain Run, KY. Jim, following graduation, became a CPA and lives in Nashville. Bob is a veterinarian in Lewes, DE. Nina, our only daughter, is a remedial reading teacher and freshman girls basketball coach at Knox Doss Jr. High in Hendersonville. Ivan, our youngest, is the owner and operator of Pedigo's Landscaping in Hendersonville.

Two years ago John and I moved to Cookeville where I am enjoying my family, which now includes four grandchildren. I also enjoy sewing, cooking, bridge and involvement in church and community projects.

My memories of WKU include The Hilltoppers (musical group), Coach Diddle and his winning basketball teams and the many friends that made college days so great.

FRANCES LYNN TAYLOR PETERS, Class of 1950, B.S. in Elementary Education, currently living in Louisville, KY.

I received 99 hours above B.S. degree, but did not finish my Masters degree.

I retired from Jefferson County Board of Education in 1981, after teaching 37 years in six different schools: Newberg, Greenwood, Rangeland, Hikes, Melborne Heights, and Klondike.

Before entering Western in 1942, I studied salesmanship at Ahrens Trade School and worked as a salesperson at Kaufmans, Stewarts, Taylor Trunk Co., and in office personnel for an insurance company and at Belkhaps Hardware. I attended the Church of Christ on 12th and Park Street and found great knowledge in Bible study.

My memories of Western include the good times we had in Mr. Wilson's Art Club, meeting lifetime friends from Park City, KY (J. Jackson, K. Toms, M. Riber).

I enjoy bowling three days a week, playing golf, swimming, exercising at YMCA. I also travel six times a year by car and have covered all of the U.S.A. except Hawaii. I am now 75 years young!

SANDRA DEMPSEY PETTITT, Class of 1959, Elementary Education Degree, currently living in Eustis, FL.

I continued my education at Rollins College and University of South Florida receiving my Masters.

I am an Occupational Placement Specialist for Tavares High School in Tavares, FL. My responsibilities are of dropout prevention.

I am President of American Cancer Society.

My affiliations include F.P.G.A. and O.S.G.A.

I am married to Carl Pettitt, Retired Superintendent of Schools. We have four children ranging from age 24 to 29. We also have two grandchildren, ages three and one.

My memories of Western include AUBREY, walking to Hunts Barbecue late at night after lock in dorm hours, Baron's Camp, Beta Omega Chi. 13ers, The Goal Post, Mr. Diddle, the old gym, Snell Hall, trying to get exams that the basketball players stole from Cherry Hall!

ANNE ROBEY PEPPER, Class of 1952, A.B. in English, currently living in Brandenburg, KY.

I continued my education receiving a M.A. and Rank I in School Counseling.

I retired in 1985 after serving as Middle School Librarian in Meade County.

I married Stuart Pepper in December of '52. We have two children: Kattie Smith, a WKU graduate, she has three children, Joseph Timothy, Sarah Katherine, and Robey Stuart; and Sarah Nelson, a WKU graduate, who has one child, Natalie Stuart.

STUART PEPPER, Class of 1951, B.S. and M.A. in Education, currently living in Brandenburg, KY.

I continued my education at Indiana University.

I currently hold the position of School Superintendent at Meade County Board of Education.

I am married to Anne Robey Pepper, who is retired. We have two children and four grandchildren.

JANE LOVELL PFINGSTON, I have taught English, speech and theatre, remedial reading and social studies at various institutions including Elizabethtown High School, Caverna High School, Alvaton High School, Union County High School, Morganfield Junior High, Owensboro Vocational School and Henderson Community College.

My interests and pursuits are extremely varied. Participation in various capacities in my professional educational organization includes state, district, and local activity. I am also a Special Olympics volunteer and coach on the local, regional and state level.

My activities include originating and establishing Kaleidoscope, a non-profit summer program for gifted students which served over 100 students in five counties. Presently, I serve as chairman of the board of Kaleidoscope, Inc.

I have also been very active in the speech and theatre field from serving on the Kentucky High School Speech League Board of Directors and the Kentucky Two-Year College Speech League Board of Directors to being instrumental in establishing the Union County Community Playhouse and serving as president and director. I have also worked with Henderson Community Theatre and Elizabethtown Little Theatre.

I enjoy the political arena and have served in many areas in my county Democratic party. I have also served as president of the Union County Democratic Women's Club and as first director of the First District of the Kentucky Democratic Women's Club. I also served on the Governor's Task force for Education. Presently I am a member of UCEA's Legislative Contact Team.

In 1986 I was named Sturgis Woman of the Year.

I spend much of my spare time overseeing the UCEA Colonel Malcolm Hart Memorial Scholarship which I helped to establish to honor a colleague. I derive a great deal of pleasure in serving as chairman of the committee and also serving my club as chairman of the Morganfield Business and Professional Woman's Club Scholarship Committee.

My husband Eddie, Union County Circuit Clerk, our daughter Julie, a Union County High School senior and I live on a farm near Sturgis and raise registered quarter horses.

The people who made such a contribution to my life constitute my fondest memories of Western: such as Dr. Miller and his Western's

Summer Theatre, Ivan Wilson the gentle man behind those marvelous watercolors, Dr. Wilson Wood, my appreciated mentor and my friend Frances Dixon.

Other memorable impressions include leading the homecoming snake-dance downtown and through Tandy's; the late night aroma of fresh-baked bread from Colonial Bakery wafting up the Hill to the steps of Van Meter; typing a term paper all night; the thrill that went up when the band played "Stand up and Cheer"; and all the strange and interesting personalities that became a part of my life as a result of being on that hilltop.

BETTY CLIFTON PILEGGE, Class of 1952, B.S. in Elementary Education, currently living in Northport, AL.

I continued my education receiving my M.A. from Marshall University in 1958, also additional work at the University of Maryland and University of Alabama.

I have been an Elementary School Principal in Tuscaloosa City Schools for 22 years. Job responsibilities include the Arcadia Elementary School with 405 students.

I was also a teacher of public schools in West Virginia for three years, Marshall University Laboratory School for six years, and Maryland public schools for four years.

I am in Delta Kappa Gamma, NAESP, and also a member of the University of Alabama Women's Club.

I am married to Dr. Joseph C. Pilegge, a Professor of Political Science at the University of Alabama. We have no children, but enjoy nieces and nephews.

My memories of Western (1948-52) include working at West Hall (in the office), getting to know so many people, favorite teachers (Miss Richards, Joe Howard, Miss Robertson, to name a few). My roommate was Sara Downing Taylor. Dero and Harriet Downing were so supportive and helpful.

LAVERNE CRAIG PINCKLEY, Class of 1952, A.B., English and History. M.A. in 1954, in Education and English, and received Rank I in 1969.

I started my teaching career in Monroe County at Gamaliel Consolidated School and taught for two years then transferred to Tompkinsville High School as an English teacher. After 14 years of teaching experience, I was promoted to the Central Office in 1966 as a supervisor of instruction a position which I presently hold and have had for 22 years. I have been with the Monroe County Board of Education for 36 years.

I have wonderful memories of Western and professors like Dr. Gordon Wilson, Dr. and Mrs. Moore, Dr. Stickles, Dr. Poteet, the meek Ivan Wilson, who called himself "Ivan the Terrible", Dr. Bert R. Smith and the "Curriculum" class in particular. The "Hilltoppers" the singing group serenading the dorms.

I am married to Thomas Bratton Pinckley, a former student at Western. He is a retired teacher. We have two daughters Teena and Pippa. They are graduates of Western. Teena is a kindergarten teacher at Tompkinsville Elementary and a part time teacher for WKU - Glasgow Campus. Pippa is a Pediatrician at Graves-Gilbert Clinic in Bowling Green.

After my work at the office and at home; I enjoy needlework, tending to flowers, working and caring for the lawn.

WILLIAM A. PLOUMIS, Class of 1954 Degree/Major: B.S. Chemistry. New Rochelle, NY. Further Education: D.D.S. U. Pittsburgh 1958 M.S.D. Fairleigh Dickinson 1966. Current position: Dentist/Orthodontist.

Since 1966 I have been practicing orthodontics in New York. Married to Athena since 1956, and have enjoyed raising four children and have two grandchildren. Traveling and sailing have been my favorite diversions.

OMEGENE POWERS POWELL, Class of '50. B.S. Elementary Education.

I started Western in the summer of 1944. Cadets still occupied the dorms. I was fortunate to get a room in what, that fall, became Diddle's Dorm for basketball boys. That fall I moved to old West Hall where I lived a full year then returned to Daviess County to teach, on an emergency certificate, the second grade at Sorgho. After the summer term in 1946, I married Thurman Powell and we both returned to Western. Thurman was on the G. I. Bill so we lived in Vet's Village. I worked and went to school, off and on, for the next four years, receiving my degree in the summer of 1950.

I was grade one thru 12 librarian in Nelson County at Bloomfield, KY for three years and after our four children - Jean, Bill, Ed and Carolyn - were all in school I returned to the teaching field as Elementary School Librarian in Webster County, retiring in 1981 with 19 years of service. Thurman retired in 1979 after 30 years with Soil Conservation Service.

Our daughters, Jean and Carolyn graduated from WKU and a son, Bill attended WKU one and half years.

I remember the thrill, each time we returned to Western, of seeing the "hilltop" from ten miles out of town; the friendly "hello" from everyone you met on campus; the beautiful walks around the hilltop; no shorts on campus; working in the old library; basketball games in the old gym; rook games with other Vet's Village couples instead of Saturday night movies which weren't affordable; a pint of ice cream each or bananas on pay day to celebrate. Those were great days!

My husband and I have square danced for 20 years. I love reading and traveling. I am a geneology "bug" and have published two family histories - Powers and Basham. I have been a Webster County Public Library Board Trustee for a total of 21 years during which time a library tax was passed and old school building renovated for library.

CHARLES L. PRICE, M.D., Class of 1952, B.S. in Biology, currently living in Hartford, KY.

I continued my education at the University of Louisville receiving my M.D. degree.

I am the Health & Chief Executive Officer at the Green River District Health Department in Owensboro, KY. I have the responsibilities as the Chief Executive Officer over seven counties (Daviess, Henderson, Hancock, Ohio, McLean, Webster, and Union), District Heath Department with 270 employees and the director of Medical Services.

Previously I was in private practice of Medicine (Family Practice) for 29 years at Hartford, KY.

I am married to Shirlye Johnson Price, a housewife. We have four children: Pamela Sue Price Koonce—B.S. in Accounting, WKU-1978; MBA, WKU-1981, CPA; Sandra Kay Price Cuzzort—B.S. in Computer Science, WKU-1982; Brenda Anne Price Perigo—BS in Computer Science, WKU-1986: Charles Lee Price, II—Freshman at WKU. We have four grandchildren: Steven Brent Koonce (six), Brian Christopher Koonce (three), Adam Price Cuzzort (four), and Laura Elizabeth Cuzzort, seven months.

I have great memories of Western, including Dr. L. Y. Lancaster, and all the other fine Professors, especially of the Biology and Chemistry departments.

WILLARD PRICE, Class of 1953, B.S. Degree, currently living in Louisville, KY.

I am a vice president and a secretary/treasurer of Cardinal Carryor.

I am married to Pat (Horn) Price who is a teacher in Jefferson County.

We have two daughters and one grandchild. They are Toni Price Ross, Pam Price Koenig, and the grandchild's name is Matthew Koenig.

PAT (HORN) PRICE, Class of 1954, A.B. Degree in Music, currently living in Louisville, KY.

I am a teacher at Jefferson County High School in Louisville.

I am married to Will Price, a vice president and secretary/treasurer at Cardinal Carryor.

I have two children. They are Toni Price Ross and Pamela Price Koenig. My only grandchild is Matthew Koenig.

DAVID M. PROW, Class of 1958, B.S. in Agriculture, currently living in Campbellsville, KY.

I am currently the Dealer District Manager for Southern States Cooperative. I set up new dealers in Western Kentucky, aid in sales, give advice on management and finance.

I am married to Mona Gayle Prow, who is a secretary for the Taylor County Middle School. We have four sons: Gregory, 32; Thomas, 30; Bruce, 24; and Brian, 22. We have seven grandchildren: Tyler, six; Paige, five; Mendi, four; James David, three; Blake, four; Clifton, two; and Taigan, one.

My memories of Western include attending basketball games in the old gym, attending the Talisman Ball, staying on campus during the summer when very few students were there,

and serving as Post Master at the College Heights Post Office my senior year.

My hobbies include houseboating, fishing, and traveling.

JAMES C. PROW JR., Wadesville, IN. B.S. '51 in Agriculture, married to Beverly.

As many of the graduates of the 50s, I entered the military service after graduation in 1951. After spending four and one half years in the Air Force during which I received my pilot's wings and spent one year in Korea I returned to civilian life. I obtained a Master's degree from the University of Tennessee in Dairy Manufacturing in 1957. The Bordon Milk Company was my employer until 1968 when I left and joined Mead Johnson and Company in Evansville, IN now known as Bristol-Myer USPNG.

As a Senior Process Engineer I am currently responsible for the process to make our Adult Nutritional products.

CAROL DICKSON PRUITT, Class of 1957, B.S. Degree in Chemistry-Math, currently living in Manchester, TN.

I furthered my education with a Masters Degree in Science Education from University of Tennessee.

I am currently and have been a teacher at Anderson County Schools for 25 years. My job responsibilities are to teach chemistry and physics.

Other important positions are to help my husband in the business office.

I am married to Murrell E. Pruitt, who is a business owner.

We have three children. They are Vernon Pruitt (middle son) graduated in 1984 from Western. His wife (Kim Duet Pruitt) graduated from Western in 1988 with a B.S. Degree in Nursing; Vernon graduated from UT Medical School in 1988. Royce Pruitt (oldest) graduated from University of Alabama in 1983. He is a

CPA in Cleveland, TN. Dean Pruitt (youngest) is a student at MTSU in Murfreesboro, TN.

My memories of WKU include the beautiful place, the hard work, the wonderful (life long) friends, the Inter-Varsity Christian Fellowship, the basketball games, and its being a friendly place.

MURRELL E. PRUITT, Class of 1957, B.S. Degree in Chemistry/Math, currently living in Manchester, TN.

I continued my education by receiving my Master's Degree n Chemistry at University of Kentucky.

I am currently President of Pruitt Management & Incorporated; Manchester, KY.

I am responsible for operating two Burger King stores.

Other important positions include working at Oak Ridge National Laboratories for 21 years.

I have been selected as a Kentucky Colonel.

I am married to Carol Dickson Pruitt who is a teacher.

We have three children. They are Vernon Pruitt (middle son) graduated in 1984 from Western. His wife (Kim Duet Pruitt) graduated from Western in 1988 with a B.S. Degree in Nursing; Vernon graduated from UT Medical School in 1988. Royce Pruitt (oldest) graduated from University of Alabama in 1983. He is a CPA in Cleveland, TN. Dean Pruitt (youngest) is a student at MTSU in Murfreesboro, TN.

My memories include the hard work, meeting the many wonderful people, and the basketball games.

My hobbies include: fishing, water sports, hunting, and kids.

BOBBY E. RAKESTRAW, Class of 1959, B.S. Agriculture, currently living in Monrovia, MD.

I am currently the Program Manager for the U.S. Soil Conservation Service which includes being manager of the National Rural Abandoned Mine Program.

I am married to the former Donna Hammers, who is a housewife. We have two children: Wendy Sue, 22 and David M., 19.

I remember my first day at Western when I met Uncle Billy Hill, who got me a room and a part time job. I worked at the Kentucky Building and it was there that I met Mr. Ivan Wilson, who was the best friend an individual could have and the water colors he displayed were outstanding.

DOROTHY AGNEW RAY (DOT), Class of '50, B.S., Mathematics and Biology. I taught

math in Owensboro, KY while my husband, Mort, was in Korea and again in Alexandria, VA while he was in Vietnam. During 20 years of Army life we lived in Red Bank, NJ twice; Adak, AK; Pittsburgh, PA; and northern Virginia (DC area). We did not get to Europe until he retired and we went on our own.

I started work at General Research Corporation (GRC) as a Technical Aid and was a Senior Analyst when I took early retirement in 1988 after 21+ years. The Logistics Directorate, Organization of the Joint Chiefs of Staff, where I worked on a contract at the Pentagon for many years, gave me "military" mementos. I had attended many such ceremonies, never dreaming I would one day receive the same honor.

When Mort retired from the Army he started his own business, Ray Electric Outboards. While in Virginia I moonlighted by being the keeper of the books. When I retired from GRC and we moved to Florida I became the full-time (?) office help. Nice to have such a lenient boss. Love the sun and water, swimming and boating.

I have been President of two Women's Clubs and of a local chapter of a national computer association. Served as national publicity chairman of the National Computer Conference in New York.

I have three children (ages 31 to 34) and seven grandchildren (ages 4 months to 9 years).

I was at Western only five months of the 50's decade, but my years from '46 - '50 will never be forgotten. Western prepared me well for my various positions at GRC and for living. Mr. Hugh Johnson, math department, will always be remembered as a guiding light.

JAMES A. RAY, Class of 1957, B.S. in Agriculture, currently living in Burke, VA.

I work for USDA/Washington D.C. I am in charge of directing the nationwide market news service for Livestock and Grain. This includes thirty-seven field offices and working with thirty State Departments of Agriculture including Kentucky.

I received Market News Reporter of the year in 1988; five certificates of Merit by USDA for exceptional service.

I have a daughter, Lisa, in law school, Mercen University, Mason, GA; a son, James, a computer programmer with Freddy Mack.

My memories of Western are meeting Nadine Pottinger at Mrs. Moore's boarding house on College Street.

NADINE SEAY POTTINGER RAY,

Class of 1958, B.S., currently living in Burke, VA.

I have a master's degree in Guidance and Counseling from Trinity University, San Antonio, TX.

I currently teach Environmental Science and Integrating Computers into the Science Program at Fairfax County Public Schools in Fairfax, VA.

I have been Science Team Leader for grade level, Science Project Workshop Coordinator (three years), and United Way Sub School Coordinator.

I was the Mini-Grant Winner for Fairfax County (twice).

I am married to James A. Ray, who is Chief of Livestock and Grain Market News. We have two children; Lisa Dianne Ray—Law School, Mercer University, Macon, GA; James F. Ray, Computer Programmer for Freddy Mac.

My memories of WKU include; Football Games, Ed Diddle losing his teeth at basketball games, Talisman Balls, and Dr. Gordon Wilson's love of birds and interest in students and their families.

My hobbies are photography, reading, and travel.

H. RANDOLPH RICHARDS, Class of 1953, B.S. Degree in Agriculture, currently living in Scottsville, KY.

I furthered my education by getting my M.S. in Agronomics at the University of Wisconsin in 1954. I received my Ph.D. in Plant Breeding and Genetics at Purdue University in 1960.

I am currently a county agent for the University of Kentucky in Scottsville. I work as an Extension Agriculturist and Resource Development.

I am a member of the Methodist Church, Rotary, and Masonic Lodge.

I am married to Hope C. Richards, who is a math instructor at WKU. We have five children: Virginia, 35; Richard, 32; Douglas, 30; Barry, 21; and Elaine, 19. We have four grandchildren: Meredith, Lindsay, Amy, and Leslie.

I enjoy farming, beekeeping, hunting and fishing.

JIM RICHARDS, Class of 1959, B.S. in Chemistry and Physics, currently living in Bowling Green, KY.

I furthered my education by getting my Masters of Arts at WKU in 1960. I did postgraduate work at Indiana University.

I am currently the Director of Alumni Affairs at WKU in Bowling Green. I am responsible for all alumni activities at WKU.

Other important positions include head basketball coach at WKU from 1971-1978, as-

sistant coach at WKU from 1968-1971, and head coach at Glasgow High School from 1963-1968. My team won the Kentucky State High School Championship, and I was Kentucky State High School Coach of the Year in 1968, and O.V.C. Coach of the Year in 1973-74 and 1975-76.

I am married to Annette Waggoner Richards, who is a math teacher at Bowling Green High School. We have two children, Steve, 25, and Ann, who is deceased.

My memories of WKU include wonderful friends, baseball team and teammates, Mr. Diddle, Dr. Scarborough, Dr. Kelly Thompson, Dr. Dero Downing (president), many superior teachers: Hugh Johnson, Math; Evan Wilson, Art; Dr. McNally, Chemistry; Mr. Lyle Sherrill, Biology; Mr. George Bennett, Biology; Mr. Sanderfur, Physics; and coaches Ted Hornback, Nick Denes, and Jack Clayton. I remember living in the basketball dorm, my roommates Willard and Wayne Smith, Ronnie Sheffer, Richard Smithson, and Ray Southerland. I remember the cheerleaders Alice Chumbley, Phyllis Robinson, Rachael Chadwick, Sandy Harrah, and others. I remember athletic contests, intramurals, great happy days and nights, McFarlands—"Wow!", winning the Courier Journal Baseball Contest and a free trip to the World Series.

I'm one of the privileged few to have had the opportunity to have worked at my alma mater for the past 20 years . . . to give back some portion of what WKU gave to me.

I enjoy golfing, being Basketball Color Commentator for WKU home games, and living life to its fullest everyday!

EVELYN BAILEY RICHARDSON, Class of 1952, A.B. Degree in English/Library Science, currently living in Russellville.

I am currently a Regional Librarian for the Kentucky Department of Libraries and Archives. I work in the ten-county Barren River Area Development District and am a consultant to public library staffs and boards of trustees.

I am a member of the Kentucky Library Association and the Southeastern Library Association.

I am married to James Richardson, who is a farmer. We have two daughters, Celia and Lynn, and two grandsons who are seven years old.

I received the 1986 Tim Lee Carter Distinguished Service Award presented by the Barren River Area Development District and I received the 1985 Outstanding Public Service Award presented by the Public Library Section of the Kentucky Library Association.

My first year at Western, 1948-49, was spent in Potter Hall. In '49-'50, we residents had first choice of living in the "New Dorm," later named McLean Hall. I remember the early morning Christmas gift exchange at the dorm. We came to the lobby in our robes and exchanged gifts with a maximum cost of ten cents. We also wore coats over our pajamas to the steps of Van Meter for Easter Sunrise Services. It was often so cold that the musical instruments would not play.

I write a weekly human interest column that I began in 1952, "Here and There," for the **Franklin Favorite**. It now also appears in the **Logan Leader-News-Democrat**. I teach the adult "Upper Room" Sunday School class at the United Methodist Temple in Russellville. I enjoy giving readings and original skits to clubs and organizations.

JOHN C. "KOKO" RICHARDSON, Class of 1958, B.S., Industrial Arts.

WKU was home beginning the summer of 1947 when parents "Johnnie" and Ann Mary worked on teacher certification. I enrolled in 1953, spent two years in the Army and returned for my Master's in 1962. After teaching in Florida and South Carolina, I finished the doctoral program at UK in 1971. I teach special education and school psychology at Clemson University. My wife, Mary Martha Blackmon, from South Carolina, completed her Master's in 1963 at WKU.

I remember early influence by Eagle Keys and Sam Short, being student trainer and playing one freshman football game, Cheerleading, Thirteeners, Desegregation, Sledding College Street snow, Hunt's BBQ beans, College Street Inn footlongs, Mac's, Mooselodge, Tandy's Chili, Hilltopper Lunch Breakfasts, Murray Campus raids, Louisville OVC Tourneys, "Whitey" Sanders' bands, my brother, Bob, "Citrus", and sister, Rosemary.

I also own a small consulting firm, EDUCATUS ASSOCIATES. I hold memberships in numerous professional organizations and regularly present invited research papers. I frequently represent schools in litigation and am an ardent advocate of neglected children.

Martha, 25, once a Presidential Scholar at WKU summer school, had my first grandson, Robert, two. Robert, 22, is an account with Elliott Davis Company in Greenville, SC. Sarah Ann, 20, will graduate in education December of 1989 and continue the teaching tradition of this family.

EMILY HUMPHREYS ROBISON, Class of '59 B.S. Education, Crestwood, KY.

I took a course in the Book of "John" from the Southern Baptist Seminary. I taught Adult Education in Oldham County 1935-1937. I was postmaster at Clermont, KY 1938-1943. I taught all eight grades in Bullitt County 1946-1972.

I belong to the Retired Teachers of Oldham and Bullitt County. I was President of Oldham County Retired Teachers 1978-1980 and 1984-1986. Now I am Vice President 1988-1990.

I taught the last two schools that was taught at Woodsdale in Bullitt County.

The Historical Society was able to acquire the building and renovate for a Museum to commemorate the one room schools in Bullitt County. It was completed in 1985.

I am a life member and secretary of the Oldham County Historical Society, the Kentucky Historical Society and The Filson Club.

I married Charles Samuel Robison. He worked at James B. Beam Distillery at Clermont, KY and Kroehler Furniture Company, Louisville, KY.

The Kentucky Building was built when I was at Western, and they had three dormitories for girls and one for boys.

My interests are genealogy and handwork. I teach an adult women's class and play the organ for the church.

RACHAEL CHADWICK ROLL, Class of '60, B.S. in Physical Education.

I have taught for 29 years, the last 20 have been at Seminole community college where I chair the Health and PE dept. Before that I taught in Auburn and Henderson, KY; Austin, TX and Evansville, IN.

I have also sponsored cheerleaders and dance teams and coached women's tennis, volleyball and softball. I'm active with the American Red Cross and Heart Assoc. and a member of FL Assoc. Comm. Coll., FL Assoc. HPER&D and AAPERD. I completed my doctorate at the Univ. of GA.

I have four sons, Chad, Chip, Chet and Chuk. I completed my Doctorate at the Univ. of Georgia.

I run, cycle and swim regularly and participate in road races and triathalons.

I enjoy remembering the fun of living in the dorm; wearing raincoats over our shorts to PE; Coach Diddle yelling at us if we cut across the football field; basketball games in the red barn; Sat. afternoon football games in the old stadium and the Cherry Hall chimes every 15 minutes.

RANDELL G. ROUTT, Native of LaRue County. Vietnam War Veteran who served in the U.S. Army 24 years. Overseas assignments included duty in Korea, Vietnam and Germany. Highest award received was the Legion of Merit. Retired as a LTC February, 1983.

Education/training: B.S. Agriculture, M.A. Economics, and the Command and General Staff College. Post graduate work also includes course work toward an M.B.A. I have completed Farm Credit Service Level I and II training.

Professional Licenses and Certification: Licensed in Real Estate, insurance, securities and hold a Rank I Teaching Certificate.

Work Experience: Field Representative for Farm Credit Services, farming, financial planning, and college professor. Currently Assistant Professor for Economics and Finance at Elizabethtown Community College.

Professional, Church, and Civic Organizations: International Association of Financial Planners, American Association of Individual Investors, Kentucky Economic Association, Kentucky Economic Educators, Midwest Economic Association, Honorable Order of Kentucky Colonels, Kentucky business Society, Retired Officers Association, Association of United States Army, Disabled American Veterans, and Elizabethtown lions Club. Member of Severns Valley Baptist Church. Director Sunday School department at Severns Valley Baptist Church, and President Elect (1989) for Kentucky Business Society and the Elizabethtown Band Boosters.

Family: Wife is the former Mary Louise Hazle of Hodgenville; daughter Allyson, sophomore at Elizabethtown High School; daughter Rhonda Witten, Recreation Director for City of Radcliff; son Stan is a Captain in the Army.

PEARL B. RUTLEDGE, PH.D., Class of '53, BS Education. Licensed psychologist and current president of the Gestalt Training Center. She conducts nationwide training workshops for professionals and maintains a private practice in Lexington, KY. Dr. Rutledge is a graduate of the University of Kentucky and the post graduate program of the Gestalt Training Center of San Diego with Erv and Miriam Polster with additional training from Jim Simkin; Alan Joe Zinker in the creative arts and Gestalt; and Stanley Krippner in dream work.

She is a member of the American Academy of Psychotherapists, American Psychological Association, Kentucky Psychological Association, and Association for Creative Change in Religious and other Social systems.

Director of R & R Associates for Human Resource Development, a consulting firm which conducts training in the field of effective communication in organizations. She is a consultant with the AMA (American Management Associations) serving management, marketing, sales and public affairs and while on the Psychology faculty of Pace University, New Your, she developed courses in Organizational Development, Group Relations and Psychology of Personal Development. she has been a trainer and consultant for 18 years in the management, mental health and educational fields, including designing training and serving as a consultant to organizations such as IBM, General Foods, M & M Mars, and Gillette Company and Hanover Brands.

Dr. Rutledge obtained her Ph.D. in Educational Psychology and Counseling from the University of Kentucky. She is a currently licensed as a psychologist by the Kentucky Board of Psychology. She is a member of the American Psychological Association, American Personnel and Guidance Association, Association for Humanistic Psychology, Association for Specialists in Group Work, and an accredited Professional trainer in the Association for Creative Change. She is listed in the 1979-1980 Who's Who in the East.

DELLA MILLER HILDRETH RUNNER, Class of 1958, Degree in elementary Education, currently living in Bowling Green, KY.

I continued my education by getting my Masters in 1964 at Western, and a Rank I in Guidance in 1980 at Western.

I am currently retired, and have been a wife, mother, grandmother, and teacher. My children are 40 and 42 years of age, and my grandsons are 14, 20, and two of them are 18 years of age.

My memories of WKU include hard work. I was raising a family and teaching at the same time that I did most of my work at Western.

HAROLD B. SALMON, Class of '50, BS, currently living in Cincinnati, OH. Further education includes real estate classes at the University of Cincinnati.

I am the owner and broker of the Salmon Realty Company and have been for the past 30 years. I have also taught vocational agriculture in Brownsville, KY in '50 and '51. I was the assistant to the sales manager, Armour Fertilizer, Cincinnati for five years.

I am married to Ruth A. Salmon, a retired schoolteacher. We have two sons and one grandson.

MARY COMBS SAMPLE, Class of '57, B.S. - Business Education.

During the first five years after graduation, I taught business education at Western's College High and completed the M.A. Degree. Later I taught at South Fulton, TN and Muldraugh, KY. Since 1966 I have been a member of the Western staff serving in the capacities of secretary to the Vice President for Administrative Affairs, secretary to the President, secretary to the Board of Regents, executive Secretary of the College Heights Foundation since 1980, and since 1982 treasurer of the Foundation and secretary to the Board of Directors.

I have a daughter, Sheila Riley, who is also a Western graduate and two stepsons, Irvin, Fr., and Robert. My life is enriched by three grandsons and a granddaughter. My husband, Irvin Sample, Sr., is retired from Naval Ordinance and is employed by Warren County Schools.

Memories of dorm life include signing out after 7:30 p.m. with destination listed and return by 9:30 p.m. except for one 10:30 during the week, going up and down the hill to B.U. for business classes, and being so homesick that first semester. Having been at Western since 1953 except for four years, Western is now home.

MARILYN MILER SANDERS, Class of 1954, B.S. Degree in Biology, currently living in Owensboro, KY.

I continued my education with a M.D. at University Louisville in 1958. My residency was in International Medicine at Methodist Hospital of Indiana from 1961-1964.

I am a physician with a private practice with my husband.

Other important positions include being selected (in 1986) the first woman president at the Daviess County Medical Society in 85 years, and a trustee at Campbellsville College—chairman 1985-'86.

I am married to R. John Sanders M.D., General Surgeon.

We have three children. They are John Christopher, an attorney; Mark Evan, an accountant; and Kathryn, a poet. We have three grandchildren.

Memories of WKU include the B.S.U. group; the thrill of the "National Anthem" and flag presentation in the old gym before basketball games; walks through the fort and to Biology labs; and apple dumplings and coffee for 25 cents at Woolworth's.

My husband and I have made four trips to teach and help in mission hospitals in Indonesia and Nigeria.

DELMA CALVERT SCHNELLEN-BERGER, Class of 1953, B.S. Degree in Home Economics, currently living in Fern Creek, KY.

I have furthered my education receiving my Masters in Education at UL and Rank I, 30 hours above a Masters at Western.

I retired on July 1, 1985 from teaching Home Economics in Jefferson County.

Memories of WKU are: Basketball games, football games, the beautiful campus, my aching legs, Miss Lottie Kay—"Miss Day Knows, Girls"—third floor of McClaim Hall, the walls ears; Princess Theater costing 25 cents; Home Management House, the walls had ears, Miss Murphy, Emma Lou, Dr. Willie, Dr. Wilson, Mom Drew, Virginia Thomas, Church.

NANCY SHAW, Class of 52, Diploma in Secretarial Science, currently living in Rabun Gap, GA.

As a life-long student, I've completed a B.S. at University of Charleston and an MBA at the University of Denver, as well as counseling certification form the Universities of Colorado, Miami, and Florida.

I retired from the State University System of Florida—most recently as Assistant Director of our Honor's Program in Teacher Education at the University of South Florida—has given me the opportunity to be a part of Foxfire's Teacher Outreach to initiate teacher networks in West Virginia and in Eastern Tennessee.

My two children John Alden and Kathryn Elizabeth are grown and on their own. I'm happy with the persons that they are becoming.

Other interests are teaching yoga, conservation work, tennis, hiking, birding, and traveling. Membership in the Conservancy, Audubon Society, Sierra Club, Friends of the Mountain, ForestWatch, Incredible Edibles, and The Mountain afford many exciting experiences.

My memories of WKU/BU include living at Moore's Boarding House, getting myself (on time!) to Joe Orendorff's Law Class at 7:00 a.m. in the dark mornings of winter and being the only female in the class, and participating in the "Miss BU" Beauty pageant—my first and last experience with pageants!

DR. WILLIAM C. SHIRLEY, Class of '58, B.A. English.

At the present, I am an Education Advisor for the U.S. Army Infantry School at Fort Benning, GA. Since leaving Western, I have been an Army Officer; a Junior/Senior High school teacher and head coach in Kentucky and Georgia; writer; Weapons System Analyst; Government Supervisor; and co-author of an educational textbook. Also, I have earned a Masters and Doctorate in Education at Georgia State University in 1972 and 1976.

The awards which mean the most to me are: Bronze Star Medal awarded for combat duty in Vietnam; membership in Phi Delta Kappa (Professional Honor Society); outstanding Government Service awards; and a softball Award/Trophy established in my name for future awardees.

My wife, the former Dianne Hogan, is a native of Georgia. We have two daughters, Melody and Michelle, plus a wonderful granddaughter, Lauren.

My hobbies include worldwide travel, reading, sports, and sponsoring/playing in a men's softball league.

Memories of Western are many and include exploring the "wild" caves surrounding beautiful Bowling Green; canoeing down the Green River; the ROTC drills; the Scrabbard and Blade socials; research in the library, midnight parties; the outstanding professors and President Thompson (my lifetime role model) and those "special" coeds.

JUNE SHORE, Class of 1952, Art/English Degree, lived in Glasgow, KY.

She died Oct. 28, 1988 of lung cancer. She had tutored in the literacy program at the Barren County Literacy Council.

She had taught school in Battle Creek, MI; Victoria, British Columbia; and in Louisville, KY.

She authored a GOOD HOUSEKEEPING novel, two books, a play, and a movie script. She won the Abingdon Award for best juvenile fiction of 1973. Two of her books were Junior Literary Guild selections.

Her surviving husband is Ken Shore. He is a senior therapist at Barren River Mental Health Retardation Board, Incorporated.

Her surviving children are: Stephen, Susan, Rebecca, Alison, Melissa. Her surviving grandchildren are Matthew O'Toole, and David Jones, both of Louisville.

GEORGE S. SIMPSON, The author was born in 1929 in Webster Co., KY. He obtained a Bachelor of Arts degree from Western Kentucky University and a Juris Doctor in Law from the University of Kentucky (1954).

He was admitted to the Kentucky Bar in 1954 and is currently a practicing attorney.

He served as a Judge Advocate Officer in the United States Air Force (1954-1956).

He is married to Sandra (Slater) Simpson, and they have four children.

He has held positions in Kentucky State Government from 1972 to 1988; those positions being: Member of the Workers' Compensation Board, Board of Claims, and he has served as attorney for the City of Sturgis.

He is the author of other biographies and local history papers. They are: The Life of Reverend John Withers (1811-1858); Tidewater to Tradewater (Reverend W.W. Wynns); Cumberland Commander (Reverend J.T. Barbee); Judge Peter Casey (1811-1812); Early Union County Roads; Early Union County Militia; Cypress Creek Christian Church; Mt. Ephriam Cumberland Presbyterian Church and Session Minutes; and Early Coal Mining of the Tradewater River from Heath Mountain to Anvil Rock. He has also compiled and edited Caseyville Merchantman Vol. I and II (1854-1855).

He is a member of the Kentucky Historical Society and the Filson Club.

ROBERT (BUBBER) E. SIMPSON, Class of 1953, B.A. Degree in English, currently living in Bowling Green, KY.

I furthered my education with a Master's Degree at the University of Louisville, and a Ph. D. at the University of Alabama, Tuscaloosa, AL.

I am currently a professor at WKU in Bowling Green, KY. My job responsibility includes being the Professor of Psychology.

Other important positions include being a jet pilot in the USAF. After the USAF I continued flying with Kentucky Air Guard and started teaching and coaching. I was head football and track coach for several years in Jefferson County.

I was selected Jefferson County Coach of the Year. I am a member of the American Psychological Association, Kentucky Psychological Association, and the Kentucky Academy of Science.

I am married to Pat Simpson, who is a secretary.

We have two children Mark, 30, and Tim, 28. Mark, married to Julie Wallace, works Defense Mapping in D.C.; Tim, opera singer, performs in West Germany.

Memories of WKU include the many friends made, classes, playing football and track, study sessions, sledding down the Hill, packing ten people in an Old Model A car to catch a movie.

My hobbies include sailing, tennis, and flying.

ANITA SIZEMORE SMITH, B.S. Home Economics, 1956.

I started Western in 1952 and lived in McLean Hall when it was a new girl's dormitory. There were only two girl's dorms at that time, McLean and West Hall. I remember especially the friendliness of all the students and the spirit of Western, which has stayed with me through the years.

My teaching career across Kentucky has included Daviess County, Fayette County, Warren County, Franklin County,and Kenton County, where I taught the last 14 yeas before retiring. When I retired, I was head of the Home Economics Department st Scott High School in Kenton County.

My affiliations have included serving on local, state, and national auxiliary boards with the Kentucky Society of Professional Engineers and the National Society of Professional Engineers. In 1975 I was named to the "Out-

standing Secondary Educators of America". At present, I am a member of K.E.A., N.E.A., Phi Delta Kappa, and Kentucky Retired Teachers Association.

I have one son, Cary, and my husband and I enjoy traveling and working with church, professional, and civic organizations.

HELEN LEET SMITH, Class of 1954, Degree in English/Education, currently living in Owensboro, KY.

I continued my education to obtain a Master's and Rank I at Western.

I am the Librarian for Owensboro High School with the responsibilities of Department Chair.

Most of my professional experience has been with the Owensboro City Schools as librarian on the elementary, junior and senior levels. In the 60's I co-coordinated the beginning of the elementary library program in Owensboro. In the 70's I transferred to the new 9-10 Center of Owensboro High School as head librarian and began that library program. Since 1982 I have been department chair at Owensboro High School which now includes grades nine through 12.

Much of my spare time for the past 15 years has been devoted to active involvement in professional organizations. I have chaired several committees at the local, district and state levels. I served as President of the Kentucky School Media Association.

This involvement gave me opportunity to work in political campaigns of state and national legislators and to lobby for education interests.

For a number of years I have taught a personal development/image building class and an audio/visual class for the Owensboro City Schools' Adult Education Program.

I am married to Alvey B. Smith, who works in retail sales. We have two children: Alvey Benjamin 33 and Carol Natalie 29, both are married. We have four grandchildren (three boys and one girl).

My memories of Western include the wonderful faculty and the support, interest friendship, and confidence they have me during my years at Western.

I enjoy bridge, golf and, of course, reading, traveling, and politics.

LEWIS E. SMITH, Class of '54, B.S. Elementary Education.

I attended Western from 1950-1954, graduating May, 1954, with a BS in elementary education. I returned for summer terms 1956-58, receiving a masters in education and history.

Later, Rank I requirements were completed in school administration.

Positions have included elementary teacher in Grayson County (KY) schools; junior high school teacher, Superintendent, and Federal Programs Coordinator/Instructional Supervisor in Leitchfield (Kentucky) Independent Schools. My current position is Chapter I Coordinator (reading ands math programs) which I have held since the merger of Grayson County and Leitchfield Independent Schools in 1972.

Special hobbies and interests include travel and amateur radio. I travel both inside and outside the United States as often as possible, and have been a licensed, active radio "ham" since 1961. Another special interest has been working with the Adult Basic Education program since 1967.

There are so many pleasant memories associated with Western that it is difficult to isolate a few. Some that come immediately to mind are attending basketball games in Western's "Red Barn," Saturday football games, student and faculty acquaintances, and Western Drive In, Western Lunchroom, and Hilltopper's Cafe.

ROBERT DAMON SMITH, Class of 1959, Degree in Agriculture/Biology, currently living in Cadiz, KY.

I continued my education at Louisiana State University to achieve my M.S. in Wildlife Management.

I am self-employed as a Wildlife/Environmental Consultant and Outdoor Writer. My responsibilities include contacting Wildlife/Environment and Outdoor News/Education.

I retired from TVA's Land Between the Lakes National Recreation Area (Nation's first Biologist on a National Recreation area).

I am a Certified Biologist, member of Lions Club, past Master of Mason's, Fox Trotting Horse Association.

I am married to Mahala Cline Smith, who is an Educational Aide. We have one daughter, MeLisa Smith Morris, WKU graduate, and a son Eric, Second Lt. US Air Force.

My memories of Western include the people, students and professors, athletics, Uncle Ed Diddle, the Duck Inn Cafe, courses and cramming for exams!

I enjoy hunting, fishing, traveling, pleasure and show horses, dogs, and church activities.

JOAN SOETE, A budding writer who corresponds frequently will find time to write.

After four delightful years I graduated in June '54.

With a B.S. in Elementary Education I

moved to Memphis, TN in 1955, There I first became involved in Special Education. I tutored a brilliant young lady (about my age) in The Home for Incurables. I evaluated the values instilled by Western Kentucky State College. With God's help I composed and typed her curriculum (fourth grade level). Still, she is my favorite tutee.

By now I have taught five or six categories of so-called Special Education.

Also, I taught four different grades - so-called normal.

First graders at church this choir member taught, (most labeled normal - one labeled Trainably Mentally Handicapped (normal to me))

I have returned to college four or five times. Since I was at Western, I have learned more from my students.

At western I learned that education is fun.

This Western Player hopes she has shared a love for Western. (A former student, now a teacher, incorporates fun.)

Right now I am tutoring "a teacher's dream". This 37 year-old man wants to read and write, etc.

Western made me a teacher by profession, not by career!

MARJORIE KELLER SPALDING, Class of 1958, B.S. in Commercial Education, currently living in Ft. Washington, MD.

I continued my education with graduate work at the University of Maryland receiving an Advanced Professional Certificate.

I am a teacher at Oxon Hill, MD with the responsibilities of Department Chairperson, Business Department.

I am a member of the faculty advisory committee.

I am affiliated with the Civic Association and Audubon Society.

I am married to Glenn R. Spalding, Director of Science and Technology (Navy Dept.). We have four children (ages 27, 25, 23, and 19), and one granddaughter, age one.

My memories of Western include the marching and concert band, basketball, McLean Hall, foot-long hotdogs at College St. Inn, T-bone steaks at Mary's.

I enjoy oil painting, antiquing, furniture refinishing, bird watching, and playing with my granddaughter.

WILMA JEAN DEPP STERLING, Class of 1951, B.S. Degree in Elementary Education, currently living in Orlando, FL.

After leaving Western I taught in Jefferson County at Prestonia Elementary in Louisville for three years. During those summers (52-54) I earned my M.A. at Peabody in Nashville, TN.

In 1954 I married Joe Sterling and moved to Florida. Joe retired two years ago from Seminole Community College where he served as basketball coach, athletic director, and chairman of Health and P.E. department for more then 20 years.

Our children are grown. Joe, Jr., 32, is in his last year as a resident in anesthesiology; Alice, 30, is already practicing as an optometrist here in central Florida and Jon, 28, is in business here in Orlando. We have no grandchildren.

Presently, I am a sixth grade teacher in social studies at Liberty Middle School. I stayed out of teaching when our children were small so I'm not quite ready to retire.

My memories at Western are many. I always enjoyed working in the Periodical Room of the Old Liberty on top of the hill. Dorm life in Old Potter Hall and later in McLean Hall was fun. Other happy memories too numerous to mention!!!

VERNON A. STONE, Class of 1951, B.A. English.

As research professor in the School of Journalism at the University of Missouri at Columbia, I conduct research, teach and write about the field I first experienced as a student of Frances Richards thorough classes and her advising the College Heights Herald, which I edited for two years.

Then came a master's at the University of Iowa; nine years in television and radio news at WHAS, Louisville; a Ph.D. in mass communication at the University of Wisconsin, Madison; nine years on the Wisconsin faculty; four years as research professor at the University of Georgia, Athens; eight years as director of the School of Journalism at Southern Illinois University, Carbondale; and since 1987, Missouri.

My writing includes two books and many research articles and convention papers, mainly on broadcast news and communication behavior. Since 1972, I have conducted national surveys under grants from the Radio-Television News Directors Association, for

which I serve as research director. RTNDA honored me with its Distinguished Service Award in 1988.

A daughter and a son are in college.

Over the years I have returned often to hometown Bowling Green and Franklin to visit relatives and friends, including Miss Richards and others who have made Western so important to me.

PATRICIA (COBB) STRADER, Class of 1960, B.S. Degree in Education, currently living in Greenville, KY.

I entered Western in the fall of 1952 after graduating from Greenville High School. After two enjoyable years on "the hill" I dropped out to get married and to begin teaching. I re-entered WKU later and earned my B.S. in 1960, I then earned my M.A. Degree in 1966, and Rank I in 1977.

The first year I was there I worked in the college cafeteria located in the basement of Potter Hall. It was a great place to get to know everyone. The next year we moved to a new cafeteria in a new building, Garrett Student Center.

My three children also attended Western; two of them earning B.S. and M.A. Degrees there.

Having taught the past 34 years in the Muhlenberg County School system, I plan to retire at the end of this year and move to the Denver, County area where I will be a substitute teacher.

ALMA LEE STEENBERGEN STRODE, I started to Western in fall of 1929. I stayed at Potter Hall (a girl's dorm) on the third floor. After one year, I taught in a one-room school in Barren County. Since it was only seven months, I went back to Western for the second semester of that year. I taught school again that fall. That was my pattern until I graduated in 1932, receiving a "Life Certificate". Teaching ten years in the rural schools, I then taught in the Glasgow City School system for 19 years. Also, I worked for the Barren County Board of Education for two years.

Going back to Western, I received my B.S. Degree in Elementary Education in 1959.

In 1967 I returned to Western and received my M.A. Degree with emphasis in Reading and Psychology. At the end of that year I was employed by the Jefferson Count Board of Education as a Reading Specialist. I did further work in Reading at Colorado State University.

After retiring from Jefferson County, I took courses from Western in real estate, poetry, and psychology.

In 1935, I was married to Joseph Denton Strode, who died in 1959 as a result of atomic radiation in World War II.

I have one daughter, Jo Ann Witt, who teaches the blind children in Owensboro, KY; also, one grandson, Skip Shaw, a junior in Owensboro City Schools.

During the Years I have done extensive research in genealogy and painting Coat of Arms.

Reading, writing, poetry and growing flowers have been my hobbies.

I have found memories of the "Old Fort" and the "Spoon Holder."

PHILIP J. STROMOWSKY, A.B. Degree, English, January 1955, Rockville, MD.

Completed M.A. in special education, George Peabody College, Nashville, in 1964, and Ed. D. degree in special education ofrm the University of Alabama, Tuscaloosa, in 1979.

Completed flight school in 1956, and served on flight crew for two years at Savannah, GA. Returned to Louisville in 1958 to begin teaching handicapped children and youth. Moved to suburban Washington, D.C. in 1964, where I have positions with Montgomery County Public Schools, Rockville, Maryland, in the field of special education.

My wife, Donna, and I are now looking forward to retirement in the near future, probably moving to the South. We have two grown children, Jay and Janie.

Indelible memories of Western include the strong spirit of kinship on the campus. Everyone knew and cared about everyone else! The roundball games in the Red Barn and the bonfire pep rallies culminating with a snake line down town will live on in my happy memories. From all my experiences at Western and in Bowling Green, I am often reminded of the truth that "the Spirit makes the Master".

J. ROGER SUMNER, Class of 1952, Degree/Major B.S. Geography/Geology, Rome, GA.

Further education, Post graduate work: University of Georgia, Purdue University, Ohio State University, General Manager, Inland Container Corporation Rome, Georgia. I direct operations of a large corrugated container plant and a sales force in Georgia, Alabama and Tennessee.

Other important positions include Director Home Federal Savings and Loan Association, Chairman of Trustees Shorter College, Member Hospital Authority of Floyd Medical Center, Trustee Georgia Hospital Association, Director Business Council of Georgia, Executive Board Northwest Georgia Council Boy Scouts of America, a Deacon, Sunday School teacher in a Baptist Church, Member of Governor's Advisory Committee to the Georgia Department of Human Resources, North Georgia Area Chairman of the National Committee for Employer Support of the Guard, Department of Defense, USA.

Honors and activities include Distinguished Service Award from Georgia Hospital Association, Silver Beaver Award from Boy Scouts of America, Listed in Who's Who in American Colleges and Universities

Married Mary Ruth Page (See her biography for our children and grandchildren).

My hobby is boating.

Memories of WKU include Leading the football parades in my 1931 Ford Convertible named the "Blue Blaze", Watching Western win almost every basketball game at home, meeting friends at the Goal Post, and many great professors including: Dr. Terrell, Dr. Wilson, Dr. Stickles, Frances Richards, Frances Anderson, Mary Marks, and Gabrielle Robertson.

MARY RUTH PAGE SUMNER, Class of 1952, Degree/Major BA English/Library. Science. Rome, Georgia.

Further education includes Master of Education in Media West Georgia College, Other post graduate work: Berry College.

Past affiliations include teaching fourth grade in Macon, Georgia after graduation, Children's Librarian in Macon public library,and in Rome, GA public library, English teacher/Librarian Thornwood School for Girls in Rome, and Media Specialist at Darlington Lower School, a private school, for 15 years.

Present affiliations include teaching a Sunday School Class of senior adult women at a Baptist church, Media Specialist of the church, Thistle Garden club, and student of art at Shorter College.

Honors include Member of Phi Kappa Phi,

an honor society and Darlington School Faculty Award for Excellence.

She is married to J. Roger Sumner (Biography included). They have three children and four grandchildren.

My memories of WKU include the intimacy of the 1200 students and the closeness of professors such as: Dr. Wilson Wood, Dr. Gordon Wilson, and the distinguished Dr. Skickles. I remember the thrilling basketball games and tall players, the antics of Mr. Diddle, moving into the beautiful new McLean Hall, walking on the snow, climbing steps to the third floor of Cherry Hall, steep hills, the old stadium, and hanging out at the Goal Post and Cedar Building.

I am presently pursuing art as a possible second career. Another interest is creative writing. Roger and I enjoy traveling. In the last few years, we have traveled to the USSR and last summer we went on a cruise to the Scandinavian capitols and to Leningrad for the second time. This year we plan to visit our daughter in West Africa.

KENNETH W. TACKETT, Class of 1953, B.S. in Agriculture, currently living in Bowling Green, KY.

I am a film actor, but not under any contract to a studio at this time.

I have played the lead in a drama about company power struggle (for Georgia ETV) and played two the Wolf Man in a TV pilot film in California.

In my memories of WKU, my junior year was happiest, hands down. If I live to be 100, I'll never forget the many laughs provided by Robt. Coppersmith, who was on Ag. Faculty that year. I also enjoyed Cherry County Life Club.

I hope to be in a remake of the film "The Mask of Kijon," which starred Erich Von Stroheim (one of my favorites).

BOYCE D. TATE, Class 1950, Degree/Major: BS - Ind. Arts., Kentucky.

Further education: BS Equivalent in Civil Engineering, Virginia Military Institute, 1959; Master of Civil Engineering, University of Virginia, 1962.

Current position: Department Head, Dept. of Industrial and Engineering Technology, Western Kentucky University until May 31, 1989. On June 1, 1989, will assume the position of Department Head of Civil Engineering Technology at the Southern College of Technology at Marietta, GA.

Other important positions: Taught in public schools at Leitchfield, KY and Covington, VA from 1950 to 1954. Was Instructor of Engineering Graphics at Virginia Military Institute from 1954 to 1959. Was Assistant Professor of Engineering Mechanics and Graphics at Virginia Military Institute from 1961 to 1965. Was Assistant Professor of Mathematics at Western Kentucky University from 1965 to 1967. Started the Dept. of Engineering Technology at WKU and served as its Head until 1981 when that Dept. was merged with the Dept. of Industrial Education and Technology to form the present Dept. which I have been Head of since 1981.

Honors/Activities/Affiliations: Licensed

Professional Civil Engineer, Licensed Professional Land Surveyor, Consulting Engineer to Palestinian University in Israel, 1980, Consulting Engineer for the US Agency for International Development Agency (US-aid) in Indonesia in 1988, Private consultant in engineering and land development since 1966.

Memories of WKU: The antics of Coach Diddle and his fabulous basketball teams of 1947-50; The dances in the basketball field house (now Helm Library); Mr. L.T. Smith as my Dept. Head and Professor; The programs at assemblies on Wednesday mornings (formerly called Chapel); The Pep rallies prior to important football games, especially on Homecoming; The "Snake Dance Parades" through town on Friday night before Homecoming; The sophistication of President Paul L. Garrett; Secretly getting married to a fellow student; The faculties concern for the students achievement and welfare; Vets Village.

AMELIA MEADOR TATE, Class of 1950, B.S. in Music.

I have been a private Piano Teacher since 1963.

Other important positions include Music Teacher for Public Schools in Leitchfield, KY; Alleghany Co., VA; Keswick, VA; and Lexington, VA from 1950 to 1963.

I have five children: Boyce D. Tate Jr. (38), B.A.-WKU, '73; Lake Worth, FL; Stephen R. Tate (36), B.S.-W.K.U., '74; Murfreesboro, TN; Sara Tate Medley (33), B.A.-Murray State, '77; Cookeville, TN; Emily Tate Taylor, (31), B.A.-WKU, '79; Fairfield, OH; and Amy L. Tate (24), B.A.-WKU, '85; Indianola, IA.

I have six grandchildren: Jason R. Tate, 13; Keith J. Tate, six; Jordan Tate, five; Amelia Bess Taylor, five; Valerie Tate, two; and William Lee Taylor, 17 months.

My memories of Western include playing with the WKU band at the Kentucky Derby, Spiders in the "Web", French under Miss Claggett, Miss Richards English Classes, Miss Redd-the Nurse, Piano under Mr. Daggett and Miss Chisholm, sneaking out of Potter Hall after hours, Aubrey's security, operating the campus telephone switch board, registration day, WOW!, and Potter Hall Cafeteria!

ARTHUR TAYLOR "KIRBY", Colonel USAF Ret., Class of '52 AB Mathematics, Minors in Physics and Industrial Arts.

MS Public Administration, The George Washington University, 1966.

A native of Butler County, I entered Western in 1948. After four years of ROTC and graduation, I entered the Air Force in 1952.

Following 15 years of operational experience as Pilot and Instructor Pilot of four engine transports and single or twin engine jets, I was assigned to flying desks in Personnel, Education and Training positions. My duty stations were spread over eight states and three foreign countries.

One of the highlights of my 27 years career was duty as Deputy Commandant of Cadets for Military Instructions, U.S. Air Force Academy, Colorado.

I retired from the Air Force in 1979 and since have been active in Real Estate and golfing near Tampa, FL.

FORESTINE SMITH THOMAS, Class of 1959, B.S. Degree in English, currently living in Bowling Green, KY.

I started Western in 1928 and received a Standard Life Certificate in 1932. I taught 41 years the last 37 in Warren Co., KY, at Rockfield Elementary, prior to that three years in Logan County and one year in Simpson Co., KY. I retired in 1972.

I have rented rooms and apartments to many Western college students. I am a Warren County Homemaker belong to the Mt. Victor Club, member of the Bowling Green—Warren County Retired Teachers Association, and a member of Kerr Memorial Methodist Church.

I met my husband Forest Thomas at Western in a history class. We were seated alphabetically, Smith-Thomas, he retired as a Civil Service employee at Ft. Campbell, KY and died in 1964. We had two sons, Forest Lee Thomas, 39, is a Western graduate and a C.P.A. in Hendersonville. He and Collen (Burch) Thomas have two children Matthew, seven, and Amanda, nine. David Michael Thomas, 37, is a Western graduate and is an employee in the Dessa Mfg. Co. in Bowling Green in the Designing Department. He was married to Sue Carol Mayhew and they have one son Quinn, six.

I have many memories of my college days at Western including many inspiring teachers, especially the Chapel Programs in the Administration Building, and trips to the Goal Post.

JOYCE FURNISH TRIVETTE, Class of 1959, B.S. in Elementary Education, currently living in Lexington, KY.

I continued my education in Graduate Courses of interest in elementary education, University of Kentucky.

I am a First Grade Teacher working for Fayette County Public Schools in Lexington, KY. My responsibilities are teaching the primary level.

I am the Corresponding Secretary, Episcopal Church Women, Diocese of Lexington. I serve as Bluegrass Area Vice President, ECW, Diocese of Lexington and I am past President, St. Michael's ECW; I received the American Red Cross Service Award for Volunteer Service to the Lexington V.A. Hospital, etc. I am a Member of FCEA/KEA/NEA.

I am married to Don Trivette, Fine Arts Director, FCPS, Lexington. We have one child, Mark Evan Trivette, 16 years old.

My memories of WKU include many friends, a happy time in life, a caring faculty, and a good education.

RUBBIE ALMA (JOHNSON) TURNER, Class of 1958, B.S. in Education, currently living in Fairfield Glade, TN. I received my Life Certificate at Bowling Green Normal in 1919.

I taught fifth grade at Paducah, KY 1919-1920, second then third grade in Franklin, KY in 1920-1922.

In 1922, I married Charles Wesley Turner a businessman.

In 1930, after our dry goods business burned we moved to his farm for a 16 year stint. I also taught in the local rural school.

In 1946 we moved back to Franklin, KY with our one daughter, Elsie Charlene born in 1937.

In 1948 to 1967, I taught 17 years, mostly my beloved first grade.

With summer school and extension courses I received my B.S. in Education the same year my daughter did, 1958. Then by 1960 I had earned my Masters in Education.

In 1966, my husband died.

In 1973, after a stroke in 1969, I moved to Fairfield Glade.

In a different situation I found life more interesting. I attended church, Republican Women's meetings and find bridge a helpful mental exercise. Thank goodness, I see, drive, go and hope to reach 105.

BETTY JO ADKINS TUTTLE, Class of 1952, Degree in Home Economics, currently living in Rangely, CO.

I continued my education at the University of Cincinnati receiving my Masters in Education in 1972.

I am currently employed by Rangely District Schools, Rangely, CO as a substitute school teacher.

I also teach classes for Colorado Northwest Community College, Rangely, CO.

My husband William is Railroad Superintendent for Western Fuels-Utah, Rangely, CO.

I have two boys Roger and Jim and two girls Christie and Donna. I also have four grandchildren Christopher, Kiera and Kalli Tuttle and Jeremy Gohr.

I loved our campus and the thought it was beautiful anytime of the year, but especially when it snowed. I remember the late winter snows and how it would hang on the trees.

I remember my chemistry with Mr. McNally. He wrote the formulas on the board with his right hand and erased with his left as he went, now you see it now you don't! A smart man, but hard to keep up with.

I remember Mrs. Drew doing room check and finding me frying apples, dorm parties with our room mates, all of the people I worked with in Potter Hall cafeteria and all the fun we had, jaunts up and down the hill.

I feel teachers at Western instilled in me a life-long desire for learning and I am glad I spent four years of my life at Western.

I'll never forget the night we were glued to the radio and heard the Hilltoppers sing, "Trying", for the very first time.

I enjoy sewing, crafts, church activities, teaching, decorating my home, and babysitting the grandchildren.

MINTA FINNEY LEWIS VERNON, Class of 1950-51, currently living in Nashville, TN.

I attended WKU and BU in 1950-51. I married in 1952 and didn't return to finish my degree until 1970. Received B.A. in 1972 and MPS in 1975.

Currently I am a Psychotherapist in Nashville at Dede Wallace Center.

I continue to enjoy campus events with my friends from the 1950s and feel more a part of that era.

SHIRLEY DEAN WAGONER, Class of 1957, B.S. in Agriculture, currently living in Williamstown, KY.

I continued my education by receiving an M.A. in Education in '66 and Rank I in '70 for Education Administration.

I am retired.

I am married to Freida Wagoner, who is a legal secretary. We have two sons, Roger Layne 27, a graduate of WKU in '83, and David Gerard 21, a student at WKU.

SUZANNE HIGGASON WALDROP, Class of 1954, B.S. Degree in Home Economics, currently living in Park City, KY.

I continued my education with a M.A. in Home Economics Education, and a Rank I in supervision at WKU.

I am a retired teacher from the Barren County Board of Education.

My job responsibilities included teaching secondary Home Economics for 30 years; one in San Diego, CA, and 29 in Barren County Schools.

I served in various positions in professional organization on the local, regional, state, and national levels; developed curriculum in Home Economics for the State Department; served on the Kentucky Education and Certification Council; National Home Economics Education Coalition; served as president of the National Association of Vocational Home Economics Teachers; and AVA Region II Teacher of the Year.

I am married to Bill G. Waldrop, semi-retired finance officer for Barren County Board of Education.

My three children are Melanie, Pamela, and Kevin. My only grandson's name is Ben.

My memories of WKU included life in the "new dorm:" (McLean); cafeteria meals in the basement of Potter Hall; hangouts—Hilltopper, Western Lunch Room, and the Goal Post.

My hobbies are enjoying freedom to become invalued in community projects; literacy program, latchkey care; traveling and entertaining friends and family; and working on special projects for the State Department relating to improving the quality of home and family life. I have a vested interest in Home Economics education and related activities.

ANNE M. WALKER, Class of 1960, Degree in Art, currently living in Owensboro, KY.

I have my Masters and Rank I in Guidance and Counseling, plus 30 hours above Masters.

I am an Art Teacher at Burns Middle School and teach 6th, 7th, and 8th grades.

My husband Mickey T. Walker is In House Director at Daviess County High School. We have two children Marty and Michael.

My memories of WKU are Beta Sorority, meeting Mickey, graduation, Mary's "Restaurant", and Coach Griffin.

My hobbies are golf, herbs, antiques and needlepoint.

CAROLE SUE (SNYDER) WALKER, Class of 1958, B.S. in Elementary Education, currently living in Glendale, KY.

I continued my education to receive an MA from Western in 1970, and achieve my certification of Art from the University of Louisville.

I currently am a wife, homemaker, mother, and nonnie (grandmother). My responsibilities are unlimited for love and encouragement!

Other important positions include Executive Board Youth Theatre of Hardin County, Advisory Committee Nolin RECC, former Art Teacher at G.C. Burkhead Elementary for eight years and Hardin Central Jr. High School for three years.

I am a member of Glendale Christian Church and Glendale Homemakers.

I am married to Robert B. Walker, who works in highway construction. We have two children, Jerry Lee Walker (29) and Barbara Sue Walker (27). We also have four grandchildren; Jessica Lee four and one-half, Ashley Blake, two, Catherine Lynn Nett and Matthew Aaron Nett, five and one-half.

My memories of Western include the Western Players and Van Metre Auditions, "Mom" Drew and McLean Hall, Beech Bend Park picnics, Mary I Cole's Ed. Classes, Mr. Wilson's Art Classes, Hunt's Bar-B-Que, Sunday night pizza at the Dixie Cafe, swimming at the quarry, and Mr. Diddle and his red towel.

JAMES H. WALKER, Class of '58.

For the past 20 years I have been associated with Jennie Stuart Medical Center, Hopkinsville, KY, with the last 15 serving as Administrator and Chief Executive Officer.

I received my B.S. in Science in 1958 and M.A. in 1961. I also completed a two year Hospital Executive Program in 1977 at St. Louis University.

My former positions include a teacher and coach at Alvation High School, Bowling Green; FBI agent; Laboratory Coordinator at Deaconess Hospital, Evansville, IN and Business Administrator at Pennyroyal MH-MR Center, Hopkinsville.

My wife, Deborah, is a retired teacher and we have one son, Eric. Eric received a B.S. in Accounting from Western in 1985.

Some of the fond memories I still have of WKU are basketball in the old red barn, Saturday football games, the Goldpost and Ogden and Snell Hall.

My major hobbies are golfing and fishing.

MATILDA WALKER, Class of 1956, currently living in Louisville, KY.

For 30 years, I taught school and now have been retired for two and a half years.

While teaching, I was a cheerleader sponsor, girls cross country coach, and girls golf coach. I managed the Louisville and Jefferson County Girls' Regional Golf Tournament and the Girls' State Golf Tournament for many years.

Now that I am retired I have been substituting and enjoy it very much. Also have been able to travel more and play a little more golf.

MICKEY T. WALKER, Class of 1960, B.S. in Geography, currently living in Owensboro, KY.

I have my Masters, Rank I and 30 hours above my Masters.

I am currently In-House Director at Daviess County High School. My job responsibilities are to supervise potential drop-outs. I am also Athletic Director, 11 years D.C.H.S., football, and golf coach D.C.H.S.A.

I am married to Ann Walker who teaches Art and we have two sons, Marty and Michael.

My memories of WKU include Coach Diddle, 13ers, football, College Street Junior, Coaches Fiex, Griffin, Elrod, Denes, and many good friends.

My hobbies are golfing and fishing.

ROBERT B. WALKER, Class of 1958, B.S. M.A. in Agriculture, currently living in Glendale, KY.

I continued my education with a Master's at Western in 1968 and Smith-Hughes at the University of Kentucky.

I am Executive Vice President of Kentucky Guard Rail, Inc., Elizabethtown, KY. My job responsibilities include over-all management of the company of which I am the major stock holder.

I am an Elder in the Glendale Christian Church, member of the Advisory Committee of Nolin RECC, member of Speciality Committee KAHC, and a member of Glendale Lions Club.

I am married to Carole Snyder Walker (former elementary and J.H. Art Teacher). We have three children: Jerry Lee, 29; Barbara Sue Walker, 27; and Catherine Lynn (Walker) Nett, 24; and three grandchildren, Jessica Lee Walker, four and one-half; Ashley Walker, almost two; and Matthew Aaron Nett, three and one-half.

My hobbies include avid bird hunting, part time cattle farmer, and gardener extrordinaire.

DOROTHY JEAN RUSSELL WALLACE, Class of 1957, B.S. in Elementary Education, currently living in Louisville, KY.

I retired as a teacher in 1973 on disability from Jefferson County Public Schools. I am currently housewife.

I am married to Clay Armand Wallace, who is a truck driver.

I am a member of Valley Station Women's Club and a member of Beth Haven Baptist Church.

ROBERT C. WALLACE (CLIFF), WKU '54, '57. I received the BS-degree in Phys. Ed. at Western ('54), and the MA-degree in Secondary Ed. ('57). I also compiled an additional 26 hours beyond my MA while I taught for 16 years. I was a football coach and baseball coach for those years I was in teaching.

In 1971, I quit teaching and became a photographer. Some may recall that I worked with the Herald and Talisman staffs at WKU as a photographer. In 1973, I started my own business in photography and have done a little of almost every kind of photography; sports, portraits, weddings, public relations, architectural, and commercial, and I have won a number of awards for my work as the photographer for Seng Jewelers in Louisville.

I married Charleen Sullivan, a Bowling Green girl, and also a graduate of Western ('53). She also has an MA in Secondary Ed. from U of L, plus her 30 hours. She has taught in the Jefferson County System since the mid-70s.

We have a family of three; one son and two daughters. Charlie lives in St. Louis, Cathy lives in Philadelphia, and Carrie lives in Lexington. Charlie and Cathy are married, and Cathy has a son, our only grandchild. Wouldn't you know? Charlie and Carrie both decided to get their degrees at the University of Kentucky! They are 31 (Charlie), 30 (Cathy), and 27 (Carrie). (You might have noticed: all of us have "C.W." as initials - it was intentional.)

Charleen and I have lived in Louisville since 1957. We bought a motor home when we got our house paid for and have toured the country from coast to coast and border to border. That's our "gig"; we like traveling and get out in the tioga on every occasion we can. Naturally, I take a few pictures along the way.

Even though two of our kids went to UK, and I worked 13 years taking pictures for the University of Louisville Sports Information Office (as a freelancer), we still have fond memories of Western. After all, that's where we met. I'm an Alabaman by birth, lived in New York City 11 years, but when I came to Kentucky, I found my "home". I've lived in Kentucky for 36 years now. No place like it anywhere.

I'll be forever indebted to Bob Cochran; he did more for me than anybody, outside my family. They used to tell us how Western folks were in demand everywhere; after 35 years of living in the real world, I know they weren't just whistling "Dixie". The "Hilltoppers" are still being played by DJ's; movie scripts are being written by Western grads; scores of our grads accounted themselves very well in defense of our country; Western grads abound in the teaching field, and the coaching field; yes, and there are more than one of us who have "made the scene" as photographers, some more so than others. I'm happy to have been one who learned that the Spirit does indeed make the Master.

BYRON C. WATKINS, Class of '56, Madisonville, KY.

Have been a professional educator for over 34 years. Retired from the U.S. Army Reserve with the rank of Colonel in 1985 after 30 years service. Began teaching and coaching at Caverna Independent Schools in Cave City, spent three years coaching basketball and teaching high school English at Sebree High School, two years as principal of White Plains School and ten years as principal of Anton School in Hopkins County before assuming my current position as Assistant superintendent for Pupil Transportation in Hopkins County. Am a member of Phi Delta Kappa, Madisonville Lions Club, E.W. Turner Lodge #548 F&AM in Earlington, KY, a Kentucky Colonel, Duke of Paducah and have been given the key to My Old Kentucky Home, was selected as the first outstanding director of pupil transportation in the state of Kentucky by the Kentucky Association for Pupil Transportation, also was recognized by the Kentucky Association of School Administrator for outstanding leadership award.

Memories of Western include putting the Herald to bed at the Park City Daily News with Bob Cochran and others, Gladys and Hubert Powell at Hilltoppers Restaurant who in their own way helped many continue in school by being liberal with the entries on the back of the five dollar meal tickets they sold. Also remember Mr. Diddle and the baseball team on which I was privileged to play.

Have three sons Byron Murray (31) who holds an AA degree from Madisonville Community College, David Hunter (30) who holds a BS degree from Western and William Gregory who holds a BS degree from Georgetown and is a grad student at Western. Also remember many other things which should remain memories without publication.

JIM WEDDLE, Since the 1957 graduation, we have lived in a number of locations. Every new city and new position has been a broader educational experience. For the most part, I have been involved with new product development for the furniture industry. I have spent a lot of time in the Far East and the Philippines developing new products and ideas. It's fun and rewarding.

I married Nancy Wilson. She has her PHD in education and is a professor on the college level. We have four children and two grandchildren. Jay Todd, age 24, lives in Virginia with his family. Anne, 21, is a senior at the University of Missouri. Eric, 19, is a freshman at the University of Missouri and Mark, 15, is a sophomore in High School.

While the rewards of business have been

great, the memories and experiences at Western are equally outstanding. I remember the basketball games in the Red Barn, exploring caves with my roommates. I remember weekends at Beech Bend Park for those who couldn't get home on weekends. I remember working for the Industrial Arts convention trips.

But most of all, I remember the closeness of friends and faculty. The Industrial Arts Department was like family. Mr. L.T. Smith, Mr. Carl Barnes, and Mr. Walter Naubach were invaluable, but Mr. H.B. Clark spent many hours moulding men from boys.

Thanks, H.B., thanks Western and may that "SPIRIT" always prevail.

MARILYN (HIGGASON) WERENSKJOLD, Class of 1957, Degree in Commercial Education, currently living in Louisville, KY.

I continued my education at MSU receiving my Master of Education Degree in 1982 and Office Management and Business Education.

I am a teacher for grades seven and eight at Community Catholic School.

I have lived in California, Connecticut, New Jersey, Virginia, Washington D.C. Florida, Guam, Tennessee, and Louisiana with our family of five sons while my husband, Gary, was in the Navy.

I am a member of Delta Pi Epsilon and educations organizations.

I am married to Gary Werenskjold, United States Navy, retired.

We have five sons, all 21 and older.

My memories of Western include my counselor, Dean Grise, our class which was the first to graduate from Western with a business degree, walking from McLean Hall (the new dorm) to BU for classes my junior and senior years, Dr. Craig's Penmanship class, I remember Coach Diddle and the great Hilltopper teams, the W Club picnics, having the same roommate for four years, and going to California to teach with Pat and Dot.

JAMES T. WEST, Class of 1957, B.S. in Agriculture, currently living in Paducah, KY.

I continued my education at Murray State University, receiving my MA and Ed.S.

I am Assistant Superintendent at McCracken County Schools. My job responsibilities include being in charge of curriculum and instruction.

I am a member of Kentucky Association School Administrators, Association of Supervision and Curriculum Development, Kentucky Association of School.

I am the Past President of Reidland Lions Club and a member of Phi Delta Kappa.

I am married to Jo Sisk West, a third grade teacher. We have two children, Sara Jo, 29 and Rae Nell, 25.

My memories of Western include fried bologna sandwiches at Duck Inn Cafe, curfew with Momma at West Hall, soils lab. in basement of Suell.

My hobbies now include outdoor activities, hiking, bicycling, fishing, and reading.

CHARLES P. WEST, Class of 1959, B.S. Physics. I began Western in 1956 and received my B.S. Degree in 1959 with a major in Physics, minors in Chemistry and Math, with a certification in Secondary Education. I received my M.A. Degree also from Western in 1960. I taught at College High in Bowling Green before coming to Vanderbilt to do graduate study.

I am presently employed with the Tennessee Department of Health and Environment as Assistant Director of the Division of Radiological Health. The Division has the responsibility of regulating the use of sources of radiation, radioactive materials and X-ray machines, throughout the State.

I am married with two daughters and three grandchildren. My wife Betty is also employed with the State of Tennessee.

My hobbies are reading and gardening, and also spending time with my grandchildren.

JO SISK WEST, Class of 1957, B.S. Degree Home Economics, currently living in Paducah, KY.

I continued my education by receiving my M.A. and Rank I from Murray State University.

I currently teach third grade at Farley Elementary School in the McCracken County School System.

I am Treasurer for Irvin Cobb International Reading Association, Vice President, Omega

Chapter Delta Kappa Gamma: member of MCEA, KEA, and NEA.

I am married to James T. West, Assistant Superintendent of McCracken County Schools. We have two children; Sara, 29, and Raenell, 25.

My memories of WKU include basketball at the Red Barn, 10:00 p.m. dates on porch of West Hall, and working in office at dorm for Mrs. Reid.

My hobbies are knitting, crocheting, hiking and bicycling.

ANN IRELAND WESTERFIELD, Class of 1958, B.S. in Home Economics, currently living in Hartford, KY.

I am Secretary-Treasurer of Westerfield Implement Inc.

I taught high school Home Economics at Franklin Simpson, Livermore and Hartford. I am active in Hartford United Methodist Church (MYF Counselor, Chairman of Council of Ministered, Trustee, and President and District Treasurer of United Methodist Women), and Junior Women's Club, President and State International Affairs Chairman. I have served as Cub Scouts Den Mother, and 4-H leader.

My husband Larry is a farm equipment dealer. We have three sons; Mike 29, Dale 27, Bruce 24; and four granddaughters Michelle six, Heater five, Britney two, and Bailey two.

My memories of WKU are standing in line waiting to get in the Red Barn to see the Hilltoppers play basketball.

My favorite pass time is playing with my granddaughters.

I taught high school Home Economics at Franklin Simpson, Livermore and Hartford.

LARRY C. WESTERFIELD, graduated from Western in 1958 with a BS degree in Agriculture.

I spent six months of active duty in the army at Ft. Benning, GA and Fort Knox. I also served a second hitch of active duty as a First Lt. with the 100th Division, during the Berlin Crisis.

In October of 1959 I bought half interest with my father in a John Deere dealership in Hartford, KY. My wife the former Ann Ireland, and I have since bought my father's interest. We are now starting our 30th year in business.

I have three sons Mike, Dale, and Bruce. All three are graduates of Western. I received my American Farmer Degree in FFA and all three of my sons have received this degree, which is a first in the state of Kentucky, for a father and three sons to receive this degree.

I am past President of the Kentucky Farm and Power Equipment Dealers Assoc.

I have been active in the Hartford United Methodist Church, serving as Sunday School Supt. for 13 years, and Chairman of the Administrative Board. I have been active in Farm Bureau and the Kentucky FFA Foundation. I am serving on Western Kentucky University Agricultural Mechanization Committee.

My most recent and most coveted award was being voted Friend of the Year for Western Agricultural Dept., and having my picture placed in the L.D. Brown Agricultural Center at Western.

RAY B. WHITE, Class of 1957, A.B. in History, currently living in Bowling Green, KY.

I continued my education at University of Kentucky.

I am self employed attorney at White and Meredith in Bowling Green.

I am married to Juanita White. We have three children: Statia White, 34, William L. White, 32, and Ray B. White II, 29.

ANNA ROSE WHITMAN, Class of 1959, B.S. in Elementary Education, currently living in Louisville, KY.

I continued my education by receiving my masters and 30 hours above in Education Administration and Counseling.

I am currently the principal at Mattie B. Luhr Elementary School. I am leading leaders to develop programs that will help children become successful. I work for grades K-5.

I have been awarded Outstanding Elementary School Counselor for Jefferson County Board of Education. I have taught in grades K-8 and served as Elementary School Counselor for the Jefferson County School Counselors.

I am married to Curtis W. Whitman who is a middle school counselor. We have three children: Brian, 28; Todd, 27; and Dean, 19. We have one grandchild Kelsi Leigh Whitman who is 14 months old.

My memories of Western include fun and follies with the girls in West Hall, working in the Education Dept. with Dr. Mary I. Cole, seeing the beautiful campus each Spring, walking up and down "The Hill" to town or the movies, and meeting and marrying Curtis W. Whitman.

ELIZABETH TAYLOR (CLIFTON) WILLIAMS, Class of 1957, B.S. in Elementary Education, currently living in Greenville, KY.

I taught at 41 schools, several years at one and two room schools and the last 12 years I taught first grade at Hughes Kirk. All schools were in Muhlenberg County.

I taught my first school in 1918 and attended the spring term at Western which was my first college experience. I continued to teach and attend Western on short term basis most every year until I graduated. During this time I married a farmer, had three children and helped with farm work, gardening, canning, etc.

By the time I graduated my oldest child, a son, had already graduated from the University of Kentucky after his first two and a half years at Western. My oldest daughter was working, after attending four quarter semesters at Western. My youngest daughter had graduated from Murray and was teaching.

I lost my husband in January 1964. I retired in May 1967 at age 70.

My children are: James T. Williams, Maddisonville, KY. He is a retired County (or Extension) Agent, married, has two sons and four grandchildren. My eldest daughter, Miss Martha Lynn Williams is single and shares a home with me. She is retired from USOA-FmHA. My youngest daughter, Nancy W. Pogue teaches first grade in Greenville. She is married and has four children, one son-in-law and one grandson. All four of these grandchildren of mine plan to graduate from the following colleges in 1990, Western, Murray, Georgetown and the University of St. Louis in Missouri.

I am 92 years old and only missed two Sundays from Sunday School and church in

1988. I was an avid reader up to age 89 when I lost my eye sight. I have had two cataract operations and six laser treatments (or surgery) on both eyes. I was the first person from Muhlenberg County to have laser surgery, approximately 15 years ago.

Since retirement I have made several cross stitch quilts, and table cloths, also latch hook rugs. I had never done this before.

I remember Western's first President, Dr. Cherry, very well. He used to get very upset with cigarette butts being thrown on the walks and campus. He wanted everyone to attend Chapel every day. Chapel programs were very interesting. I once had a bird watching class at Western. The teacher and students would meet on the steps of Van Meter Hall just before sunup. We would walk down behind the building into a wooded area and watch for birds and listen to them sing at day break. We would make a list of the various birds we would hear or see. It was a very interesting class.

MARY LOU TAYLOR WOOD, Class of 1956, B.S. in Home Economics, currently living in Russellville, KY.

After graduation I taught Home Economics in Indiana and at Seneca High in Louisville for four years before moving to Russellville in 1961. Have also enjoyed being a decorator for Sherwin-Williams.

In 1986 I received my Real Estate License and am enjoying my work as Sales Associate with Shaker Realty.

Other important positions include secretary, treasurer for Russellville-Logan County Board Realtors.

I received Who's Who Among American Women in 1987-88.

I have four children. Elizabeth is a staff writer for a newspaper in Atlanta. Pamela is an auditor for the Legislature in Nashville, and

Diane and Christopher are both students at University of Kentucky.

My daughters and I have enjoyed many successful years of showing horses. I also enjoy bridge and traveling.

My memories of Western are the fun of living in a dorm and Saturday football games in the old stadium.

FONROSE E. WORTHAM, JR., Class of 1959, B.S. Degree in Elementary Education.

I started my teaching in Jefferson County where I stayed for 28 years as a teacher, elementary principal and later as Executive Director of Elementary Administration. I spent one year in Frankfort in the Department of Education.

I married Sally Coker, 1960, and have two children, Anne, a WKU graduate and math teacher in Jefferson County and Tom, a sophomore at Western.

I retired in July of 1988 and am working part time at the Anchorage Country Store and plan to be a tour escort.

I have many fond memories of WKU, especially my working in the bookstore, Beech Bend, Pi Lambda Alpha and the warm, genuine "spirit" which pervaded the entire hill.

COLONEL ARVIN LEO WRIGHT, Class of 1956, Degree in Business Administration, currently living in Hawesville, KY.

I furthered my education with Command & General Staff College, U.S. Army; and Financial Management Training Program, General Electric Company.

I am currently a USA and European Audit Manager of CRA Services, LTD of Melbourne, Australia, Corporate Auditing responsibilities for Australian Holding Company in the USA and Europe.

Other important positions include: Manager, Cost Accounting, General Electric Com-

pany; Controller, Gould Corporation; Division Controller, Microdot Corporation; Colonel, United States Army Reserve, 33 years service with Active and Reserve Components.

I am affiliated with Reserve Officers Association, Internal Auditors Association, Hancock Company Industrial Foundation, and EDP Auditors Association.

I am married to Joyce, a housewife.

We have two daughters, Angela Laposki, 30; and Susan Bell, 28. We have three grandchildren, Woody Laposki, 11; Cory Bell, 8; and Casey Bell, 4.

My memories of WKU include: Bill Hardin's, Beach Bend; swimming pool, long study hours, RA Fraternity, "Maudie's" for food; "Hoad" Holland's accounting class; and Mrs. Cates "Statistics" class.

My hobbies include: golfing, hunting, fishing, and jogging.

KATHRYN DANIEL YATES, Class of 1950, B.S. Degree in Elementary Education, currently living in Metamora, IL.

Although now my position is in Domestic Science, I taught fourth grade in Peoria, IL. My responsibilities are to keep in shape to continue to be a ten speed mon in a ten speed world.

I am active in First United Methodist Church in Peoria and Prison Ministry (volunteer).

I am married to Lyle F. Yates, Engineer with Caterpillar Inc. We have four children: Carol 31, Daniel 26, and Lori and Martha (twins) 22. We also have one granddaughter, Lyndsey, four and one-half.

I remember coming to Western at mid-term of '48-'49. I lived in Potter Hall and later in McLean Hall. Dorm life was fun but strict by today's standards. Basketball games were the greatest and I still marvel how coach Diddle could control the crowd by waving his red towel.

Glyna (Meredith) Gallreins

Marvin Logsdon

M/M EARL AARON
MR. PRESTON R. ACREE
MR. BILLY M. ADAMS
ORLAND N. ALFORD
VERNIS M. ALKIRE
JOSEPH C. ALLBRITTEN
BEATRICE W. ALLEN
RACHEL S. ALLEN
MR. DAVID ALMAND
MATTIE CATHERINE ALVIS
DR./M ARTHUR N. ANDERSON
DR. HALBURN C. ARNETT
M/M KENNETH L. ARNOLD
IMOGENE ASHBY
MRS. LOUISE ASHBY
MR. KENNETH ASHLEY
MARY VIRGINIA AVRITT
M/M CLARENCE BAKER
M/M DAVID EDWARD BAKER
DON BALE
DR. COY E. BALL
DR. FRED. D. BARLOW
MARY PORTER BARNES
PAULINE BASHAM
M/M DARYL F. BATES
MARGUERITE BATES
M/M THOMAS M. BATTLE
M/M LEWIS BEAN
MR. CLAUDE BEGLEY
DR. PHILLIP E. BINZEL JR.
MRS. BLAKENEY BLAKENEY
LOUISE B. BLAKENEY
M/M JAMES E. BOHANNON JR.
MR. THOMAS E. BOONE
ARTHUR W. BOONE JR.
MR. GEORGE E. BOURNE
ALICE I. BOWDON
MARY BIRD BOWLES
SAM S. BOYD
MRS. JUNE BRADLEY
MR. JOHN W. BRATSCHI
MR. JOHN R. BROWN
ARTHUR W. BROWN JR.
MR. WADE H. BROWN JR.
MR. THOMAS WILLIAM BRYANT
EDNA K. BURBANK
DR. WILLIAM JOSEPH CALLISON
WILLIAM O. CAMERON
HERBERT CARROLL CAMP
DONNA H. CARPENTER
M/M KAMOS CARPENTER
M/M WILLIAM A. CARR
IDELL CARTER
DR. OVAL H. CARTER
ELLEN M. CATHER
M. BELLE CHANDLER
MR. MARK B. CHANDLER
MABLE D. CHEEK
MR. BUDDY A. CHILDRESS
M/M WILLIAM S. CHILDRESS
JACK T. CHISM
MRS. TOM CLAGGETT
M/M FRED R. CLAYTON
M/M GEORGE COKER JR.
DR. W. FRANK COLE, JR.
MARTHA C. COLLETT
MR. GREG COLSON
REV. ABBOTT EUGENE CONNER
DR. ROY G. COOKSEY JR.
MR. WALTER E. COOPER
DR. JACOB D. CORRIHER
MRS. MARGARET CORRIHER
MRS. ELEANOR COWAN
BETTY W. COX
DR. CLOVIS CRABTREE
FRED T. CRAWFORD
COL. EDWARD H. CURTIS
M/M BOWMAN DAVENPORT
HELEN A. DAVIS
MR. MITCHELL DAVIS
MR. RALPH O. DAVIS
MARGARET B. DAWSON
LULA S. DEMAREE
MR. NICK C. DIACHENKO
CHARLES W. DOOLEY
MR. THOMAS S. DOOLEY
JOSEPH W. DOUGHERTY
GEORGE DOWNING
DR. JAMES R. DRAKE
VIOLET L. DRAKE
M/M JOSEPH F. DRIESLER
LLOYD F. DRIVER
MERLENE DUNLEAVY
MRS. J. L. DURBIN, III
M/M JOHN B. DURHAM
DR. AUBREY L. EMBRY
RUTH Y. ENNIS
ALINE FARRIS
M/M FAYETTE FIELDS

WILLIAM B. FISHER JR.
MR. BILL FLAHERTY
LOUELLA J. FLATT
CONNIE H. FLOWERS
DR. THOMAS B. FOLLIS
BARBARA ANN FORD
LILLIAN M. FOREMAN
MR. RAY G. FORGY
CHARLES M. FORSYTHE
MARGARET W. FOX
JEAN FRENCH
JAMES M. FRENCH JR.
RAYMOND FULKERSON
ETTA F. GAMMON
MR. BOBBY G. GARRETT
MR. JOHN GIVENS JR.
THURMAN LEE GODBEY
M/M GLENN H. GOFF
RAY GRAHAM
VERNA P. GREGORY
BETTYE B. GRUBBS
ARNOLD GUESS
DENNIS C. HAMMER
MR. DARREL C. HAMPTON
MR. GEORGE M. HANKS
MRS. GRACE W. HARDIN
DR. ALICE J. HARPRING
FRANCES T. HARRIS
M/M SKILES B. HARRIS
MRS. ZELMA W. HARRISON
MR. JACK D. HARTSOCK
MR. WILLIAM KENNETH HARVEY
NANCY H. HAYES
MR. MAURICE HENDERSON
JOE G. HENDRICKS
JOSEPHINE R. HEPBURN
MARION E. HIGGS
MARY EDNA HODGE
M/M R. TURNER HOGAN
DR. CHARLES PHILLIP HOLLAND
MR. KENNETH H. HOLLOWAY
MR. CLAUDE HOPPER JR.
J. RALPH HORNING
RUTH P. HOWARD
MR. CHARLES E. HUDSON
MRS. OPAL HUDSON
HELEN HUFFMAN
JOHN B. HUGHES
JAMES ORR INGLE
SHELBY JOHNSON
WILLIAM JOHNSON
MR. ROBERT L. JOLLY
BARBARA I. JONES
MR. CHARLIE T. JONES
COLUMBIA F. JONES
MRS. JEAN JONES
DR. WILBURN C. JONES
MRS. WILLIAM JONES
MR. WALTON JONES JR.
CARRIE S. KELLY
MARILYN KIEL
ARMAND M. KING
M/M THOMAS E. KINSER
MR. FRANK E. LAMBIRTH
MR. BENJAMAN K. LANE
MRS. ELIZABETH LANIER
M/M JOHN LANIER
MR. JAMES W. LARMOUTH
M/M WILLIAM B. LASHLEE
M/M ROBERT WILLIAM LAVOY
MR. RAY LAWLESS
OLETA LAWSON
MRS. GLENN LAYMAN
DR. ALBIN L. LEE
L. HAROLD LEE SR.
HELEN LEET SMITH
MARY LEWIS
BRIG. GEN. W. D. LEWIS
MR. DENNIS E. LILLY
JOHN R. LITTLE
MR. MARVIN LOGSDON
MR. FRANK LOUDERMILK
MRS. GEORGE W. LOY, JR.
M/M WALTON LUTTRELL
DR. H. LUTZ
CAROL LYNN
GEORGE W. MANLEY JR.
M/M CHARLES EVERETT MARTIN
ELIZABETH MARTIN
FRANK F. MARTIN
HENRY E. MARTIN
MR. ROBERT LEE MARTIN
THOMAS C. MAY
DOROTHY J. MAYR
FRANK A. MCCRORY
MRS. BEATRICE A. MCDUFFIE
MAUDE M. MCGREGOR
LEWIS S. MEADOR JR.
MRS. RUSSELL MEARS

ALLEN S. MEDUS
MARY CORRINE MEEKS
LOUIS A. MIAZZA
GRACE EVELYN MILLER
BARBARA ANN MILLS
M/M THOMAS L. MONTGOMERY
DR. CLEMMIE E. MOORE
M/M ROBERT RIVES MOORE
MR. MARVIN R. MOORMAN
MRS. HELEN MORGAN
MRS. NINA K. MORGAN
LT. CARL E. MORRIS
MR. GEORGE MORRISON
MARY JANE MORRISON
SANDRA E. MORRISON
NANCY R. MOUSER
LYMAN L. MOUSER JR.
FRANCES A. MULQUIN
MR. BEN R. MURPHY
HAROLD DEAN MURPHY
ELBERTA NALL
MR. CLIFTON B. NEWMAN
DR. WILLIAM L. NEWMAN
GOEBEL W. NEWSON JR.
MR. GLYNN E. PAGE
JAMES R. PALMORE
HAZELLE M. PARKER
ROSSEE PARKER
REV. ELIZABETH M. PAUL
RUTH IVA PAYNE
JAMES M. PEAK JR.
BERNARD PERKINS
MS. FRANCES T. PETERS
MR. J. THEO PHILLIPS
T. PLAIN
LAWRENCE ARTHUR POTTER
MRS. OMEGENE POWELL
WILLIAM R. POWELL
MAXINE PRYOR
MRS. DOROTHY L. RAY
MR. FRANK A. RAY
AMY READ
MR. DONALD RAY REDDICK
JUDGE CHARLES H. REYNOLDS
EDITH RICHARDS
MR. MARK S. RICHARDSON
MILDRED RICHARDSON
NANCY M. RICK
C. RILEY
ALTIE RIVES
MR. JAMES L. ROBERTS
JEANE ROBERTSON
ARNOLD ROBINSON
CHARLES O. ROBINSON
CATHERINE G. RODGERS
THELMA S. ROGERS
M/M CHARLES ROSS
MARGARET J. ROSS
MRS. BYRON ROVINE
MR. EARL RUSSELL
MRS. KATHERINE RUSSELL
KENNETH RUSSELL
DR. MARVIN RUSSELL
M/M WILLIAM R. RUSSELL
MR. HAROLD B. SALMON
DR/MRS. J. SANDEFUR
BEN SANDERS
EVERETT G. SANDERS
LT. COL. RALPH DALE SCHRENK
WILLIAM FRED SCHUCK JR.
M/M DELBERT D. SETTLE
MR. JAMES T. SHAW
EARL R. SHEPPARD
MR. ROBERT E. SIMMONS
MR. CARROLL D. SIMPKINS
GENE T. SIMS
MR. HILTON SISK
M/M JAMES R. SKAGGS
BARBARA SMITH
CHARLES RAYMOND SMITH
MR. FRANK E. SMITH
MR. HOWARD E. SMITH
MR. JAMES T. SMITH
SARA J. SMITH
M/M THOMAS SMITH
MR. COOPER R. SMITH JR.
M/M HENRY P. SMITH JR.
DOROTHY S. SNYDER
MR. WOODSON W. SOSH
J. B. SPARKS
MRS. SPEARS
CORA JANE SPILLER
DR. EUGENE STEINQUEST
HAZEL STEPHENSON
DR./M. JULIUS STEPHENSON
DR. W. D. STRODE
JAMES STURGILL
THOMAS P. SUMMERS
MRS. MARY RUTH SUMNER

JESSE W. TABOR
M/M T. Y. TABOR
NOLA B. TALBOTT
MR. OSCAR K. TALMAGE
AMELIA TATE
M/M BOYCE D. TATE
MRS. ROBERT L. THARP
ALVA RAY THOMAS
CARL G. THOMAS
DIMPLE THOMPSON
MR. J. CLIFFORD TODD
MR. GEORGE G. TSOUKATOS
SAM P. TUGGLE JR.
DENNIS G. VAUGHN
ROLAND V. VILLIERS
M/M GEORGE T. WADE
JOANNE M. WALLACE
STANLEY LEE WALTERS
M/M DANIEL V. WARD
DR. ROBERT E. WEDEMEYER
JAMES BERNARD WELBORN
MR. THURAL EUGENE WEST
MR. WALLACE WHALIN
M/M RONNIE R. WHEAT
JOHNIE CARLISLE WHITE
COL. RAYMOND E. WHITE
DR. JOANN WHITSETT
MR. RALPH V. WILLIAMS
FLORABELLE WILSON
RAY C. WILSON
WAYNE K. WILSON
WILLIAM O. WILSON
ROY L. WINCHESTER
LEVY G. WOOD
W. G. WOOSLEY JR.
FRANCIS WORTHAM
GEORGE D. WRIGHT
MR. JAMES E. WRIGHT
LUCY ANN YANCY
KATHRYN D. YATES
MRS. LYLE F. YATES
MRS. NANCY ANN YOUNG
MR. WILLIAM YOUNG
JAMES GILL YOUNG JR.
FLORENCE H. ZOELLERS

'51 GRADS
MISS MARION L. ADAMS
MR. GENE ADKINS
MR. ROBERT S. ALLEN
M/M EUGENE COLEMAN ALLEN SR.
PANSY ALLISON
BETTY JO ANDREWS
FAYE R. ATHERTON
MR. JERRY E. BAKER
MR. THOMAS H. BARTON JR.
DR/M HUGH M. BASKETT
BETTY SUE BATES
REV/M THOMAS F. BEARD
MILDRED BURNS BECK
HAROLD K. BELLAMY
M/M ANDREW M. BIRD
MR. WILLIAM C. BOGDAN
MR. WILBUR F. BOGGESS
MRS. JUANITA BOGLE
DOROTHY D. BOOTH
RAYMOND BOTTOM
HOWARD BOWMAN
MRS. FRANKLIN BOYER
HAROLD D. BRITT
M/M FRED BRIZENDINE
B. B. BROWN
MR. ARTHUR PRESTON BURKE
M/M GEORGE C. BURNETTE
EMMA W. BYBEE
M/M JONATHAN CARPENTER
M/M JOSEPH R. CARRICO
ETTA JOYCE CASH
M/M WILLIAM B. CATE
MR. GEORGE TERRENCE CAVANAUGH
OSCAR CHAPPEL
MR. DAVID CHASE
DR. ROBERT D. CHENOWETH
MS. RUTH B. CHURCHILL
MR. CARL M. CLARK
M/M JAMES F. CLONINGER
MRS. HELEN D. CLOUTIER
HELEN D. CLOUTIER
DR. JAMES COKE
WILLIAM F. COKER
DOROTHY AGNES COMBS
E. COMBS
RUTH A. COMFORT
MR. ROBERT GENE CONNELLY
M/M CHARLES E. COOKE
MR. LEE E. COOKE
LT. JOSEPH H. COWLES
MR. THOMAS J. COX

M/M CHARLES E. CRAFT
MAURICE P. CRAIG
ANDREW CRAWFORD
LEONARD PRESTON CURRY
MR. CHARLES MARTIN DAVIDSON
DR. JAMES C. DAVIES
MR. JACK R. DAY
LARRY A. DEWESE
MR. EDGAR A. DIDDLE JR.
BEVERLY DOCKREY
MR. ALLEN L. DODD JR.
MR. WILLIAM H. DOLAN
ROY L. DOSSEY
M/M WALTER N. DOWNS
MRS. A. DRAKE
SARA LEE DUNN
MR. VERNON N. DWYER
MR. BILLY K. DYE
MR. ROY L. EMMICK
WILLIAM FRANKLIN ENNIS
MR. ROBERT A. ESKEW
MR. STEVE FRANKLIN ETTER
MR. CHARLES G. FALK
MRS. POLLY B. FARMER
T. H. FARMER, III
CORBETT FARRIS
MRS. COLLEN FEIER
BGN/M KENNETH FLEENOR
WILLIAM T. FULKERSON
M/M JAMES R. GALBREATH
DR. LOUIS W. GARRETT
MR. CARL H. GIBSON JR.
DAPHNA GILBERT
BETTY JO GILL
EDNA GLENN
EUGENE R. GLOD
AUSTIN V. GLOVER
WILLIAM ARLIE GOAD
MR. JOHN P. GOODMAN
DR. PRENTICE L. GOTT
DR. STANLEY H. GRADY
ROBERT E. GRANTHAM
DR. ALBERT RAY GREEN
HUGH G. GREENE
MR. HUBERT D. GREGORY
LTC/M HARRY T. GRESCHEL
M/M MORRIS HARDWICK
WILLIAM D. HARGETT
HELEN P. HARRIS
MILDRED EVELYN HARRISON
JULIA S. HAYDEN
MABEL B. HAYDEN
MR. RALPH W. HAZELIP
MR. JACK NORTON HENNINGER
JOYCE ANN HEPPLER
ROBERT LEE HIGGINS
MR. THOMAS EUGENE HILL
MS. MYRTLE L. HILLENBRAND
MR. J. GENE HOGGARD
RHODA HOLMES
MR. HENRY D. HOLT JR.
ADA HOPKINS
M/M CLYDE C. HOPKINS
MR. LEWIS C. HOPPER
MARJORIE L. HOSKINSON
THOMAS E. HOWARD
MR. JOSEPH P. HUDSON
JULIA P. HUGHES
MRS. W. HYDEN
MR. JOHN IPOCK
L. D. IRISH
M/M CHARLES R. IRWIN
MRS. NELDA R. JAMES
MR. JAMES D. JENKINS
MARION C. JENKINS
ISHMAEL E. JOHNSON
DR. JOHN T. JOHNSON
MR. JAMES LAMAR JONES
NELLIE KARNES
DR./MRS. HITE Q. KENNADY
JEAN KENNADY
MS. LOIS C. KIRKPATRICK
WILLET D. KIRKPATRICK
MRS. WILLIAM K. KRAUS
M/M CHARLES LABHART
MR. LEROY LAMAR
MRS. MARY EVELYN LAND
MR. CLARNECE WALTER LANGE
M/M CLARENCE LEE
MR. LEWIS C. LIKINS
GROSS C. LINDSAY
MR. JAMES L. LITTLEFIELD
DR. ROBERT E. LIVELY JR.
DR. DAVID W. LIVINGSTON
JEWELL W. LOGAN
MRS. GEORGE ANN LOWE
MARY ANNA LOWE
PAUL W. LUSTER
MR. JAMES A. LYLE

91

M/M PAUL MANNING
WENONAH MANNING
MR. HARRY L. MARKHAM
MR. HOWARD R. MARKS
ELLEN MASON
HOWARD R. MCBROOM
ROBERT E. MCBROOM
MARY LUCILLE MCCARTY
M/M CHARLES E. MCDONOUGH
MR. EDWIN B. MCGARY
BOBBY MCGUIRE
ROBERT MCKENZIE
MRS. ANTHA MCKINNEY
M/M RALPH C. MEADOR
DEBELOU I. MEARS
MR. CHARLES JOSEPH MELLOTT
ROBERT K. MEREDITH
MR. KENNETH E. MIDDLETON
MR. GORDON N. MILLER
MRS. WILLIAM T. MILLER
E. J. MILTON
DR. WILLIAM G. MONAHAN
AUBREY L. MOONEYHAM
MR. REED NULAND MOORE
M/M WILLIAM T. MORAN
DR. L. MORGAN
LORIECE MORRIS
MR. EDWARD BOTTS MYERS
MRS. LUCY OCKERMAN
DR. ROBERT N. PACE
MINNIE LEE PAULSEN
EDWARD E. PAYNE
WILMA C. PAYNE
M/M STUART PEPPER
MRS. JOHN L. PERGUSON
M/M JAMES I. PERKINS
LETA K. PERKINS
MR. HAROLD L. PHILLIPS
HAROLD L. PHILLIPS JR.
ROBERT POLSTON
DR. SAM POTTER
MR. JAMES C. PROW JR.
MR. RAYMOND E. PRYOR
THOMAS S. REDFORD
IRENE M. REECE
RAYMOND B. RENEAU
JOHN T. REYNOLDS
MR. GEORGE F. REZICH
MR. CLIFTON E. RHODES
MR. ROBERT R. RICH
M/M JESSE RICHARDS
HAZEL T. RIGSBY
FRANCES ROADY
MR. JAMES E. ROBARDS
MR. CHARLES T. ROSS
ELLIS WADE RUST
RAY M. RUTHERFORD
MARJORIE SAGABIEL
MR. EARL O. SAULMAN
PATSY A. SCENT
EARL J. SCHULTZ
MR. WILLIAM P. SCHULTZ
M/M WILL O. SEGO
M/M PERRY L. SHARER JR.
EMMA B. SHEELEY
DOROTHY L. SHELTON
DR./M. VINCENT SHERRY
J. D. SIGLER
MR. STANFORD L. SIMMONS
M/M W. H. SIMMONS
GEORGE B. SIMPSON
MISS IMOGENE SIMPSON
JOAN T. SIMPSON
WILLIS B. SIMPSON
MRS. ALICE RENEAU SMITH
M/M CLYDE SMITH
MR. WILLIAM ALDON SMITH
MR. JOE A. SOSTARICH
GERALDINE SPARKS
TROY E. SPEAR
PATRICIA ANNE SPERRY
PARRY B. STEELE JR.
M/M MARSHALL R. STEPHENS
WILMA DEPP STERLING
M/M HUGH M. STEWART
DR. WILLIAM M. STOKES
DR. VERNON A. STONE
CHARLES G. SULLIVAN
ROBERT L. SUMMERS
ELLEN THOMAS
M/M JOHN H. THOMAS
WILLIAM BRADLEY THOMAS JR.
MRS. JOANN THOMPSON
MR. JACK THORPE
ARMON E. THURMAN
REV. E. THURMAN
M/M ROBERT TINCHER
CLOYD E. TIPTON
J. K. TRAVELSTEAD
MARGARET ANN TUTEN
CARROLL MYRON UPTON
MR. JAMES RAY VAUGHAN
M/M FRANK J. WALLHEISER
KATHLEEN WALTER
M/M THOMAS WARD

MYRTLE M. WHEELER
AUDIE L. WILBURN
MR. WILLIAM WILSON
RANDOLPH C. WILSON JR.
COL. RONDELL K. WOOD
MR. JAMES R. WOOTEN
MR. CHARLES D. ZUTT
'52 GRADS
CHARLIE AKINS
M/M SAMUEL ALEXANDER
CALVIN ALFORD
MR. JOSEPH W. ALLEN
M/M NORMAN LEE ALLISON
CPT. DANIEL F. ANDERSON
SUE H. ANDERSON
WELDON D. ANDERSON
VIRGINIA APPLE
CHRISTINE H. ATWOOD
REGINALD AYERS
LTC. HUGH D. BAILEY JR.
DR. GEORGE S. BEARD
MR. LEIGH ROY BELL
MR. LUTHER S. BELL
M/M CHARLES O. BLAIR
MR. JAMES T. BLAKEY
OWEN LEE BLANTON
M/M HOLLAND E. BOAZ
MRS. POLLY ANN BOAZ
MR. RICHARD G. BORCHARDT
WILLIS B. BORDEN
MARSHALL BOUCHER
ERNEST P. BRAKE
ESTILL J. BRANHAM
DR. NORRIS EDWIN BRANSON DMD
DOROTHY BRENT
M/M ROBERT ALLEN BRENT
DR. EDWARD S. BRIDGES
KATHERINE BROOKS
RUTH BROWN
M/M JOSEPH BEN BROWNING
BOBBY L. BUCHANAN
MARY HELEN BURNETTE
MRS. VIRGINIA G. BURRES
DR. JOHN C. BURRIS
EVA BYBEE
ARTHUR L. CALHOUN
RONNIE CARNES
MICKEY CARRICO
MR. BRUCE HARRISON CARTER
DR. LILA HARGAN CARTER
LT. ROBERT H. CARTER
DR. WILLIAM W. CARTER
DR. JOE D. CASON
MISS MARGARET M. CATHER
VIRGINIA RUTH CHAPMAN
MR. FRANK A. CHEEK
ANNELLE H. CHERRY
M/M RODNEY N. CHERRY
MR. JAMES E. CLARK JR.
WILLIAM L. COLEMAN
BILLY L. CONLEY
LT. COL. DORAL G. CONNER
BARBARA E. COUCH
DR. RAYMOND L. CRAVENS
DEXTER CRAWFORD
WINIFRED P. CRAWFORD
EDITH HOUSTON CROPP
ED D. CLAUDIA D. CRUMP
BARBARA C. CURRY
ALLEYNE H. DANHAUER
DR. FIELDING W. DANIEL
M/M JAMES W. DANIEL
MARY T. DANIEL
PANSY B. DANIEL
MR. CARL LEE DAVIS
EITHAL DAVIS
MARION E. DAVIS
MR. DAVID E. DAWSON
JEANNE R. DEFILLIPO
M/M BILL R. DELPH
LOGAN DEVASHER
INA T. DICE
MR. BERT B. DILLIHAY
MISS CLARICE DINWIDDIE
MAE DIXON
M/M D. W. DOCKREY
ROSEMARY DODDS
CHARLES DRAKE
WILBUR B. DRAKE
LOUIS E. DURBIN
RUTH H. DUVALL
ANNA R. DYER
MR. JOHN W. EATON
WILLIAM R. EDWARDS
RUTH EMERINE
LT. WILLIS R. ENGLAND
MRS. MARY H. EPLEY
M/M WILLIAM DAVID FEILD
COL./MRS. WILLIAM FORD
M/M SHELBY C. FORSYTHE JR.
CALVIN FULKERSON
MRS. CLARESE M. FULLER
JACQUELINE B. GALLOWAY
JAMES P. GALLOWAY JR.

WILLARD C. GARNER
LAWRENCE H. GRAHAM
RAY D. GREENE
MR. JOHN W. GRIFFIN
ESTIL GRIFFIS
M/M WILLIAM M. GUTHRIE
WIILIAM HAEDTLER
MR. ROBERT M. HALE
RUTH B. HALE
M/M KENNETH E. HALL
JAMES R. HARDIN
MRS. EDITH HARDISON
MR. WILLIAM H. HARDISON
JOE HARDY
JAMES T. HARRALSON
M/M JAMES DAVID HAYDON
WILLIA A. HAYS
MR. NORMAN HEAD
EDWIN S. HEATH
MR. J. LEON HENRY
M/M VIRGIL L. HENRY
MORGAN D. HENSGEN
MR. FLOYD T. HENSLEY JR.
BERNIE J. HERMANN
BASIL O. HIGGS
BETTY SUE HILL
M/M ROY D. HINA
M/M BOBBY S. HINES
MRS. ROWENA HINES
MR. JAMES E. HOBDY
MR. JOHN J. HOLLER JR.
DR. BILLY B. HORRELL
MRS. IMOGENE PAGE HOSKINS
M/M TOMMIE HOUK
VIOLET HOUK
ROSCOE W. HOWARD
MR. JOSEPH L. HOWELL JR.
MALISSA HUMPREYS
ROBERT K. HUNT
JEANETTA A. HURT
MARY JAMES
COL. JOHN G. JAMESON JR.
MR. WILLIAM JENKINS
M/M JOHN S. JEWELL
ALMA JEWELL JONES
CHARLES FRANCIS JONES
M/M HAROLD JONES
WANDA D. JONES
EVELYN JUDY
MR. BILL M. KEEGAN
WILLIAM J. KIMBROUGH
JEANE KIMMEL
NANCY B. KING
DR. NORMAN K. KIRBY MD.
MARGARET A. KNOX
HERBERT L. LACY
IRENE LANCASTER
MR. FRED L. LEWIS
EVELYN LINDSEY
DIXIE LOIS LOGAN
W. LOWE
MR. ALBERT M. LUTHER JR.
BETTY MAGERS
MR. LEO J. MAGERS
MR. JAMES G. MARION
JEAN MARTIN
BEVERLY MASON
MR. TOM PRYOR MASON
DR. MARTIN A. MASSENGALE
REV. HOWARD L. MATTHEWS
M/M JAMES C. MCCHESNEY
GLEASON MCCUBBIN
CONRAD L. MCCULLEY
ALICIA R. MCFARLAND
M/M ROGER MCGINNIS
MR. DOYLE EUGENE MCGUFFEY
M/M CHARLES E. MEEKS
DR. RONALD A. MEEKS
M/M DAVID H. MEFFORD
LEWIS MEYER
JOYCE C. MILLER
COL. BILLY JAMES MILLS
SUZANNE MOORE
DELLA MORGAN
MR. THOMAS C. MORGAN
MRS. J. D. MORRIS
MR. ROBERT MORTON
MABEL W. MOULDER
IRIS JUNE MURPHY
MR. STANLEY NALL
EMILY R. NAMKEN
JOHN KENNETH NANCE
RICHARD E. NEEL
JAMES H. NEWBERRY
DOROTHY W. NOBLETT
MRS. LEHMAN H. NOFFSINGER
MRS. MELVIN NUNN
PAULINE OVERFELT
M/M LOUIS DAVID OWEN
M/M SAM C. PALMER
M/M RHEA S. PEDEN
ANNE PEPPER
MR. JAMES MALCOLM PETTY
GLORIA H. PHILLIPS
DR. CLAUDE E. PICKARD

M/M JIM PICKENS
BETTY C. PILEGGE
LAVERNE PINCKLEY
CHARLES P. PING
MRS. MARGERY PLUMMER
M/M WALTON DALE PLUMMER
DR. CHARLES LEE PRICE
MARY M. PUCKETT
M/M ANDREW RENICK
GENE RHODES
T. RICHARDS
MRS. JAMES RICHARDSON
PATRICIA C. ROBERTSON
MR. CHARLES RUNYAN
CLARENCE RUSH
MR. ROBERT D. RUTLEDGE
SARAH A. SANDERS
LOUISE SARTIN
M/M GEORGE P. SAUNDERS
SUANITA SAVELY
O. E. SCHOW
ROBERT D. SEARCY
HUGH D. SHANNON
NANCY SHAW
JUNE SHORE
SAM OTIS SHORT
ANNA LEE SKILLMAN
HOWARD T. SOWARDS
ELISABETH STANDIFORD
MR. CHARLES E. STEWART
M/M JOSEPH H. STEWART
MRS. CAROLYN STRODE
FRANK SUMMERS
M/M JOSEPH ROGER SUMNER
COL. ELLIOTT P. SYDNOR JR.
COL. EUGENE TANNER
M/M ARNOLD G. TAYLOR
COL. ARTHUR TAYLOR
L. RHEA TAYLOR, JR.
LESLIE B. THOMAS
MARSHALL L. TUBBS
BETTY TUTTLE
MRS. CAROLYN BOTTO VERTRESS
LEALON ARLES WEAVER
BARBARA ANN WEBSTER
MRS. DOROTHY G. WHITESIDE
MR. ROBERT H. WHITSON
M/M CARL WILLIAMS
KATHLEEN WILLIAMS
MARY H. WILLIAMS
REID V. WILLIAMS
EDNA MAE WILLIS
GRACE WINSTEAD
JAMES M. WOOD
GEORGE WOODCOCK
BEN WYATT
MRS. EDITH L. YOUNG
'53 GRADS
EMMA ALEXANDER
DR. JAMES ESTILL ALEXANDER
ABBY JEAN ALLENSWORTH
DR. THOMAS ALLENSWORTH
MR. JAMES W. ANDERSON
JESSE T. ANDREW
M/M ALLEN ANTHONY
JOHN NEILL BAKER
PAULINE GREEN BARKER
DOLYCE C. BARNES
GLADYS S. BARNETT
CHARLES J. BASSETT
DORIS J. BEARD
M/M MOORMAN "MONIE" BEARD
BEULAH MAE BENNETT
DORETHA BENSENHAVER
MARY LOYCE BIRD
WILLIAM E. BIVIN
MARY BLAIR
BILLIE SUE BLAKEMAN
ADELINE BOONE-EDRINGTON
MRS. ANNABELLE W. BRASHEAR
JOSEPH PAUL BROCK
MRS. TERESA D. BROOKS
PATSY R. BUNCH
FRANKLIN BUSSA
LOIS MARIE CAMPBELL
EDNA R. CARDWELL
MR. DONALD A. CHAPMAN
DR. WILLARD F. CHUMLEY
MR. GERALD T. COHRON
GEORGIA FULLER COLE
MR. LAWRENCE W. COLE
MRS. WILSON A. CONNER
MR. TOM CORNWELL
MR. GARLAND C. COTTRELL
ELVA B. COWLEY
RUTH C. CREWS
MR. THOMAS B. DABNEY
HELEN DANIEL
MARY SUE DAY
DONALD DEARING
MR. THOMAS K. DECKER
MR. CHESTER A. DOSS
PAUL DOWNS
NORMA DRANE
MRS. ORENE DRUEN

JOSEPH W. DURBIN
ROBERT A. EIMER
DENNIS H. ELGIN
MR. LESLIE D. ENGLER
IRENE MAE ERSKINE
M/M THOMAS LEON EUBANK
M/M BILLY GEORGE EVANS
MR. CHESTER R. FANCHER
MR. MELVIN E. FARLEY
DR. RICHARD M. FIELDS
M/M OSBURN R. FLENER
MR. CHARLES W. FORD
MR. EDWARD R. FOSTER
MARY RUTH FULKERSON
DR. WILLIAM R. FUQUA
DORIS E. GARRISON
BLANCHE H. GRAHAM
BOBBY GREEN
MARGARET GREEN
M/M WALTER W. GREEN
EULA RICE GREGORY
MRS. RUBY GUNN
DR. VERA G. GUTHRIE
MR. JIMMY HALE
MARY ALICE HANSON
NORMA J. HARDAWAY
DR. PHILIP E. HARNEY
LT. JOHN N. HARRIS JR.
DORIS F. HAUK
M/M CECIL P. HAVEN
BROWNIE HAYES
MR. HENRY HAYES JR.
DORIS J. HEFLEY
MYRTLE H. HEPLER
CLAUDE HIGHTOWER
MR. CHESTER LOWE HOLLINS
OVA M. HOLLINSWORTH
CHRISTINE HORNE
MR. KEN HUDGINS
MRS. MARCIA W. HUME
MR. WILLIAM O. JACKSON
M/M RAYMOND F. JEFFRIES
MRS. JAMES R. JENSEN
MARY ELIZABETH JONES
MR. JOHN MARVIN KAVANAUGH
JESSE G. KEOWN JR.
DOROTHY W. KERLEY
M/M JESSE KIMBROUGH
MR. RICHARD LARIMORE JR.
MR. GEORGE D. LAWSON
M/M GENE A. LAWTON
HELEN B. LAWTON
M/M WILLIAM T. LEACH
DICKIE SUE LEE
MRS. VICKIE SUE LEE
DR/M CHARLES DOUGLAS LENEAVE
WILMA JUNE LEWIS
MRS. BEN LINDSEY
CHARLES A. LIVINGSTON
VERA LONDON
MILLS M. LOWE
THELMA LOWE
GERTRUDE L. LUCAS
J. DON LUIGS
THELMA G. LYON
M/M ROBERT LYONS
DR. NOEL B. MADDOX JR.
MRS. ROBERT MAGGARD
GEORGIA SUE MARSHALL
DR. KEITH MARTIN
CHARLES W. MARTIN JR.
M/M JOHN W. MCCLENDON
REV. CARL MCCUBBIN
FLORENE MCDANIEL
J. MCINTOSH
CHARLES MCWHORTER
CHARLOTTE LOUISE MEARS
MR. JAMES LEE MERCER
MR. JAMES E. MEYER
MR. BERNARD L. MILLER
JESSIE D. MILLER
NANCY A. MILLER
NANCY LEE MILLER
PEARL MILLER
RUSSELL B. MILLIKEN
JOANNE HEDGES MOFFATT
MRS. ALMA MOORE
DR. JOSEPH MURPHY JR.
LINDA H. NEALY
BARBARA NEWMAN
WESLEY A. NICKS
MARGARET OBANNION
DR. WILLIAM J. OLIVER
MRS. JOYCE PALMER
MRS. ANNA L. PARHAM
MR. ROBERT ALVA PATE
MR. WAYNE PATTERSON JR.
MRS. JOHN A. PEDIGO
M/M JOHN A. PERKINS
MARY JO PHILLIPS
JAMES T. POLLEY
WINNIE PULLIAM
JUDGE LUKE QUINN
ROBERT RAND

MRS. ORENA A. RENFROW
ROY D. REYNOLDS
MR. H. RANDOLPH RICHARDS
DR. RANDOLPH RICHARDS
MRS. ANN MARY RICHARDSON
MR. ROBERT RICHARDSON
HUGH RIGHTMYER
MR. RAYMOND M. ROBERSON
ANN ROSS
LINNIE ROWE
MRS. SUE RUE
DR. NELSON B. RUE JR.
MRS. FAIRY B. RUNNER
WANDA F. RUSH
M/M WILLIAM RUTHERFORD
M/M ED RUTLEDGE
MRS. ANN SACCA
M/M JIMMY SACCA
M/M JOHN SARANCHAK
DELMA SCHNELLENBERGER
MR. DAVID A. SCHROEDER
REV. CHARLES SHIELDS
MRS. BETTY A. SHORT
STELLA B. SIMPKINS
DR. ROBERT E. SIMPSON
CYRUS T. SMITH
COL. DEWEY L. SMITH
MRS. ROBERT SNOWDEN
WANDA SOLLIS
M/M JOHN H. SOWDERS
GARNET DALE SPEAR
SY SPIEGELMAN
ROBERT STEINBERGER
MR. JAMES C. STICKLES
MR. DAVID STINSON
MRS. EMMA LOU STOCKTON
DR. JOSEPH D. STOKES
GRACE P. STONE
JEAN STONE
M/M WILLIAM D. STRICKLAND
MRS. ALICE SWAN
MRS. JEAN R. SYDNOR
ORENE DRUIN TABB
MR. KENNETH TACKETT
COL. JOHN H. TAYLOR
MARY FRANCES TAYLOR
SYLVIA TAYLOR
LT. COL. HARRY G. THOMAS
MR. THOMAS C. TICHENOR
M/M WILLIAM T. TRACY
MR. ROBERT M. TURNER
MR. HAROLD P. WALDEN
MR. DONALD C. WALKER
MARY WALKER
CHARLEEN WALLACE
GORDON WARD
DR. WILLIAM G. WARD
MARVIN E. WARREN
MR. RILEY H. WATSON
WILLIE F. WATSON
LAURA S. WEATHERFORD
CHLOIE WEBB
M/M JAMES ALLEN WHEAT
JUDITH WHEAT
M/M ROBERT J. WHITMER
CHARLES N. WILCOX
NANCY B. WILDER
M/M CLAUDE M. WILKERSON
MR. LEWIS P. WILLIAMS
MARIE P. WILLIAMS
WARREN B. WILLIAMS
MISS INA J. WILLIS
MARTIN W. WILLSON
M/M BOBBY T. WILSON
L. RICHARD WILSON
JOYCE R. WISE
NELLIE MAE WOODRING
RAY WOODRUFF
JOSEPH L. WOOSLEY
MRS. MARCIA WRIGLEY
SARAH M. WYNDHAM

'54 GRADS
JOHN PAUL ADAMS
M/M NOBLE ALLEN
BERT C. ANDERSON JR.
CHARLES D. ANDERSON JR.
ELIZABETH ANTHONY
MR. ROBERT J. ARCHIBALD JR.
DR. THOMAS BAIRD
DR. CHARLES H. BALL
PATRICIA MERCER BALL
KENNETH D. BARTLEY
MR. JAMES P. BATES
ROBERT E. BAULCH JR.
PAUL LEE BEAUCHAMP
MARY L. BENSON
PHYLISS BLAKEMAN
RICHARD BLANKENSHIP
BETTE A. BLOSS
M/M JAMES M. BOOKER
KENNETH K. BOONE
JAMES H. BOWLING
SHERMAN BOYKEN
M/M RICHARD G. BRANDON
M/M MYRL BRASHEAR

MRS. JEAN B. BREWER
LILLIE C. BROWN
LT. ROBERT R. BROWN
SHIRLEY J. BURIJON
MARY E. BURNS JOHNSON
ROBERTA B. BURRESS
JO ANN CABLE
DAVID CALDWELL
AGNES CARNES
MR. JAMES A. CARPENTER
FRANK D. CATES
M/M JAMES B. COE
M/M MAURICE COLE
VIRGINIA P. COLLINS
M/M BOBBY COMBS
WILLIAM L. COOK
LO. COL. JAMES W. COOPER
COL. JOHN T. COOPER
THOMAS J. CORUM
THELMA CRAWFORD
M/M HAROLD H. CREEKMUR
EUNICE F. CROPPER
CLARA E. CROUCH
EVERETT W. CUNNINGHAM
THOMAS E. CUNNINGHAM
MRS. EDITH O. CURRY
RUBY D. DANIEL
DR. BILLY H. DARKE
DR. WALLACE DAWSON
MR. JACK L. DAY
J. DICK
MRS. REBECCA MAXINE DIMKE
WILLIAM F. DITTO
M/M HARVEY J. DIXON
DON DODSON
M. DOROTHY DORR
MR. JOHN NEAL DRAKE
MISS SARAH F. DRAKE
M/M JAMES ELKINS
MRS. SHIRLEY B. ELKINS
MR. JOHN J. ENGBERSEN
HAZEL C. ENGLAND
MRS. VELMA C. ENGLAND
PATSY ROSE EVANS
JIMMY FEIX
LTX. E. FINLEY
MR. FRANCIS FLEENOR
MR. SAMUEL A. FLETCHER
M/M THOMAS G. FLORENCE
NEVA S. FLOWERS
JEAN B. FORTUNE
IMOGENE FOSTER
JESSE FRANKLIN
MRS. MACIE A. FRANKLIN
MRS. JANET FREDERICK
JANET D. FREDERICK
DR. PHILIP LEE FUSON
MR. DICKEY GALLOWAY
LURENE GIBSON
MR. RAYMOND A. GISH
RODNEY K. GIVENS
MR. EDWIN A. GOODMAN
DR. E. DEVERRE GOURIEUX MD
JOHN R. GREGORY JR.
M/M ALBERT H. GRIFFIN
LINDY C. GUNDERSON
ELOISE W. HADDEN
MR. EUTRE NOEL HAMMETT
JACK A. HANKS
MR. WILLIAM C. HARLIN
MRS. WILDA C. HARNE
M/M ROBERT L. HARRIS
ANN M. HENDRICK
KATHLEEN HENDRICK
DAVID M. HIMMELHEBER
DR. PHILIP HITCHCOCK
MRS. QUINN HOLLAND
SHIRLEY R. HOLLAND
DR. M. HOOD
MR. GEORGE MAURICE HUDSON
VERNA LOIS HUMPHREY
MR. DONALD R. HUNDLEY
CHARLES S. HUNT
HELLEN M. HURD
EDWARD LEON JACKSON
MISS MAXINE JACOBI
NINA M. JARVIS
MARGARET M. JOHNSTON
MR. PAUL G. JOHNSTON
EMMA G. JOINER
M/M WILLIAM J. JONES
M/M DONALD A. KANE
OLEN KERNS
CHRISTINE R. KOENEN
MR. PAUL RUSSELL KOENEN
BARBARA L. LAMB
COL. WILLIAM FRED LANE
DR./MRS. NATHANIEL R. LAYSON
MR. ROBERT A. LEACH
MRS. NANCY W. LEE
M/M GENE E. LEESON
M/M HERBERT H. LEGRAND
MR. ROBERT J. LIPSCOMB
AMY L. LOBB
ELIZABETH LOGSDON

MARTHA JACOB LOWE
MAJOR BURLIN LOWRY
MR. ROBERT R. LUSTER
ANN LYONS
NORMA LUCILLE MAGERS
LORENE MANNING
WILLIAM P. MANSFIELD JR.
DR. MARY HELEN MARSHALL
JIMMIE D. MARTIN
M/M GLEN C. MASSENGALE
MR. WENDELL H. MASSENGALE
MR. CARL L. MATTHEWS
L. RUDOLPH MAYS
MR. BILLY G. MCCLOUD
GUY F. MCCOY
M/M DON K. MCGUIRE
WILLIAM Y. MCKENZIE JR.
B. MEFFORD
SHIRLEY K. MEREDITH
M/M SAMUEL MESERVE
LORRAINE MILLER
MR. WILLIAM R. MILLER
LT. COL. JAMES D. MITCHELL
MRS. MARY S. MONTEITH
MALISSIA MORRIS
ATHYOLINE MOSS
M/M RAY V. NEELY
WILMA B. NELSON
JEANNIE W. NICHOLS
DR. JAMES L. NICHOLSON
MR. HUGH A. NOFFSINGER
LILLIAN COLE NOLAN
M/M RAY NUTTER
HOWARD ROWE OAKES
DR. CHARLES M. OLIVER
LT. CMDR. JAMES J. OLLIGES
ROGER H. OTTEN
MRS. IDA MARIE H. OWEN
M/M LAWRENCE S. OWENS
EVA JANE PARKER
M/M WILLIAM JERRY PARKER
COL. ROBERT PATE
JAMES SAMUEL PELL
ALICE PHILLIPS
DR. JAMES E. PHILLIPS
DON O. PICKERILL
DR. WILLIAM A. PLOUMIS
M/M JOHN H. PORTER
JEAN WRAY POYNTER
M/M ROBERT L. PRESTON
PAT PRICE
M/M WILLARD PRICE
DR. DILLON HUGH PUCKETT
DR. FRANK W. RANDALL
CHARLES M. RAWLINGS
MARTHA G. REAPSOME
RUBY P. REDFORD
BILL RICHESON
JOANNE P. RILEY
VERNON C. RODGERS
CRICKET ROEMER
M/M ROBERT L. ROEMER
PAULINE RONE
EDNA LUCILLE ROSS
DR. MARILYN M. SANDERS
MILDRED JEAN SATTERLY
MR. GEORGE E. SAUER
DR. SAMUEL ELBERT SCOTT
PAULINE B. SHARP
MRS. ELIZABETH D. SHEA
DR. JAMES G. SILLS
M/M ROBERT L. HARRIS
JANE SISK
LEWIS E. SMITH
PATRICIA MOORE SMITH
MISS T. JOAN SOETE
M/M HENRY A. SORRELS
MARGUERITE W. SOSH
M/M ROYCE A. SPECK
ANNABEL J. STEEN
M/M EDWIN N. STEEN
DR. WILLIAM D. STEPHENS
CPT. LOWELL A. STEWART
MRS. MARY JUANITA STOCKTON
LOIS T. STRANGE
MISS LONETA SUBLETT
MRS. PIATT C. SULLIVAN
M/M HAL TAYLOR
LOUISE TERRY
M/M RAYMOND TERRY
LTC. JAMES L. THOMAS
ROBERT E. THOMAS
MR. RONALD TINSLEY
NEAL R. TUCKER
M/M JACK D. VALZ
LINDA VINCENT
LTC. MAURICE R. VINCENT
SUZANNE H. WALDROP
WANDA LEE WALKER
MR. FRANK L. WALLACE
NELLIE L. WALLACE
M/M ROBERT CLIFTON WALLACE
MR. THOMAS G. WALLACE
BETTY V. WATSON
MRS. ANNA L. WEAR

MARIAN WEBB
M/M MARION H. WHITE
MEARLENE H. WHITE
MR. RICHARD LEE WHITE
M/M WILLIAM W. WHITE
MAGALENE WINSTEAD
MARGARET PEET WOODCOCK
IMOGENE P. WOODS
COL. DOUGLAS YATES
MARY WOOD YEARY
JAMES R. YEISER
MRS. AURORA P. YOUNG

'55 GRADS
J. ADAMS
MARY ADCOCK
MR. EARL A. AMOS
LENETTE AMOS
BETTIE W. ANDERSON
ROBYE E. ANDERSON
WALTER L. ANDERSON
MAJ. JAMES A. ARY
MRS. PATRICIA A. ARY
MR. THOMAS A. ATCHISON
BARBARA C. ATWELL
MR. DONALD W. BACHMANN
MR. LEONARD RICHARD BAKER
GERTIE G. BARGER
M/M WILBUR K. BARNES
SILAS RUDY BASKETT
LENORICE BAUGH
JAMES E. BAZZELL
DOROTHY P. BEARD
MR. ROBERT NORMAN BEATY
JANE MAGAN BELL
M/M ROBERT E. BELL
DR. WALLAS N. BELL
MARY P. BENZ
MARY S. BEWLEY
MR. ROBERT E. BILYEU
KERMIT BINKLEY
MR. JERRY C. BISHOP SR.
M/M CHARLES T. BLACK
MR. CHARLES H. BOZARTH JR.
M/M JAMES M. BRADFORD
JOANN BRADFORD
MARCELLA BRASHEAR
CLIFTON E. BRATCHER
M/M ROBERT BRISTOL JR.
JOSEPH C. BROCKMAN
MRS. CLYDE C. BROWN
EDITH BROWN
JAMES BRYANT
GLENDA BUSSELL
M/M GILBERT CALHOUN JR.
DR. JAMES R. CALLISON
MYRTLE S. CALVERT
MR. BOB L. CAMPER
JAMES W. CHAMBERLAIN
M/M JACK L. CHAMBERS
JAMES M. CHAMBERS JR.
MR. RODNEY MITCHELL
CHAPMAN
CAPTAIN MARION E. CHESNUT
MR. GERALD CLAYPOOL
MR. JAMES H. CLAYPOOL
CHARLES E. CLAYTON
MARGARET CLEMENTS
M/M ROBERT M. COLEMAN
JOE M. COMBEST
JEAN COMPTON
M/M ROBERT M. CONKIN
EVA P. CONNER
GEORGIANN CONNER
ROSE K. COOK
MRS. OGILVIA E. COOKSEY
MR. ROBERT GENE COX
MRS. MILLIE L. CRAFTON
C. L. CUTLIFF
DOUGLAS F. DAUGHERTY
MR. WILBUR W. DAUGHERTY
MR. HERBERT C. DAVIS
CORTEZ N. DAVIS JR.
WILLIAM M. DELK
ZELA N. DEVASHER
MRS. RUDOLPH DONOHO
NANNIE MAE DOSS
MRS. GEORGE C. DOWNING
BILLY HERMAN DOYLE
MARY E. DRISKELL
MR. HARRY E. DUNCAN
WENDELL M. DUNCAN
WILLIAM K. DWYER
M/M CHARLES F. DYER
JUDY K. ECKER
M/M TOM ECKER
MR. SHIRLEY RALPH EGGEN
META L. ELDER
KENNETH GENE EMBRY
M/M KEITH O. EMERINE
MOLENE C. EMMERT
M/M JESSE J. EVANS
MR. DONALD EVERSOLE
JACK B. FITZPATRICK
ANNE D. FORD
REYBURN W. FORD

M/M WILLIAM E. FORD JR.
M/M LAYNCE FORSYTHE
R. H. FORSYTHE
M/M ROYCE F. FORSYTHE
MRS. DON RAY FOWLER
DR. JAMES C. FRANKLIN
M/M LAWRENCE R. FRENCH
VERA FRENCH
BOBBYE LEA GALVIN
MRS. CAROLYN GARRETT
FERN GEER
MR. GEORGE D. GILLESPIE
M/M CLEMON W. GILLIAM
MRS. RUBY I. GILLIS
M/M JOHN P. GILLION JR.
LT. JOHN W. GLENN
M/M JAMES A GOAD
MRS. IRIS G. GOODIN
JOSEPH L. GOODMAN
COL. JAMES M. GREER
NADINE P. GREGORY
MS. THELMA W. GRIDER
DR. FRANK J. GROSCHELLE
LILLIAN GROSS FEGHALI
M/M JAMES E. GUNNELL
LT. GERALD D. GUTHRIE
M/M CHARLES A. HARDCASTLE
DR. WILLIS K. HARRISON
JOREEN H. HENRY
MR. WILLIAM HIX
FRANKLIN H. HOLLAND
MR. ESTIN HOLTON JR.
RUDOLPH A. HOLZKNECHT
CHRISTINE HOOD
MRS. ROSE H. HOOD
COL. CHARLES H. HOOD MD
CATHERINE HOPPER
M/M ROBERT J. HORNE
BUSTER E. HORTON
LEAMON O. HUCKABY
NATHANIEL P. HUFFMAN
PHYLLIS B. HUFFMAN
MR. BOBBY L. HUMES
M/M GRADY E. HUNDLEY
CORDELIA KING JACKSON
MRS. VERNA S. JAGGERS
GROVER D. JEFFERSON
DR. THOMAS JEFFRIES
KENNETH R. JOHNSON
DR. RICHARD H. JOHNSON
WALTER L. JOHNSON
MAJ J. KEPLEY
HELEN KEREIAKES
MRS. PATTY W. KINSLOW
WILLIAM E. KISTER
JANE S. KRICK
MARIE LANDRUM
BEVERLY L. LANGLAND
JUNE L. LANIER
M/M THOMAS F. LANIER
MARY E. LASWELL
LTC. WILLIAM T. LINK
M/M DONALD B. LOCKE
M/M CURTIS A. LOGSDON
MR. JOSEPH W. MANLEY
MR. HAROLD MARKLE
JOSEPHINE MARRIOTT
MAJ. DONALD G. MASON
M/M ALAN DEAN MASTIN
SGM. PATRICK P. MASTROLED
DAN H. MCCLENDON
MELVIN MCINTOSH
N. FAYE MILLER
RETHA M. MILLER
MR. CHARLES A. MITCHELL
MRS. FERN C. MORRIS
JOHN B. MURPHY
TOM MURPHY
MARILYN MURRAY
RUTH T. MURRELL
M/M L. HOWARD NICAR JR.
M/M ARNOLD S. OAKEN
DR. LARRY J. PACK
MARY LEE PAGE
MRS. GARNET PARE
RICHARD L. PARK
JERRY PASSAFIUME
MR. DONALD THOMAS PATERSON
MR. EDGAR R. PAYNE
LT. COL. WILLIAM M. PAYNE
MATTIE PELLOW
ALMA PERKINS
GENEVA PERKINS
MR. JAMES D. PHIFER
M/M DON PORTER
JANICE PORTER
SHIRLEY B. PRITCHETT
R. G. PUCKETT
MRS. TAFT RAMSEY
CAESAR A. RICCI
ROBERT E. RILEY
LTC. O. D. ROBERTSON
MARIE S. ROBINSON
M/M LAWTON ROGERS
RUTH E. ROGERS

JOSEPHINE B. ROTEN
ELIZABETH W. SADLER
WILLIE L. SALSMAN
M/M CECIL SCHIRTZINGER
M/M LOUIS F. SCHNEIDER
M/M ROBERT C. SHEA
MILLARD G. SHIRLEY
ROYCE SHIRRELL
MS. DELORES ANN SHOEMAKER
SHIRLEY SISK
GRACE H. SKAGGS
LEONARD E. SLACK
SUE CAROLYN SMITH
MR. WILLIS R. SNYDER
HARRY L. SPIRES
REV. LINDBERGH STEPHENS
M/M ROGER M. STEVENSON
ARTHUR SHELBY STEWART
DR. RAYMOND H. STONE JR.
DR. PHILIP STROMOWSKY
MARIE B. SULLIVAN
M/M ALMON SULLIVAN JR.
MR. CHARLES R. SUMMERS
JOSEPH M. TALLEY JR.
JOHN W. TAPSCOTT
EVA TARTER
MR. WILLIAM F. TATE
MR. JAMES FRANK TAYLOR
IONE C. TEETERS
MR. MARION M. THOMAS
MR. HOYT THREET
JUDY S. TROUT
MR. JAMES T. VEST
MR. BRUCE L. VICE
MRS. GAYLE L. WAGGENER
M/M ROY H. WALKER III
NANCY J. WARF
DOLLYE W. WEBB
LTC/M LEONARD W. WEBB
ELAINE T. WILKERSON
HENRIETTA S. WILSON
DR. DEWEY WOOD
MRS. ROSE LEE YOUNG

'56 GRADS
NONA CHRISTINE AKRIDGE
REGINA ALEXANDER
MARY ETHEL ALLEN
RUTH STOTTS ALLEN
SALLY W. ALLEN
DAISY B. ALTON
JAMES D. ALVEY
MRS. HARVEY ANDERSON
MRS. JOYCE P. ARMSTRONG
DR. HILDA ARNOLD
M/M WILLIAM M. ARNOLD
MR. DOUGLAS BALL
M/M HERBERT BARNARD
MICHAEL W. BARNARD
MRS. JEANNE BASKETT
CELOSTINE T. BELCHER
AVIS BELL
MR. DONALD BELL
AILEEN LIKENS BENNINGFIELD
COL. HUBERT M. BERTHOLD
MR. CARSON D. BEVIL
LONNIE L. BEWLEY
MARY C. BINKLEY
MR. ROBERT R. BOONE
ANN GORIN BOTTLER
MRS. CARMON BRADLEY
DR. RAYMOND PAUL BRAUGHARD
DR. JAMES L. BREWER
MARY RUTH BROWN
JOAN M. BRUNSON
H. BUCHANAN
MR. RAY B. BUCKBERRY JR.
REBA KATHRYN BULLEN
MR. WILLIAM E. BUREN
ALENE C. BURKS
MRS. NANNIE BURKS
MRS. HILDEGARDE CANNON
MRS. AUVERGNE CARNEAL
MISS ANN DEAN CARR
JANE W. CARR
M/M SCOTT B. CARR
ROBERT R. CATES
BILLIE COOPER CLARK
MR. JOHN THOMAS CLARK
LLOYD B. CLAYCOMB
ALICE S. COBB
DR. HAROLD I. COE
CHARLES M. COLE
ZELMA COMPTON
MRS. ALAN COOKE
MRS. ETHEL W. COOKE
MR. JAMES H. COOKE
WANDA L. COOKSEY
MRS. VICIE PAULINE COOP
WENDELL F. COUTS
ELLEN F. COWHERD
COL. WILLIAM T. CRAFTON III
ANN P. CRAVENS
MRS. ROBERT CRENSHAW
BILLIE W. CUMMINGS

MR. JOHNNY CUMMINGS JR.
SARAH ANN CUNNINGHAM
RUTH ANN CURTIS
BARBARA DALTON
BARBARA F. DALTON
M/M CARL E. DALTON
GUY DALTON
SHELLY H. DANTZLER
MISS WINIFRED DAVIS
DAVID D. DAVISON
KATIE LEE DAY
ROENA F. DEARING
BRENTS DICKINSON III
M/M JAMES V. DITMORE
MRS. ROLAND L. DIXON
JOHN NEALY DOSSEY
MRS. SHIRLEY DOUGHERTY
MRS. JANELLE E. DOWNS
ALTON L. DUNBAR
WANDEL L. DYE
GERRY DYER
RONNIE GAY EASTER
M/M WARD ELLIOTT JR.
LTC/M JAMES C. EMBRY
OTTIS W. EPLEY
ELIZABETH T. FERGUSON
MR. GEORGE W. FIELDS
BARBARA JO FIRKINS
EVA S. FORSYTHE
MR. HARRY FRAIM
LOIS H. FRANKLIN
SARAH FRANKLIN
RUTH GARRISON-COOK
MR. JOHN A. GASH
M/M LAWRENCE B. GILBERT
MRS. MARY P. GILBERT
MR. HERBERT G. GILLEY
MRS. JAMES F. GILLIGAN
MRS. PATRICIA W. GILMAN
EMMA JANE GOLLOTTE
INA GREGORY
NELLESA E. GRINESTAFF
LT. COL. BILLIE R. GROVES
MARJORIE HANDY
MRS. JOHN W. HANES
DR. OLETA ELIZABETH HARDEN
M/M RICHARD P. HARDING
HELEN C. HARRALSON
MR. ALVA T. HARRELL
JAMES I. HARRINGTON
NOVELLA HARRISON
ELIZABETH H. HAYES
E. HAZELWOOD
M/M ROBERT B. HENSLEY
DELANO HESTER
COL. DAVID B. HIGHTOWER
M/M WILLIAM F. HILSMEIER
MR. KENNETH B. HINES
M/M VIRGIL PHILIP HOFFMAN
M/M ANDY C. HOLLAND
MARJORIE HOLMES
M/M CARTER KOON HOOKS
SHERRY D. HOOKS
PHILIP E. HOSKINSON
M/M CLARENCE H. HOWARD
JAMES E. HUGHES
MRS. NANCY H. HUGHES
ANDREW J. HUSSEY SR.
DON H. IGNATZ
MR. GORDON JACKSON
MRS. JESSIE M. JACKSON
HAROLD DEAN JAGGERS
MRS. LETTY JAMES
MARY LOU JARVIS
M/M EDWIN JOHNSON
ELSIE P. JOHNSON
ROSEMARY R. JOHNSON
MS. BEVERLY F. JONES
MR. BILLY K. JONES
HELEN B. JONES
MARGARET "PEGGY" JONES
MRS. ORA LEE JONES
HAZEL BANDY JORDAN
MRS. CORNELLA JURLING
RAYMOND KALDENBACH
BILL KEMP
DR. SPERO KEREIAKES
WYONIA KIMBROUGH
MR. JOHN J. KINNARNEY
M/M JAMES EDWIN KIRTLEY
JACK T. KLEIER
JOANN F. KOEHLER
RUBY E. LAW
MR. WINDEL H. LEWIS
JAMES R. LINDLE PH.D.
MR. EDWIN C. LOBB
MRS. VERA LONG
MARIE LOWE
HELOISE B. MARSH
JOHN C. MARSH
MR. RUSSELL A. MARTIN
PEGGY J. MATTINGLY
NAOMI J. MCAFEE
MOLLIE R. MCCARTY
EARLENE MCCUBBIN

EARLINE A. MCCUBBIN
MARILYN MCCUBBIN
M/M W. HARDIN MCLANE
LUCILLE MCNEALY
MRS. T. MIDDLETON
M/M GERALD W. MILLER
MR. ROBERT L. MILLER
MR. WILLIAM DAVID MILLER
VIRGINIA HELEN MOORE
ANN LYNE MORGAN
M/M K. LYNN MORGAN
JAMES W. MULLINS
ESTELLE CLARK MURRELL
MR. THOMAS J. NALL
GERALD J. NASSANO
MR. DONALD B. NELSON
GUY NEWCOM
MR. ROBERT K. NUCKOLS
MR. BARNEY C. OLIVER
M/M GEORGE S. ORR
HELEN V. ORRENDER
MARY M. PACE
DOROTHY E. PARK
GLEN D. PARRIGIN
M/M WILLIAM T. PAUL
E. PAYNE
GEORGIA PAYNE
KATHERINE H. PEARCE
JEAN PEBDYCOART
MRS. BARBARA A. PENN
CHRISTINE ALLISON PERKINS
BARBARA PETTEY
M/M EARL J. PETTEY
DOROTHY PHELPS
MR. WILLIAM POLLARD JR.
ELEANOR B. POTTER
JESSIE PRESTON
REV. BILL PRICE
DR. RONALD E. PRICE
VIRGINIA PRIDE
MR. EARL S. REID
PAULINE E. REYNOLDS
MRS. FRANCES RICE
RUBY R. RICE
DR. BILL W. RIDEOUT
RONALD LEE RIGGS
MRS. NORMA J. ROACH
MRS. GERALDINE H. RODDA
BARBARA M. RODGERS
MARTHA F. ROGERS
MR. JERALD L. ROSE
NORMA J. RUBLE
JOANNE F. RUFF
DELLA M. RUNNER
M/M JOHN W. SAGABIEL
M/M ROBERT SALLEE
MR. WILLIAM W. SANDERS
M/M EWELL SCOTT
SARA SCOTT
DR. WALTER N. SCOTT
MRS. MARION SHANNON
MRS. ANN W. SHARP
M/M ORVIE J. SHARP
BARBARA EUBAND SHELBURNE
LARRY B. SHELTON
MARGARET JEAN SHEPLER
MR. JAMES A. SHERRARD
MR. DENNIS G. SHIRLEY
MRS. MARGUERITE M. SIMMONS
ELIZABETH SIMON
ELAINE SIMPSON
RICHARD SMALL
MRS. ANITA A. SMITH
M/M GILBERT H. SMITH
MRS. LAGATHA J. SMITH
NORA ANN SMITH
M/M WILBERT H. SMITH
M/M PAUL SPARKS
LOUISE L. SPIRES
MRS. SHERI LYNN SPRUELL
RUTH ELLEN STANLEY
M/M WILLIAM C. STAPLES
EULA B. STEENBERGEN
M/M WALTER LEE STEVENS
BERTHA L. STEWART
LULU M. STICE
MRS. MARY VIRGINIA STILES
MR. BOBBY L. STRATTON
M/M HARBARD SUGG JR.
M/M WILLIAM SUMMERHILL
MR. VERNON SUTER
LINNIE EARL TATE
M/M JOHN H. TAYLOR
REV./MRS. ORIEN P. TAYLOR
DAISY W. THALER
CAROLL W. THOMAS
VIRGINIA SUE THOMAS
ELLISON TUBB
DORIS JANE TUCKWELL
ROY SAMUEL TURNER
LAURA E. UNDERWOOD
DONALD E. UTLEY
RONALD K. UTLEY
MAE VAN PETETT
DANE WALDEN

MRS. ROSA R. WALDEN
MRS. ANITA R. WALKER
MR. JOHN L. WALKER
MATILDA WALKER
MRS. BERNICE D. WALLACE
MARIE J. WARD
REV. RAYMOND WARD
CLAY M. WARE
M/M BYRON C. WATKINS
M/M CHARLES WATKINS
DR. JAMES YANCEY WATKINS
LONNIE A. WELLS
MRS. ESTHER P. WHITE
YVONNE WHITSON
MRS. SHIRLEY WIGGINTON
LACY WILKINS
JUDITH C. WILLIAMS
ROGER T. WINN
DEBORAH WITHERS
MARTHA F. WITHERS
HARRELL E. WOOD
MARY LOU WOOD
MRS. ELSIE C. WOODWORTH
M/M CHARLES RAY WOOSLEY
ROYCE S. WOOSLEY
MR. WILLIAM E. WORLEY
DON THOMAS WRIGHT

'57 GRADS
BETTYE ANN ADAMS
GENEVIEVE ADKINS
ALICE B. AHMED
MRS. ALICE P. AHMED
GERTRUDE ALKIRE
NANNIE C. ALLEN
M/M DONALD R. ALWES
MRS. EDNA ANN ALWES
MS. EDWINA H. ANDERSON
VALERIA ANDERSON
MR. JOSEPH A. ANTHONY
JAMES H. ATCHISON
JANE S. AUSTIN
MARGARET ANN G. BAIC
MR. BENNETT D. BAIRD
MARY LOU BAIRD
CARIDAD BAKER
ALVIN BARBEE
MAY G. BARNARD
DENVAL P. BARRIGER
BETTY BASKETT
MR. CLARENCE H. BATES
CLYDE T. BAUGH
RUBY LEE BAUGH
MRS. MARY E. BEAMS
EZBON B. BEAUCHAMP
JAMES SCOTT BETHEL
RALPH BLACKWOOD
MARIE HORD BLOYD
HELEN P. BOON
MR. LEONARD BOOTH
DELORES BRANDON
M/M PHILIP S. BRANDON
JAN C. BRANSTETTER
MR. BILL BROGAN
EDITH D. BROOKS
MR. BEN F. BROWN
NANCY O. BUCHANAN
DR. KENNETH BURCH
MAX CAMBRON
ELAINE CARROLL CAMPBELL
DOROTHY R. CAPPS
MR. JOHN E. CARR JR.
MURIEL H. CARTER
RUBY T. CASWELL
FRANCES H. CATLETT
DR. RAY A. CAVE
DR. JOHN M. CHAMBERLIN
DR. BILLY H. CHANDLER
CAROL CHEAL MOLLYHORN
DR. JOSEPH H. CHEATHAM
VALERIA NELL CISNEY
MARY P. CLABORN
M/M RONALD W. CLARK
MS. BARBARA E. CLAY
MRS. ESSIE L. COBB
BERTHA COOMER
MARY B. COPAS
RUFUS E. COURSEY
LAURA CRAFTON
LTC. WILLIAM R. CRAWFORD
MR. JAMES W. CRISP
GERALDINE DAME-STONE
M/M BOB DANIELS
ROBER L. DAVIS
MARY PATRICE B. DEATON
RITA DEES
VIRGINIA D. DEPP
MRS. VERONICA DIEMER
LORVETTA DILLARD
DOROTHY ANN DOBBS
MR. HAROLD DONTA
COL/MRS. JAMES E. DOUGHERTY
CLARA W. DUGAN
LEON DUNAGAN
LUELLYN DUNBAR

DIXIE M. DUNCAN
MRS. MATTIE R. DUNCAN
JUNE DURBIN
M/M HAROLD E. DWYER
MRS. NELL S. EATON
DR. ROBERT H. EDWARDS
CLORA EUBANK
MRS. MARY COX EVERETT
DOROTHY FARMER
MR. FLOYD RAY FARMER
RUE E. FOE
MRS. LUCY B. FORBES
MRS. CORRINE M. FORTNEY
DR. ROBERT B. FOX
MRS. EARL E. FRANCIS
MALORIA FUQUA
BETTY GREEN GARDNER
DOROTHY GARRETT
M/M THOMAS D. GARRETT JR.
NELDA GARY
BETTY GILLASPIE
MR. WILBUR G. GILLEY
ETHEL GRAY
MARY EVELYN GRAY
DR. HARRY B. GRAY JR.
LOUISE GREENE
M/M WILLIAM T. GRIFFIN
M/M WINTON HACKER
MRS. MCIVA HALE
MR. STOKLEY B. HALL
M/M A. HAMMONDS
LESLIE HARDISON
G. VAN HARLAN
IRENE HARRINGTON
TRESSIE B. HATCHER
M/M GLEN HAWKINS
NANCY Y. HENDERSON
NOVA B. HICKMAN
BETTY J. HILL
GLADYS HILLYARD
M/M HOLLIS HINTON
MRS. INA N. HODGES
REGGIE HOFFMAN
M/M CARL HOLLAND
MR. HARRY E. HOLLAND
M/M MONTROE HOLLAND
VIRGINIA M. HOLLOMAN
PATRICIA J. HOLT
M/M WILLIAM J. HOLT
MR. NORMAN D. HOPPER
MRS. LELAND HUFFER
MRS. BETSY ROSS HUGHES
LUCILE G. HUGHES
HELEN K. HUNT
MR. EARL D. HUNTER
MARTHA HUNTER
OLIN JENT
ALMA C. JOHNSON
JACKIE F. JOHNSON
M/M KEMBLE F. JOHNSON
LAVINIA OAKES JOHNSON
ROBERT SCOTT JOSLIN JR.
MR. JOSEPH DEAN JOY
MONTRA M. KEEN
M/M NELSON L. KELLEY
MR. GEORGE EDWARD KELLY
M/M JOHN E. KEMKER
M/M ALBERT J. KIEL
AMELIA MAE KING
MR. EDWIN L. KING
DR. JAMES KING JR.
MRS. CECIL KINNAIRD
MR. MAURICE W. KISER
DR. DONALD RICHARD KNARR
MRS. JOANNE KRATZERT
MR. SAMUEL C. LAWRENCE
M/M OWEN LAWSON JR.
HAROLD DEAN LEE
GARY E. LESLIE
HAZEL GREEN LIKINS
HOWARD P. LINDSEY
CAROLYN F. LIPPO
M/M JOE LIPPO
GARY E. LITTLE
MRS. JEAN J. LITTLE
M/M JOE LONES
DR. VIRGIL WAYNE LOWE
M/M WARREN E. LOWE
JOYCE L. LUKROFKA
BERTHA G. LUNDY
HELEN R. LYLE
MRS. ERSIE CARTER LYON
PATRICIA A. MARSH
EVELYN MARSHALL
M/M PAUL H. MARTIN
MRS. SAM MARTIN
NELL F. MATTHEWS
MR. BILLY R. MAYES
JUNE D. MAYHEW
MR. HUGH L. MCCLURE
DR. WILLIAM M. MCCORMACK
ELIZABETH MCKIBBEN
DORIS MAXINE MCKINNEY
MAE MEFFORD
SAMUEL C. MEFFORD

94

CLARA L. METZMEIER
MRS. ANNA F. MEUNIER
DAVID H. MILLER
DENCEL WAYNE MILLER
ROSS MILLER
LAURA Z. MILLS
COL. WILLIAM F. MOHR JR.
CORINNA H. MOORE
MR. GUY E. MOORE
JOHN F. MOORE
LANNY SMITH MOORE
MRS. ELLA W. MORGAN
M/M MARION O. MORGAN
PAULA MORGAN
TRACY MORIARTY
LTC. ROBERT K. MORRIS
JOSIE C. MORROW
JUANITA J. MOSS
M/M WILLIAM E. MOSS
ELAINE K. MURPHY
MISS ALMA F. OLGES
MR. CREED ONEY JR.
VIRGINIA T. PAGE
MR. LARRY PARDUE
NANNIE PARRIGIN
M/M BENNIE T. PAXTON
GEORGIA PAXTON
V. WAYNE PEDIGO
M/M JOE A. PERKINS
ALLEN B. PERRIN
MRS. LOUISA M. PETRIE
MR. WILLIAM RAY POPE
MRS. MARY R. POYNER
MRS. GENOLA L. PRATHER
MR. WALLACE E. PRICE
MRS. BANNA PROFFITT
MRS. ELTA S. PROWSE
CAROL PRUITT
M/M MURRELL PRUITT
WILLIAM A. PRYOR
MRS. WILMA B. RABOLD
MARY RACHEL RAMSEY
GROVER C. RAY
M/M JAMES A. RAY
DR. DOROTHY E. REEVES
M/M CHARLES A. REID
PATRICIA REID
M/M THEODORE R. REVACK
MR. GERTHA LEONARD
REYNOLDS
M/M J. LEE ROBERTSON
M/M WILLIAM M. RUSH
MR. GARNETT E. RUSSELL
JO ALICE RUTHERFORD
M/M A. B. SANDEFUR
MILDRED P. SANDUSKY
MRS. RAYMOND C. SCHNUR
MARYLAND H. SCOTT
GUSTAVA SHAIN
MR. CLAYTON E. SHANNON
CAPT. JOHN SHANTON
MR. JAMES B. SHAW
PATSY ANN SHIRLEY
M/M WILLIAM L. SHORT
BETTY SHOULDERS
KATHLEEN SHREWSBURY
DOLLY SMITH
EVELYN C. SMITH
HELEN L. SMITH
VIRGINIA M. SMITH
MRS. J. E. SOMMERS
CARROLL L. SPEER
WILLIAM V. SPENCER III
PEGGY LOU ST. CLAIR
JEAN STARK
JULYN G. STEINBECK
M/M GEORGE A. STEINBERGER
MARY SUSAN STEPHENS
GENEVA STEPHENSON
MR. SAM D. STEWARD
MRS. LINDA STONE
MR. WILLIAM J. STRAWN
MR. JOHN C. STUART
FRANCES E. STULTS
AVO SYMPSON
ERSIE C. THOMAS
MRS. NEA THOMPSON
RACHEL THOMPSON
RONALD D. THORNBERRY
A. THRASHER
MRS. LAURA S. THURMOND
M/M BEN TOPMILLER
LEON TOWNSEND
ANNICE TRACY
MRS. BELMA TRAYLOR
HELEN S. UNDERWOOD
MARY M. UTLEY
GERTRUDE VANCE
M/M CARROLL T. VANHOOSER
GLADYS H. VINCENT
SHIRLEY D. WAGONER
MRS. DOROTHY J. WALLACE
DR. THOMAS WATSON
MISS FLORA PAULINE WAYNE
SUSAN M. WEBBER

JAMES A. WEDDLE
MR. JAMES R. WELLS
MR. JOE WELLS
M/M MARVIN WELLS
MARILYN H. WERENSKJOLD
M/M JAMES T. WEST
MR. DENNIS C. WHEELER
RAY B. WHITE
MR. JERRY WHITSELL
JOYCE W. WHITTAKER
M/M WILLIAM W. WILKERSON
MRS. ELIZABETH T. WILLIAMS
LTC/M GLEN W. WILLIAMS
MR. KENNETH A. WILLIAMS
LOU MAE WOOD
BERTHA WOODWARD
BOBBY GENE WOOTON
MRS. IVAN L. WORTHAM
MR. HOWARD G. WREN
COL. ARVIN LEO WRIGHT
BARRY ZEITLIN
'58 GRADS
M/M FOREST ABLE
MRS. MARLENE ABLE
BEEGIE ADAIR
NANCY ADAMS
JOSEPHINE AKIN
DORIS B. ALBANY
MILDRED ALEXANDER
MRS. JONELL ALFORD
ELVA R. ALLEN
MRS. SHIRLEY M. ALLEN
MARGARET ALTMAN
WILLIAM H. AMOS JR.
MARY ARMSTRONG
MARIE ARNEY
MACAULAY LEE ARTHUR
HAZEL A. ASHBY
MR. PAUL G. AUSTIN
MR. ERIC L. BACK
M/M EARLE BAKER
M/M HULET G. BALE
MARJORIE BALE
MR. DAVID F. BARKER JR.
M/M KENNETH R. BARRETT
M/M BOBBY R. BARTLEY
MR. VICTOR T. BEACH
DR. AARON E. BEALS
M/M BYRON H. BELL
M/M JAMES BOYD BELL
MARTHA LOUISE BELL
NOVELLA E. BELL
M/M RICHARD J. BELL
SARA BELL
LOUISE A. BENNETT
MRS. SANDRA L. BERDUX
BYRNA BEWLEY
MRS. ROBIN B. BIDEAU
MR. WILLIAM R. BIRDWELL
MARY ALICE BLACK
MR. RALPH BLALOCK
SHIRLEY M. BLANCK
MRS. RUTH ROBINSON BLAND
MR. WILLIAM BOOK JR.
MRS RUTH T. BOSWELL
MR. J. DAVID BOYKEN
M/M ROBERT O. BOYLE
LOWELL BRADEN
MR. LARRY F. BRANTLEY
WILLARD R. BRAWNER JR.
MR. JAMES DON BRENT
MR. JOHN C. BRITT
GRACE C. BROWN
MRS. GRACE M. BROWN
MARGARET BROWN
MARY D. BROWN
MARY V. BROWN
MR. JOHN E. BRUNNER
MARTHA BUDD
MR. JAMES S. BURNS
MRS. RUTH S. BUTLER
MRS. L. E. CAMPBELL
MR. CHAS P. CAMPBELL, SR.
MR. ROBERT A. CARTMILL
MARTHA G. CHAMBERLAIN
JAMES R. CHAMBLISS
MRS. JOAN J. CHOATE
MARY C. CHRISMON
MRS. AVIS CHRISTIE
JEAN SMITH CLAIBORNE
JOAN CLARK
VIRGINIA P. COLE
M/M E. COLLINS
M/M EDWIN G. CONNER
IRENE P. CONYERS
DR. PAUL B. COOK
ROBERT C. COOKSEY
EUGENE COOP
DR. CHARLES L. COOPER
THELMA E. COOPER
MRS. FRANKIE CORBETT
M/M RUSSELL C. CORNELIUS
SHIRLEY H. COTTON
CHRISTINE COX
MARY CRAIGHEAD

ALMA T. CRENSHAW
ROBERT D. CRENSHAW
DR. WADE A. CROWDER
MR. JOE N. CUNNINGHAM
M/M BERNARD D. DAVIS
PATRICIA P. DAVIS
ANN DENES
ERSIE DICKERSON
JOHNNYE F. DIEMAR
MRS. DORA L. DOUGLAS
JUDITH S. DOUGLAS
BARBARA J. DRUEN
TINA DURBIN
BILLY F. DUVALL
M/M JAMES W. EDWARDS
LUCY H. EDWARDS
MARY KATHERINE EDWARDS
M/M TOM EMBERTON
BEDFORD ESTERS
MR. ANTHONY F. FARGNOLI
MRS. VIRGINIA C. FENDELL
LORENA FENTRESS
DR. HAROLD A. FERGUSON
M/M JAMES F. FITZPATRICK
IZORA M. FORD
DR. SCOTT FORD
MRS. LOUISE B. FORSYTHE
RUBY FOUTS
RUBY CECIL FRANCE
MRS. VONNIE J. FRANCE
PAT FREDERICK
M/M ROBERT A. FREDERICK
JAMES C. FREY
JOYCE FROGGETT
JOYCE C. FRYE
M. GABEHART
MRS. RUSSELL GADDIE
LEWIS R. GARDNER
MR. BOBBY E. GARMON
WANDA MARKHAM GENTRY
WILLIE R. GETTINGS
MRS. CELESTINE W. GIBBS
M/M HERBERT GINGER
MRS. CHARLENE T. GLAZIER
SARA HELEN GLEAVES
EDITH GORY
ROBERT GOVER
MRS. ELSIE N. GRAY
MR. MAURICE GRAYSON
JOHN R. GREEN
DOUGLAS G. GRIFFIN
FRANK GRIFFIN
MR. GEORGE ROBERT GUMM
DR. CHARLES S. GUTHRIE
LARRY P. HACKLER
LINA LOUISE HADDEN
DR. ROBERT S. HALL
M/M WARREN V. HANCOCK
LILLIAN L. HARNED
M/M EDWARD D. HARPER
MARGARET L. HARPER
CHARLES EDWARD HARRIS
LORENE HARSTON
ANNA LOU HATCHER
MR. ROBERT LEE HAYS
ANN T. HAYWOOD
MARCELLA HEADRICK
MRS. DORIS ANN HENDRICK
TALMAGE L. HENDRICK
GORDON HENDRIX
M/M WILLIAM E. HENSLEY
MR. WILLIAM C. HICKERSON
ALICE M. HIGHTOWER
MARYBETH HILFER
MARY V. HILLS
IRENE HINTON
JUANITA B. HIRE
CARROL HOAGLAND
ANNA F. HOGUE
JAMES S. HOLCOMB
MOLLY HOLLAND
MOLLY C. HOLLAND
MRS. DELORIS HOLLOMAN
M/M JOHN F. HOLLOMAN
PATSY I. HOOPER
MR. BOBBY G. HOUK
M/M PAUL R. HUDSPETH
MR. JOHN ALLEN HUGHES
MARIE S. HUGHES
MRS. GERTRUDE HUMPHRIES
MRS. JESSIE R. HUNT
MAXINE INGRAM
M/M MORRIS INGRAM
AILEEN JACKSON
M/M FERRY JACKSON
VIRGIA IRENE JAMES
ROBERT U. JOHNSON
DELILAH MAE JONES
GORDON O. JONES
M/M TERENCE E. KELSAY
HILMAN F. KEY
JEAN P. KING
M/M ALVIN L. KLEIN
M/M L. D. KNIGHT
MARTHA FAYE KNIGHT

M/M ROBERT H. KNIGHT
MR. HERMAN D. LANE
MR. ROBERT A. LANE
MRS. CAROL H. LAW
MR. RAY LAW
DORIS LAWSON
LTC/MRS. OWEN D. LAWSON
ERBA T. LEE
CARL J. LEISURE
MARGARET K. LENTZ
DR. ROY LESTER
LUCY S. LEWIS
FRANCES LITSEY
MARY RUTH LITTLE
ANNE H. LOCKE
MRS. C. R. LOCKHART
DR. JOHN A. LOGAN III
MR. RICHARD A LOVELADY
PATRICIA H. MANNING
DR. DONALD L. MANSFIELD
M/M RONALD MARKWELL
DR. JERRY WAYNE MARTIN
M/M YANDELL H. MARTIN
GERALDINE MATHERLY
BETTY ZOE MAY
ELMA MCDERMOTT
M/M GENE MCFADDEN
ERNEST W. MEADOR
MR. JAMES E. MEADOR
EDWARD MILLER
MRS. MARY H. MILLER
DR. RONALD MILLER PH.D.
LEONA W. MONEY
MRS. FELIX E. MONTGOMERY
M/M BALLARD J. MOORE
BLANCHE W. MORAN
M/M DUVALL MORRISON
CLARA W. MORROW
BETTY S. MORTON
BRYAN R. MUFFETT
ROBERT D. MURPHY
DR. BRADFORD E. MUTCHLER
LOIS T. MYERS
MARGARET NANCE
MS. LOIS K. NANTZ
ROXIE NEELY
FRANK P. NEWBERRY
BEVERLY JANE NEWMAN
M/M GLENDAL M. NEWMAN
MRS. DAPHNE M. NICAR
MRS. ALICE O'NEIL
M/M GREGG O'NEIL
MRS. JACKIE C. OATES
HELEN ORNDORFF
MRS. BERTHA OSBORNE
MR. JAMES W. OWENS
BOBBY GENE OWSLEY
EDRA PAGE
SANDRA F. PATTERSON
M/M TWYMAN L. PATTERSON
JONELL W. PAYNE
WILLIE L. PENNER
ROAN PERRY
MRS. JANE PFINGSTON
M/M ROGER PHELPS
ELSIE S. PITCOCK
M/M JAMES C. PORTER
MARJORIE C. PORTER
MRS. HELEN PRICE-RABY
MARGUERITE PROCTOR
MR. DAVID M. PROW
ANN MILLER PURNELL
M/M WILLIAM PURNELL
JULIUS EDWARD RATHER
NADINE RAY
VIRGINIA B. RAY
RUBY REAMS
M/M JAMES V. REESOR
M/M EDWIN R. RENDER
LT. CLARENCE C. REYNOLDS
HELEN F. REYNOLDS
DR. JOHN C. RICHARDSON
LT. COL. GARY A. RIGGS
ELLIS C. RILEY
MR. HARRY T. RIVES
THERESA ROBERSON
M/M RALPH ROMANS
DR. SAM J. ROSS, JR.
MRS. ELIZABETH H. RUSSELL
JEANETTE SALLEE
TIMONS SANDEFUR
MR. JOSEPH M. SCHURECK
MRS. OLLIE R. SCOTT
ARLENE M. SETTLE
MR. BRADLEY R. SHAW
ROLLIN R. SHAW
SOPHIA SHIPLEY
ELDON B. SHIRLEY
DR. WILLIAM C. SHIRLEY
MRS. WILLIS SHORES
MRS. JACKIE SIDDENS SHELTON
REBECCA P. SIMMONS
LUCY H. SISK
MARIE L. SKAGGS
HELEN C. SKEETERS

NANCY LEE SLAUGHTER
MR. ELDON J. SMITH
HEBRON L. SMITH
MR. JACK H. SMITH
PATRICIA SMITH
MRS. KATHLEEN L. SOKOLITSKY
MARJORIE K. SPALDING
MR. MICHAEL E. SPECK
NAOMI SPENCER
MR. HAROLD J. STAHL
CELESTE E. STAPLES
RICHARD GREGORY STAPLES
BEULAH B. STEPHENS
MRS. JAMES A. STEPHENSON
ROBERT G. STONE
MRS. VIRGINIA A. TALLEY
M/M LAWRENCE W. TANDY
WILLIAM B. THOMAS
MRS. LUCY LEE THOMPSON
MR. S. THOMPSON
DONALD THORNBERRY
REV. BILLY R. TICHENOR
SHELBY C. TILFORD
JAMES E. TITTLE
MR. VENSIL A. TRIMBLE
M/M DON TRIVETTE
ALMA J. TURNER
M/M DAVID P. TURNER
MRS. NANCY P. TURNER
SAMUEL E. TURNER
KENETH WAYNE UTLEY
LT. COL. DAVID P. VANHOOSER
MR. HERMAN L. WAGGONER
MRS. CAROLE S. WALKER
M/M JAMES WALKER
MARY EVELYN WALKER
M/M ROBERT B. WALKER
MRS. SUSAN R. WALKER
MR. ROBERT BRUCE WATERS
MRS. BEVERLY H. WATHEN
MR. PERRY C. WATSON
ANN WESTERFIELD
M/M LARRY C. WESTERFIELD
ALTON B. WHITE
M/M LAROY M. WHITEHEAD
J. R. WHITEHEAD JR.
JEANETTE WHITLOW
GERTIE MAE WILCOX
BARBARA BLANCHE WILEY
JERRY O. WILLIAMS
RECA WILLIAMS
HELEN H. WILSON
VERNON KENT WILSON
COL. DAVID M. WINKLER
GRACE WOOD
MARY FRANCES WOODSON
NANCY LEE WRIGHT
M/M AUBREY D. YOUNG
DAREL YOUNG
'59 GRADS
M/M DONALD ACTON
MARY ACTON
DORRIS ADAMS
MARY H. ADAMS
MR. EARL ALBRIGHT
MRS. MARGARET L. ALFORD JR.
M/M NEIL ALLEN
HERMAN WAYNE ANDERSON
JOYCE M. ANDERSON
RACHEL APPLING
BETTY ARMSTRONG
OWEN G. ARNOLD
DR. J. ASHLEY
MR. JOE E. AUSBROOKS
CLARENCE W. AUSTIN
MR. FRANK M. BACON
MR. BEN DAVID BAIRD
MAJ. NORVAL BAIRD
NELLIE B. BAKER
JAMES R. BANTON
MR. GLEN O. BARRETT
MRS. OPAL E. BARTLEY
NELLIE BARTON
LOUISE BAUGH
M/M CLUSTER R. BELCHER
IRVING LEE BELL
MR. RICHARD BERNARD
INEZ BERRY
CHARLES BERRYMAN
EUNICE BEWLEY
NORMA JEAN BEWLEY
DR. HERMAN A. BLAIR
MR. JOHN T. BLAIR JR.
RUSSELL N. BLOWERS
MARJORIE M. BONDS
GOLDA G. BOOHER
MR. THOMAS H. BOSWELL
MARTA BOYLE
DR. BILLY S. BRADEN
ALICE M. BRADFORD
ROBERT L. BRADFORD
M/M ELDON W. BRADLEY
EVELYN PEARL BRAGDON
DIMPLE H. BRANSTETTER
MR. WENDELL J. BRANSTETTER

IDA FRANK BRATTON
LOIS P. BRAY
M/M JOSEPH F. BRITT
BETTY K. BROCK
MR. JAMES CLYDE BROWN
MAGGIE NAN BROWN
MRS. MARY DOYLE BROWN
MARY M. BRUCE
WENDELL D. BRUCE
RALPH E. BUCHANAN
MRS. NANCY H. BUCKINGHAM
BARBARA BURCH
MRS. PEGGY W. BURDEN
LELIA ANN BURROW
REBA M. BUSH
M/M CECIL W. CALVERT
MRS. KENNETH CALVERT
MARION J. CANARY
RUTH R. CARLO
J. CARNEAL
DR. FAYE CARROLL
FREDA CARROLL
WILLIAM G. CASE
M/M CHARLES E. CECIL
THOMAS M. CECIL
MR. JAMES G. CHAPMAN
MR. JAMES R. CHAPMAN
DR. CARL P. CHELF
JOSEPHINE R. CHINN
MRS. BETTIE J. CHRISTOFOLI
MR. JAMES LEON CHURCH
MR. JAMES EARL CLARK
DR. JAMES H. CLARK
OLA MAE CLARK
MR. ALDERSON CLARK JR.
ANN B. CLARY
LEONA L. CLEMONS
MR. CHARLES ALAN COLE
PHYLLIS R. COLE
TOMMY R. COLLINS
LORENE S. COLVIN
MAYME S. COOK
M/M S. JOHN COOMBS
EVELYN JANE COOPER
MRS. FRANCES COOPER
GRACE MARIE COPAS
MRS. CALAIS M. COPPAGE
RONALD E. COULTER
JAMES E. CRABTREE
MR. MORRIS C. CRAIG
MAJOR CLARENCE CRIGLER
RUTH M. CROSTHWAITE
MARY G. CULVER
MR. LEWIS D. CUTLIFF
MR. ROBERT M. DALE
MRS. PATSY ANN DALTON
JOYCE MOSLEY DAVIDSON
M/M JAMES R. DAVIS
MRS. IRENE DAVIS
MARGARET BELL DAVIS
MR. ROBERT M. DAWSON
MR. RONALD L. DAWSON
M/M WILLIAM W. DESKINS
IVA L. DICKERSON
M/M DONALD L. DOBBS
M/M WILLIAM R. DORRIS III
KAY DORRIS-SCHUMANN

M/M JAMES D. DOSSETT
MR. JOHN W. DOUGHTY
EDWARD L. DREIKORN JR.
EMMA LOU DUNCAN
M/M JAMES H. DUPREE
WILLIAM J. DUVALL
M/M BILLIE R. EARLE
NELL A. EDMONSON
MR. JAMES B. EDWARDS
WILLIE RUTH ELLIS
BILLY EVERETT
MRS. ELLIS FAIR
MRS. MARY S. FARRIS
BESSIE A. FLEET
M/M PHILLIP FOOTE
HELEN C. FORD
MR. JAMES EARL FORD
M/M WILLIAM S. FORESTER
MR. GORDON FOSTER
M/M BILL C. FRANCIS
VIRGINIA FULTS
GLYNA M. GALLREIN
DR. MICHAEL GARDONE JR.
M/M ERNEST H. GARNER
MRS. VIRGINIA GARRETT
CAMILLA GATEWOOD
WENDELL GENTRY
MR. KENNETH O. GIBSON
JAMES D. GILLIAM
M/M ROBERT E. GILLION
LETHA C. GIVENS
LAURA J. GLENN
MRS. DOROTHY LOU GRAY
JAMES E. GREER
FRANCES GREGORY
WANDA LOU GREGORY
M/M DAVID GRIGGS
M/M LARRY D. GUMM
EVELYN HAKE
ARTIE MAE HANKINS
MR. HOWARD K. HARDIN
M/M JAMES HARDIN
CLAUDETTE R. HARRIS
JEAN HARRIS
MR. WILLIAM J. HARRISON
ALICE JO HARWOOD
MR. FRANK R. HATFIELD
M/M LARRY HATFIELD
OVALETA HAVEN
M/M ADRIAN E. HAYES
MR. HOWARD STANLEY HEAD
AUDREY JAGGERS HEATH
GLENNIS N. HENSLEY
M/M JAMES R. HICKS
ALICE F. HIGGASON
EUGENIA HIGGASON
MR. ALLEN E. HILSMEIER
MRS. JEAN B. HITCHCOCK
M/M BILLY J. HOAGLAND
MARGARET P. HODGE
MR. MARK LEE HOFFARD
MARY K. HOLLAND
M/M BOBBY P. HOLMAN
AILEEN C. HOOD
MRS. ERMAN B. HOUCHIN
VIRGIL W. HOWARD
MRS. GOLDA G. HUDDLESTON

NETTIE B. HUDSON
MR. BILLY L. HUNT
MR. RONALD W. HUNT
REV. DONALD JAMES HURST
OPAL JAGGERS
MR. JEWEL JAMES
MRS. VIRGINIA F. JANES
J. LEE JENKINS
MR. JEFF H. JENKINS
DR. MARTHA JENKINS
RAY JENNER
M/M CRAWFORD L. JENT
MRS. MILDRED A. JENT
DR. JAMES S. JOHNSON
JIM JOHNSON
LAURA J. JOHNSON
M/M MERLE M. JOHNSON
MRS. OLA JOHNSON
THOMAS F. JOHNSON
JO NELL JONES
DR. JOHN EDWARD JONES
RICHARD R. KEMP
BARBARA KILGUS
MR. JOHN TAYLOR KING
M/M BILLY B. KINSLOW
GEORGE ALFRED KINSLOW
PAUL R. KNOOP
JO ANN KURTZ
MR. JAMES W. LAMBERT
M/M NOEL LANE
NORMAN DOW LANE
WILLIAM S. LAPADULA JR.
THOMAS HARRIS LASSITER
BOB G. LAW
M/M JEFFREY CORY LAWHON
ORA JEWELL LAWSON
M/M WILLIAM B. LAWSON
RHEA P. LAZARUS
ROSIE L. LEE
DOTTYE LINDSEY
WALTER LITKE
MRS. GEORGE LITTLE
JOSEPH A. LITTLE
ROBERT HARDIN LITTRELL
MRS. MELVIE LIVELY
NANCY LONG
MICHAEL J. LONGO
SARA B. LOWE
JOHN S. LYON
MR. BILLY MADISON
BILLY G. MADISON
MR. JOSEPH A. MAGRUDER JR.
VIRGINIA S. MARDIS
NANCY W. MARSHALL
MARY DELL MARTIN
ELLA MASON
MR. JAMES L. MASON JR.
DR. ROBERT B. MATHENY
HAROLD T. MATTHEWS
CHARLA JEAN MAUZY
M/M JOHN D. MCCLEARN
M/M FLOYD MCKIBBEN
NORMA MCKINNEY
MR. HAROLD LINDEN MCLELLAN
WILLIAM R. MCRAE
REV. HAROLD MEERS
MR. BENNIE S. MILLER

CAMILLA K. MILLER
DR. JAMES E. MILLER
MARY P. MILLER
STELLA J. MILLER
WILLIAM FERREL MILLER
M/M JAMES R. MILLER III
M/M JOE M. MITCHELL
NONNIE P. MOBLEY
HILDA J. MOHLER
M/M RONALD W. MOHLER
MR. WILLIAM J. MONIN
DOROTHY Y. MONROE
M/M CHESTER MONTGOMERY
M/M BURL C. MORRIS
JAMES A. MOSS
GLENDA NAPIER
VIRGINIA NEATHERY
JOE BEAUCHAMP NEELY
JAMES N. NEVEITT
DR. JOHN F. NEWPORT
RANDAL EARL NIX
MR. THOMAS E. NUTTER II
M/M BOBBY E. O'NAN
MR. DAVID ODEN
ROBERT T. OFFUTT
M/M HERBERT OLDHAM
MRS. FRANCES OLIVER
JAMES O. OLIVER
JUANITA PARK
MR. AUBREY L. PENDLEY
MARIE PERKINS
M/M LARRY B. PERRY
M/M ROBERT R. PERRY
MR. FRANK M. PETETT
SANDRA D. PETTITT
MR. BRUCE NEAL PHELPS
ANNA N. PIERCEY
MR. FRANK M. PITTMAN
CONNIE POLSTON
MAUREEN PORTER
MR. ALTON L. PREVATTE
SHIRLEY G. PRICE
DORIS S. PRUITT
MRS. EARLENE I. QUEEN
DOROTHY QUISENBERRY
M/M GORDON QUISENBERRY
BOBBY E. RAKESTRAW
MILDRED REVIS
M/M WINFRED B. RHOADES
M/M JAMES S. RICHARDS
MRS. MARY S. RICHARDS
MR. GERALD RICHARDSON
GLORIA ELAINE RICHARDSON
MADALENE S. RIHERD
M/M CHARLES ROBERTS
MISCH C. ROBERTS
MR. JAMES ROBINSON
EMILY I. ROBINSON
BROWNIE WILSON ROCK
DR. JAMES F. ROLD
LTC. RANDELL G. ROUTT
MARY E. SAMPLE
GENE G. SANDEFUR
LORETTA SANDERS
MARILYN J. SAUDER
CHARLES E. SCHAFROTH
JOHN EARL SCHNEIDER

GUY T. SCHROETER
JANET M. SCHWARZKOPF
M/M ROBERT SCHWARZKOPF
MRS. JENNIE SEYMOUR
MRS. CLYDE LEHMAN SHAVER
MRS. WILLIE W. SHIPP
MR. WM. E. SHOCKLEY
ROBERT B. SIDDENS
M/M F. DELANE SIMPSON
FREDA THOMAS SMITH
MR. JAMES H. SMITH
M/M ROBERT D. SMITH
MR. WAYNE N. SMITH
WILLARD N. SMITH
MR. RICHARD A. SMITHSON
DORIS ELAINE STEELE
DR. HARRY C. STEPHENSON
MRS. FREDA STEVENSON
MR. HENRY DAVID STONE
ALMA L. STRODE
WILLIAM HALL STRODE III
MRS. GLENN L. SUMMERS
M/M HARRY B. TATE
M/M CHARLES K. TAYLOR
JOSEPH P. TAYLOR
FORESTINE S. THOMAS
MARTHA S. THOMAS
REV. WALLACE E. THOMAS
RUTH THOMPSON
KENNETH THRASHER
MR. ROBERT W. THUM SR.
ALICE TRAYLOR
MRS. JOYCE F. TRIVETTE
ZORA IRENE TUCKER
DALMA S. TUNKS
M/M BILLY WALDROP
DOUGLAS WALDROP
MR. J. RICHARD WALKER
M/M MICKEY T. WALKER
FANNIE WASHER
DR. BILL L. WEAVER
DR. JOANN WEAVER
RAYMOND M. WEAVER
MAJ. RAYMOND P. WEBER
PAULINE B. WEBSTER
WILLIAM L. WEEDMAN, SR.
MR. GERALD WELLS
MR. MARVIN LEE WENZ
MR. CHARLES P. WEST
M/M JULIAN L. WESTBROOK
WILLIAM A. WETHINGTON
GEORGIE WILSON WHEAT
M/M HARLIE T. WHITE JR.
ANNA WHITMAN
PATRICIA W. WHITTINGHILL
HAZEL WILKERSON
M/M RAYMOND WILLIS
MR. ROBERT G. WILSON
ALICE L. WONG
MRS. CARLENE WOOD
MR. DON S. WOOD
EARL RICHARD WOOD
M/M JAMES ROBERT WOOD
M/M FONROSE WORTHAM JR.
MR. WILLIAM P. YOUNG

9 781681 622361